THE UNITED STATES OF THE WORLD VS. THE UNITED NATIONS

THE UNITED STATES OF THE WORLD VS. THE UNITED NATIONS

CAN GLOBAL UNITY AND NATIONAL SOVEREIGNTY COEXIST?

JD ROSSETTI

Copyright © 2025 by Juxtapolitico

Juxtapolitico.com

All rights reserved.

No part of this book may be reproduced in any form or by any electronic or mechanical means, including information storage and retrieval systems, without written permission from the author, except for the use of brief quotations in a book review.

For Humanity

We are not waiting for permission to create a world of rights, justice, peace, and shared responsibility.

We are claiming our place in the great work of humanity's repair, reimagination, and moral awakening.

FOREWORD

**The United States of the World vs. The United Nations
Can Global Unity and National Sovereignty Coexist?**

In a world on the brink—where climate disasters ignore borders, digital monopolies transcend laws, and billionaires command more wealth than nations—*The United States of the World vs. The United Nations: Can Global Unity and National Sovereignty Coexist* delivers a bold, urgent question: **Can humanity govern itself without sacrificing either sovereignty or solidarity?**

This groundbreaking book offers a sweeping yet actionable vision for a **hybrid global governance model**, one that honors cultural identity and national autonomy while enforcing shared responsibility for our planet and species. Juxtaposing the United Nations' multilateralism with the United States' history of nationalist expansionism, the book explores why both models fall short—and how a third path is not only possible, but necessary.

From a global parliament and enforceable universal rights to digital sovereignty, ecological reparations, and a binding framework for the world's wealthiest elites (The Trillionaire Club), this book proposes a radically democratic system of planetary governance—designed not for empires, but for **everyday people, commons stewards, cities, tribes, workers, and future generations.**

Structured with clarity and vision, it includes:

- A detailed manifesto across five parts,
- Four implementation appendices with legal frameworks, policy scorecards, and charters,
- A call to action for governments, NGOs, activists, and ordinary citizens alike.

Written in the voice of a bestselling contemporary author and political scientist—with wit, rigor, and heart—this is not just a book.

It is a **blueprint for building the world we need,** before collapse becomes our only teacher.

Read it. Share it. Use it. The future is still unwritten—and this may be the map.

PROLOGUE

Prologue: The Planet at the Crossroads
Let me tell you a story. It begins not with a war, a protest, or a dramatic United Nations vote—though we'll get to all those things in due time. No, this story begins with something far more ordinary: a conference Zoom call gone terribly wrong.

There were 47 world leaders on the line. One thought their camera was off while flossing. Another muted themselves right when they were supposed to vote. A third confused the background feature and appeared to be Zooming in from a scene in *The Lion King*. You could almost hear someone humming "Circle of Life." The chat feature exploded. Someone typed in all caps: "THIS IS WHY WE CAN'T HAVE NICE THINGS."

Now, of course, I'm being playful. But beneath the chuckles is a serious truth: the modern world is trying to operate on a system designed for a far less connected, far less complicated era.

The planet is facing truly global problems—climate change, artificial intelligence, economic inequality, water scarcity, misinformation, mass migration—but solving them is like trying to play a multiplayer game where everyone refuses to follow the same rulebook. Each nation is using its own controller, and some insist the game doesn't exist at all.

So what do we do?

Do we throw up our hands and retreat into national silos, pretending that the ocean between us is wide enough to keep the wildfires, viruses, and cyberattacks at bay?

Do we tear down our borders and submit to a single world government, hoping that unity will finally bring peace—even if it means surrendering control over our unique cultures, customs, and tacos?

Or is there something in between? A hybrid? A new architecture of global cooperation that respects sovereignty while solving collective problems?

That's what this book is about. A middle path. A *both/and* approach to the *either/or* problem that has paralyzed global governance for decades. It's not about choosing between "America First" or "Globalism Forever." It's about designing a model where the U.S.—and every country—can be proud, independent, and cooperative all at once.

When Borders Can't Stop Smoke

Let's take a breath—hopefully not a smoky one. In 2020 and again in 2023, wildfires in Canada sent thick plumes of smoke cascading across the northeastern United States. Air quality in cities like New York dropped to levels comparable with industrial Beijing. You could barely see the skyline. I had a colleague in Boston who claimed the smoke got so bad, he couldn't see his own self-importance—and this is a guy with tenure.

But seriously, this was nature's blunt reminder: smoke doesn't need a passport.

Nor does a virus. Nor rising sea levels. Nor disinformation. Nor economic shockwaves from a collapsing bank in a different hemisphere. Our problems do not respect borders, and yet our institutions are still married to the idea that sovereignty is sacred above all.

That worked when threats were mostly local or regional. But in a globally networked world, where a cyberattack launched from a basement in Minsk can disable a hospital in Minneapolis, the model breaks down.

Yet people don't want to hand their fate to some faceless, global bureaucrat who has never tasted their food, shared their values, or voted in their elections. That's where the resistance comes in. People want solutions—but not centralization. Unity—but not uniformity.

And that's the core tension this book tries to untangle.

Why the United Nations Needs an Upgrade (and Maybe a Sense of Humor)

Now, before the purists come for me with their blue-flag-waving righteousness, let me say this: I love the United Nations. It has done extraordinary work in peacekeeping, health, development, and human rights. I would never say the UN is useless. But let's be honest—it's a bit like an aging smartphone running 27 apps on a 10-year-old battery.

The Security Council structure, with its five permanent members (the U.S., Russia, China, France, and the U.K.), is a relic of post–World War II power dynamics. It's as if someone decided the seating chart at your family reunion should be based on who won the potato sack race in 1945.

Meanwhile, the General Assembly operates on

consensus that often takes longer than the life cycle of a sea turtle to achieve. The UN can issue bold resolutions—but struggles to enforce them. It's great at **calling** for peace, less effective at **creating** it. It's the global version of your friend who plans to run a marathon but hasn't jogged since high school.

So what do we need? Not to scrap the UN, but to supplement it. Rethink it. Strengthen it. Build **around** it—not **over** nations, but through voluntary integration, creative diplomacy, and new frameworks of accountability that work in a hybrid way.

America: The Reluctant Globalist

The United States occupies a unique place in this story. It is both the architect and the destroyer of many global structures. It built the UN, NATO, the IMF. It led in drafting the Universal Declaration of Human Rights. It spearheaded the World Bank. And yet, it also withdrew from the Paris Agreement, torpedoed the Trans-Pacific Partnership, and skipped town on the UN Human Rights Council like a rock star ghosting a sound check.

Why? Because the U.S. is torn between two instincts: the desire to lead the world and the fear of being governed by it.

Americans have a complicated relationship with authority—even our own. We'll cross oceans to stop tyranny, but throw a constitutional tantrum if you suggest limiting Big Gulp sizes. We love freedom so much, we make it a brand. But that very love for liberty is what makes global cooperation such a hard sell domestically.

Yet here's the paradox: no country *benefits* more from global order than the United States. Our corporations, our military alliances, our trade dominance, even our pop culture—are all supercharged by a stable, interconnected world. We just don't want to admit how much we're married to the system we built.

THE HYBRID MODEL: *Lead, Don't Rule*

Here's the twist: this book doesn't propose tearing down nations. It doesn't propose abolishing borders or instituting some kind of planetary parliament where 8 billion people vote on what's for lunch. (Spoiler: it would still be pizza.)

It proposes a **hybrid model**—a new way of thinking where nations retain sovereignty but agree to **shared standards, goals, and enforcement mechanisms** on key issues that affect us all.

Think of it like the European Union on a global scale—but with less bureaucracy, more adaptability, and a Bill of Rights that even autocracies can't veto. Think of it like the U.S. federal system—but scaled outward, where countries are like states: self-governing but united in mutual interests.

In this model:

- The U.S. can still choose its path, but when it signs on to global treaties, it follows through.
- Trillionaires aren't just celebrated; they're **activated** into a *Trillionaire Club* responsible for solving water scarcity and hunger—because if you've conquered capitalism, you can probably spare a glass of clean water for someone in Sudan.
- The UN doesn't just wag its finger at genocide— it has the **legal and military authority** to stop it.
- Global AI governance doesn't rely on tech barons

in Silicon Valley doing the right thing—it's codified in international law.

This is what the hybrid model is about: making global leadership effective again—without making it tyrannical.

A New Social Contract—With the World

This book is structured to walk you through this concept in five parts:

1. **The Foundations of Global Order** – how we got here, what sovereignty and globalism really mean.
2. **The American Dual Identity** – why the U.S. is both a barrier and a bridge to a new world model.
3. **The Case for a Hybrid System** – including real-world frameworks that could work today.
4. **The Trillionaire Era and Future Cooperation** – yes, billionaires are powerful, but trillionaires will be planetary actors—and we'd better have a plan.
5. **A Call to Action** – policy recommendations, moral imperatives, and a hopeful look at what's possible if we get our act together.

Why It Matters (and Why You'll Laugh Anyway)

Look, I get it. Global governance sounds about as exciting as a subcommittee on stapler regulations. But this is about more than institutions—it's about survival, justice, and imagination.

You'll laugh. You'll disagree. You might even yell at me in all caps (it happens). But by the end of this journey, my goal is that you'll **see a way forward**—a path where we don't have to choose between **cooperation and freedom**, but instead, embrace both in a smarter way.

Because if we don't figure this out, the next Zoom call may not just be embarrassing—it may be the last one we're able to schedule before the internet, the climate, or civilization itself collapses under the weight of our inability to act together.

And if that doesn't motivate you... well, we'll always have pizza.

1

A WORLD DIVIDED, A WORLD UNITED

THE GREAT TUG-OF-WAR – NATIONALISM VS. GLOBALISM

Imagine Earth as a massive, blue marble spinning through space, tethered together by invisible threads of technology, trade, language, and climate—yet also fiercely pulled apart by flags, anthems, and historical grievances. That, in a nutshell, is our current geopolitical predicament: **a civilization connected like never before, but reluctant to act as one.**

We're in the middle of what could best be described as **a planetary identity crisis.** Are we global citizens or proud patriots? Do we belong to humanity or to our homelands? And why, after decades of globalization, is there such a powerful resurgence of nationalism—border walls, trade wars, isolationist rhetoric, and sovereignty-first doctrines?

Let's begin by acknowledging the obvious: both globalism and nationalism are not fringe ideologies or temporary trends. They are deep, enduring philosophies about how power should be distributed and how human beings should organize themselves. They arise from very different understandings of history, culture, morality, and survival.

And in our present moment, they are locked in a global tug-of-war with consequences that ripple across continents.

This book opens with a simple but vital question: **Can unity and sovereignty coexist?** Can we build systems of cooperation strong enough to address collective challenges—while still honoring the independence and identity of nations?

The Story of a Pandemic and a Passport

Let's ground this abstract question with a painfully recent memory: COVID-19.

The virus didn't care about your passport, your religion, your national anthem, or your allegiance to fried dough over flatbread. It didn't check in at customs or wait for a visa. It spread with ruthless efficiency not because the world was connected—but because the world was *unprepared to cooperate.*

While scientists collaborated across borders to sequence the virus in record time, **governments defaulted to nationalism.** Borders closed. Vaccine hoarding began. Some nations ignored WHO warnings; others expelled foreign journalists or refused to share data. Even within supposedly unified blocs—like the European Union—member states scrambled to protect their own first.

In the age of a global threat, our response was **profoundly national.** And yet the virus, like climate change, AI, and water scarcity, was a **problem without a passport.**

If ever there was a wake-up call to the limits of sovereignty in the face of planetary challenges, this was it.

. . .

*Defining the Terms: **Globalism and Nationalism***

Before we go further, let's define our terms with precision—and a dash of humility, because few words have been so abused in modern discourse.

Globalism, broadly speaking, is the idea that nations are—and should be—deeply interconnected economically, politically, and culturally. It supports the development of global institutions (like the UN), international treaties (like the Paris Agreement), and shared standards for human rights, environmental protections, and trade.

Globalism doesn't mean one world government (though some dream of it). Rather, it's an acknowledgment that **our fates are linked**, and that cooperation is not optional—it's survival.

Nationalism, in contrast, asserts the primacy of the nation-state. It values independence, self-governance, cultural identity, and borders. It insists that each country should act in its own interest, protect its own citizens, and resist global encroachments on sovereignty. Nationalism ranges from benign patriotism to dangerous xenophobia, depending on how it's wielded.

When balanced, these forces can coexist—national pride alongside global responsibility. But in practice, they often collide.

*The Post-Cold War **Mirage***

After the Cold War ended, there was a euphoric moment where many believed that **globalism had won**. The Soviet Union collapsed. The European Union was expanding. China joined the World Trade Organization. American popular culture—blue jeans, Big Macs, and *Baywatch* reruns—seemed to conquer the world.

Francis Fukuyama even declared the "end of history," arguing that liberal democracy and free markets had triumphed as the final form of human governance. (To which history promptly replied: "Hold my beer.")

But beneath this optimism lurked tensions:

- Globalization brought wealth—but concentrated it unevenly.
- Technology connected us—but also amplified disinformation and division.
- Migration accelerated—but triggered cultural backlash.
- Trade expanded—but eroded local industries and working-class security in many countries.

In short, **the spoils of globalization weren't evenly shared**, and the backlash was swift.

Enter Brexit. Trumpism. Erdoğan's populism. Modi's Hindu nationalism. Bolsonaro's Brazil-first politics. These weren't aberrations—they were signs of a deeper discontent with globalist promises unfulfilled.

Interdependence without Integration?

We now live in an age where:

- A semiconductor shortage in Taiwan disrupts car manufacturing in Detroit.
- A war in Ukraine spikes food prices in Nigeria.
- A meme from an American teenager sparks a protest in Tehran.
- A virus that jumped species in Wuhan shutters businesses in Milan.

This is **global interdependence**. But it is not **global integration**.

We are connected, but not coordinated. Bound together, yet still pulling apart.

And here lies the paradox: our **problems are global**, but our **tools are national**. Climate change isn't going to pause while we debate jurisdiction. AI doesn't need a passport to disrupt your job market. Water scarcity doesn't wait for bilateral talks. And no amount of national pride will stop the next variant from spreading at the speed of flight.

The Ticking Clock

So why does this matter? Because we're running out of time.

This book is being written at a moment of profound global transition:

- Climate tipping points are approaching.
- AI development is accelerating beyond national control.
- Inequality is deepening—both between and within nations.
- Democracy is in retreat in dozens of countries.
- Authoritarianism is rising—with state actors defying global norms.

If we don't develop a **new model of cooperation**, we risk entering a century of fragmentation, resource wars, digital totalitarianism, and environmental collapse. Sound dramatic? Perhaps. But so did the idea of a global pandemic, right up until we were all wiping down our groceries and comparing quarantine bread recipes.

This chapter—and this book—asks you to think beyond the nation, without erasing it. To imagine a **world system that preserves identity but shares responsibility.** A framework where sovereignty is not sacrificed, but guided—like a solar panel, angled to capture the light of mutual interest.

Humanity's Interdependence vs. the Persistence of Borders

If you take a flight from Paris to Nairobi, or Beijing to Sydney, you'll pass over national borders that were drawn—sometimes with care, sometimes with a colonizer's cocktail napkin—and yet you won't see a single one of them from 30,000 feet. No walls, no checkpoints, no flashing neon signs saying "Welcome to Sovereignty." Just clouds, mountains, rivers, and coastlines.

From space, we look like one united planet. But from the ground, the world is an elaborate patchwork quilt of flags, checkpoints, languages, laws, and rivalries. That tension—between the unity of our shared humanity and the persistence of our territorial divisions—is the heart of our political moment.

And it's not going away anytime soon.

Why Borders Still Matter (and Always Have)

You might think that globalization would have made borders irrelevant by now. After all, multinational corporations don't recognize them. Viruses ignore them. Climate change laughs at them. Social media makes communication instantaneous across continents. So why are we still so obsessed with drawing, defending, and policing them?

Simple: **borders create identity**.

They tell us who we are, who we're not, what laws we obey, what language we speak, what holidays we celebrate, and, for some, even which side of the road to drive on. Borders are both literal and symbolic—they're about **territory, yes, but also culture, memory, and fear**.

And while global interdependence may be our reality, **psychological and emotional sovereignty remains deeply entrenched**. Most people don't wake up in the morning thinking, "Today, I am a citizen of the world." They think, "I'm American. I'm Indian. I'm Nigerian. I'm Brazilian." It's not just geography—it's belonging.

Moreover, for nations with histories of colonialism, occupation, or forced dependence, sovereignty is not just a preference—it's a **sacred assertion of dignity**.

The Rise of the "Sovereignty Shield"

In the past decade, we've witnessed a remarkable resurgence of nationalist rhetoric and policy—all under the banner of "taking back control."

- **Brexit** wasn't just a critique of EU bureaucracy; it was a spiritual return to the idea that "Britain governs Britain."
- **The U.S. withdrawal from international agreements** (the Paris Accord, the Iran nuclear deal, etc.) was often framed as a defense of American interests, not a rejection of international norms per se.

- **Hungary and Poland** have used EU funds to finance domestic policies that openly challenge EU liberal values—all while defending their "right to decide."
- **China's rise** comes with a distinct rejection of Western-led global governance norms, in favor of a new model of state-led sovereignty with "Chinese characteristics."

What all of these examples have in common is the **"sovereignty shield"**—a kind of political firewall nations use to justify rejecting external pressures, even if they belong to multilateral frameworks.

And frankly, there's logic behind the shield.

Global institutions, for all their ideals, can feel distant, elitist, slow, and unaccountable. Citizens don't elect UN officials. WTO rulings can supersede domestic policy. IMF conditions can force austerity on democratically elected governments.

So when leaders invoke the sovereignty shield, they're not always being cynical. Often, they're tapping into **genuine fears** that local voices are being drowned out by global consensus.

The Inconvenient Truth of Global Interdependence

But here's the catch: **sovereignty doesn't stop interdependence.** It only complicates it.

We're facing what might be called a **"governance mismatch"**—our problems are global, but our responses are local. And this mismatch creates friction, finger-pointing, and paralysis.

Let's take three quick examples:

1. Supply Chains

A factory shutdown in Vietnam delays iPhone production in California. A drought in Brazil raises coffee prices in Berlin. A shipping bottleneck in the Suez Canal causes a furniture shortage in New Zealand. You get the idea. Economies are **deeply intertwined**, and yet most trade policy is negotiated bilaterally or regionally, with little global coordination on worker rights, environmental sustainability, or corporate tax evasion.

2. Climate Change

It doesn't matter if one country meets its emissions targets while the rest of the world burns coal like it's on sale. The atmosphere doesn't care who polluted it. The consequence? Countries don't want to go first. They demand assurances others will follow. But without an enforcement mechanism—or trust—progress stalls.

3. Migration

Whether it's conflict in Syria, gang violence in Central America, or economic hardship in sub-Saharan Africa, people move to survive. And when they do, **borders become flashpoints**. Host nations resist, transit nations panic, and the international community issues statements that no one really enforces. There is no comprehensive, cooperative framework for human migration on a global scale. Only fences and fear.

A Planet Divided... Until the Internet Buffer Spins

There's a bizarre irony in all this. We are more globally connected than at any point in human history, and yet we can't seem to **act like it**. Our financial systems are synchronized, but our values are not. Our technologies are global, but our laws are national. Our memes cross continents in seconds, but our treaties take decades.

One nation's disinformation becomes another's electoral crisis. One company's carbon footprint becomes another country's flood. One hacker in Eastern Europe can drain bank accounts in Ecuador.

We're entangled. Like it or not. And while nationalism may help people feel secure, **it cannot solve problems that are borderless by nature.**

Let's put it bluntly: **Sovereignty is necessary—but insufficient**. It provides order, identity, and agency—but not always solutions. And yet, dismissing it as outdated or reactionary is both dangerous and ignorant of political reality.

That's why this book argues for a **hybrid model**—one that keeps what's good about borders, but transcends what's bad about them.

The Emotional Gravity of the Homeland

Still, we must tread carefully.

Because sovereignty isn't just about government—it's about memory. Language. Struggle. Pride. It's the grave of your ancestors. The sound of your national anthem at the Olympics. The rituals that make life feel rooted.

And that's why global solutions must never ask people to give up **who they are**. We don't need uniformity to achieve unity. We need empathy, design, and a political imagination that can **hold both truths at once**: the need for belonging, and the need for cooperation.

We must stop thinking in binaries. National vs. international. Patriot vs. globalist. Strong borders vs. no borders. These are false choices.

The real challenge is to **build systems flexible enough**

to honor sovereignty and firm enough to enforce shared obligations. Systems that allow national governments to speak in their own voices—but sing in harmony when it matters most.

Aligning Sovereignty with Solidarity

Let's begin with a bold and perhaps uncomfortable truth: **globalization is not optional anymore.** The toothpaste is out of the tube, and no amount of nationalism will cram it back in without causing a mess.

But here's the twist—**neither is sovereignty obsolete.** In fact, it's more emotionally and politically resonant than ever. It's not a question of whether we'll have globalization or nationalism. The question is **how we reconcile them without imploding.**

Because the world we're living in is not a tidy binary. It's not a courtroom where one side argues for open borders and the other for barbed wire. It's a chaotic, overlapping, multidimensional Venn diagram of overlapping challenges and identities. And the truth is: **most people live in the overlap.**

They want their nation to thrive *and* the planet to survive. They want their leaders to be accountable *and* their lives to be secure from global instability. They want culture to be protected *and* innovation to flourish.

What we need is not less sovereignty or more globalization—but a **re-engineered global architecture.** One that matches the complexity of our time. One that operates like a **federal system**, where global authority exists *only where necessary*, and national authority is protected *everywhere else*.

That's the hybrid model. And to get there, we need to first understand why our current institutions are failing.

. . .

The Structural Trap: Sovereignty Without Responsibility, Globalism Without Teeth

Let's unpack what I call the **sovereignty paradox**. On one hand, we have nearly 200 nations that jealously guard their right to self-rule. On the other, we have urgent global problems—climate change, pandemics, artificial intelligence, ocean acidification—that no one nation can solve alone.

Yet here's the trap: most of our global institutions—like the United Nations—are built on **voluntary compliance**. That means countries can sign on to treaties, agreements, or declarations and then... well... do nothing.

For example:

- **The Paris Climate Agreement** allows countries to set their own targets. There's no enforcement mechanism. You can show up, smile for the photo op, and then ignore your pledge while building a few new coal plants.
- **The International Criminal Court (ICC)** aims to hold war criminals accountable—but powerful countries (like the U.S., Russia, China, and India) aren't even members, and can veto actions.
- **The World Trade Organization (WTO)** can adjudicate disputes but relies on member states to enforce rulings—and has seen its appeals body paralyzed by political gridlock.

Meanwhile, **global corporations operate in legal limbo** —able to extract resources from one country, pay taxes in another, hide profits in a third, and lobby in a fourth. They're sovereign in everything but name.

In short, we've built a system where **nations claim the right to act freely**, but **decline responsibility for shared consequences**. At the same time, we've created global institutions that aspire to solve problems but **lack the power or legitimacy** to do so.

It's like asking your neighborhood watch group to police international crime rings—using a paper megaphone and a half-empty suggestion box.

Real-World Juxtaposition: **The U.N. vs. U.S. Expansionism**

This brings us to a vital comparison: the **United Nations** and **United States foreign policy**—two of the world's most powerful symbols of governance, yet so often in tension.

- The **UN promotes cooperation, consensus, peacekeeping, treaties, and international law.**
- The **U.S. often bypasses these norms in favor of unilateral action, sanctions, military power, and selective diplomacy.**

To be fair, the U.S. does engage globally. It funds (funded) the WHO. It leads NATO. It helps write trade deals and broker peace accords. But it also **reserves the right to ignore, veto, or withdraw** from global institutions the moment they conflict with domestic interests.

This isn't hypocrisy—it's strategy. And it's a strategy rooted in the belief that **sovereignty must be supreme**.

But here's the twist: the U.S. model, for all its contradictions, may actually offer the very **blueprint the world**

needs. A hybrid model—where cooperation is conditional, sovereignty is retained, and shared goals are pursued without erasing national identity.

We'll explore this idea further in **Part II**. But for now, let's imagine what this looks like on a global scale.

Hybrid Governance: What Might It Look Like?

Think of a system with **three nested spheres of power**:

1. **Local Sovereignty** – Nations retain full control over their culture, education, internal policies, and legal systems.
2. **Regional Federations** – Similar to the European Union or African Union, regional blocs manage trade, infrastructure, defense coordination, and regional conflict resolution.
3. **Global Stewardship Mechanisms** – These govern issues that cross all borders: climate, oceans, global health, artificial intelligence, space, and fundamental human rights.

Each level operates under the principle of **subsidiarity**—the idea that **power should be exercised at the most local level possible, but no lower than necessary.** If a problem can be solved nationally, it stays national. If it must be solved globally, then there must be a mechanism—binding, democratic, enforceable—to do so.

This isn't world government. It's **world cooperation, with boundaries.**

And in this system:

- The UN is reformed to be more agile, accountable, and democratic.
- Billionaires and corporations are taxed globally when they operate globally.
- Treaties include enforcement teeth—not just good intentions.
- Human rights are protected even when nations don't want them to be.
- Global crises get rapid, coordinated responses—not bureaucratic delay.

It's a system where **sovereignty is real—but solidarity is stronger.**

The Moral Case for Balance

Now, some may ask: Why complicate things? Why not just let each nation handle its own affairs?

The answer is both practical and moral.

Practically, as we've seen: no nation, no matter how powerful, can stop a virus, a wildfire, a cyberattack, or a heatwave on its own. Global threats require **global coordination.**

Morally, we are one species. One planet. One biosphere. And it is an absurd cruelty to say that a child in Yemen deserves less water, medicine, or education than a child in France because of an invisible line on a map.

Sovereignty without compassion is just selfishness. And globalism without respect for diversity is just empire with a smile.

The hybrid model aims to transcend both extremes. It says: **We can lead together. We can govern wisely. And we** can stay true to who we are—without leaving others behind.

A Bridge to History

To get there, though, we need to understand **how we got here**. The nation-state wasn't inevitable. It was invented. Sovereignty wasn't always the norm—it was a reaction to empire, war, and revolution.

So in the next chapter, we'll travel back to the **Peace of Westphalia,** to Enlightenment philosophers and post-colonial revolutions. We'll see how the idea of the sovereign nation took root, why it gained such power, and how it became both the **guardian and the jailer** of human progress.

Because to build a better system, we must first understand the one we've inherited—and why it commands such fierce loyalty, even in a borderless age.

2

THE RISE OF SOVEREIGN NATIONS

From Empires to Borders – The Westphalian Revolution

LET'S rewind history for a moment. Way back. Long before CNN, Twitter, or debates about TikTok diplomacy. Long before the United Nations, NATO, or the European Union. In fact, let's go back to a time when your political identity was less about what nation you belonged to and more about **who owned the land you lived on, who taxed you, and whose banner hung above your village square.**

You didn't wake up and think, "I'm a citizen of Spain" or "a loyal subject of France." No, in the early modern era, politics was more about **dynastic allegiance**, feudal relationships, and a lot of nobles wearing too much velvet.

What we now call **the nation-state**—a sovereign political entity with clearly defined borders, a centralized government, and a sense of shared identity—**did not**

exist in the form we know today. It had to be **invented**. And like many inventions, it was born out of crisis.

The Thirty Years' War: Europe's Original Multiplayer Disaster

One of the most important catalysts for the rise of sovereign nations was a blood-soaked period known as the **Thirty Years' War** (1618–1648). This conflict wasn't just long—it was *catastrophically* long, especially for a continent that still thought leeches were cutting-edge medical technology.

The war started as a **religious conflict** between Catholics and Protestants in the Holy Roman Empire but quickly devolved into a **geopolitical free-for-all**. France fought Spain, Sweden fought Bohemia, and mercenaries fought... well, anyone with a coin purse.

By the time the smoke cleared, an estimated **8 million people** had died—making it one of the deadliest conflicts in European history. Cities were razed, crops destroyed, populations decimated. But in the rubble emerged something new: **a recognition that perpetual war, justified by religious absolutism and dynastic claims, was unsustainable.**

Europe needed a better system. Something more stable. Something more... sovereign.

Enter: **The Peace of Westphalia.**

1648: The Birth Certificate of the Modern State

The Peace of Westphalia wasn't just a series of treaties. It was a **philosophical revolution**. Negotiated over four years by dozens of European powers, it enshrined principles that would eventually become the foundation of **modern international relations.**

Here's what made it revolutionary:

1. **Territorial Sovereignty**
2. Every prince, king, or ruler was granted **exclusive authority over their own territory**—no more outside meddling by religious authorities or foreign crowns.
3. **Non-Intervention**
4. States were now expected to **mind their own business**—a polite way of saying: "What happens in Bohemia stays in Bohemia."
5. **Legal Equality Among States**
6. Large or small, powerful or weak, every state was given equal legal standing in diplomatic affairs.

These principles flipped the script. No longer would religion dictate politics. No longer would external empires dictate domestic law. The world was moving toward a **system of bounded, sovereign entities**—each one a master of its own fate.

It was the end of empire-as-default, and the beginning of **borders as legitimacy.**

Sovereignty: A Secular Savior

Sovereignty emerged from Westphalia as the **antidote to chaos.** After decades of bloody conflict rooted in universalist ambitions—Catholic or Protestant, imperial or dynastic—sovereignty promised **order, predictability, and peace.**

In a way, it was the world's first "Terms and Conditions"

agreement: you rule your territory, I'll rule mine, and we won't hack each other to pieces over doctrinal differences. Sound good? Great. Check the box. Let's move on.

This new system didn't guarantee peace—but it **redefined the rules of war and diplomacy**. Wars were now fought over territory, not theology. Borders became sacred. And within those borders, rulers could do as they pleased—tax, govern, conscript, worship—without external interference.

The sovereign state was born.

From Sovereigns to Nations

But there's a catch: early sovereign states weren't really **nations** as we understand them. They were **kingdoms, principalities, duchies,** often ruled by monarchs with more interest in their family trees than their subjects' rights. The idea of a **nation**—a community of people bound by shared language, culture, and destiny—would come later.

So how did we go from kings and castles to constitutions and countries?

That brings us to the **Enlightenment**—the intellectual upheaval of the 17th and 18th centuries that injected new ideas into political thought: liberty, consent, representation, natural rights, and the social contract.

Thinkers like **John Locke, Jean-Jacques Rousseau,** and **Montesquieu** began arguing that sovereignty didn't belong to monarchs—it belonged to the people. The state wasn't divine—it was contractual. And legitimacy came not from lineage, but from **popular consent**.

These ideas didn't just stay in dusty books. They lit the fuse for revolutions.

- The **American Revolution** (1776) declared that governments derive "their just powers from the consent of the governed."
- The **French Revolution** (1789) proclaimed the sovereignty of the nation and the rights of man.
- The **Haitian Revolution** (1791–1804) extended these principles to formerly enslaved people, demanding not just independence, but **human dignity**.

Thus, the modern **nation-state** took shape: a sovereign entity whose legitimacy rested on **peoplehood**, not just territory.

The Colonial Twist: Exporting Sovereignty, With a Catch

Of course, this glorious vision had its double standards. While European powers were busy crafting nation-states at home, they were also busy **colonizing the rest of the world**—denying sovereignty to millions.

The modern concept of sovereignty may have been born in Europe, but it was **denied to most of the planet** until the mid-20th century. Colonized peoples in Asia, Africa, the Middle East, and Latin America were **ruled without representation**, their borders drawn by imperial cartographers who didn't care much for cultural continuity or historical legitimacy.

The result? When these nations finally achieved independence, they inherited **boundaries not of their own making**, often designed to divide and conquer, not unite and govern.

And yet, despite these injustices, the **sovereign nation-state model remained dominant**. Why? Because it was the only political framework recognized by global institutions like the UN. If you wanted to sit at the table of nations, you had to have:

- A flag.
- A capital city.
- A government that claimed legitimacy over a population inside defined borders.

Sovereignty had become the **ticket to international legitimacy.**

The Invention Becomes the Default

Fast forward to today, and the **nation-state is no longer a novel experiment—it's the default operating system of the world.** There are 193 UN member states. Nearly every corner of the globe is claimed by some government (sorry, Antarctica).

Each nation is treated as legally equal—even if one has nuclear weapons and the other has more goats than GDP.

Borders are monitored. Flags fly. National anthems are played before soccer matches and space launches. Passports are sacrosanct. And international law is built on the assumption that each state has the right—and duty—to govern itself.

In the span of just a few centuries, the world went from **feudal fragmentation to sovereign standardization.** And this system, for all its flaws, has **stabilized the global order** in ways unimaginable to earlier generations.

But now—under pressure from planetary-scale problems—it is showing its age.

Why Sovereignty Became the Gold Standard of Global Political Identity

THERE's a reason you don't walk into your local coffee shop and hear someone say, "I identify primarily as a global citizen of the Earth, ordering a decaf with almond milk." No, you say "I'm American." Or "I'm Nigerian." Or "I'm Thai." Then you argue about whether the almond milk was steamed correctly, and you go on your way.

That sense of national identity—that inward pride or political reflex—is a relatively modern phenomenon. And yet today, it's so deeply entrenched that we rarely stop to consider where it came from or why it commands such powerful emotional allegiance.

To understand how sovereignty became the **gold standard of political life**, we have to look at how it evolved from **a diplomatic principle into a philosophical ideal, a legal doctrine, and a cultural touchstone**. Sovereignty is more than just who controls what territory—it's become shorthand for legitimacy, justice, and self-respect.

Let's break down the ingredients that transformed it into such a powerful force.

SOVEREIGNTY AS LEGITIMACY: *The Law of the Land*

One of the earliest and most lasting developments after Westphalia was the idea that **sovereignty equals legitimacy**. In other words, if a government controls a territory, it gets to decide how that territory is run—no questions asked.

This meant:

- If you had a dispute with your neighbor, your local government settled it—not the Pope.
- If your country collected taxes, it was your king's treasury—not Rome's or Madrid's.
- If your leaders made laws, they didn't need approval from some foreign empire.

This might seem obvious now, but at the time, it was **revolutionary**. It gave **structure and predictability to power**. You knew who ruled you, and that ruler had internationally recognized authority.

Over time, this grew into a system of **international law** where:

- Each nation is treated as **equal in legal standing**, regardless of its size or power.
- **Borders are considered sacrosanct**, protected by norms and treaties.
- Nations may sign agreements—but they are **not subordinate** to higher laws unless they consent.

In a world where power had previously flowed from God, dynasty, or conquest, this legal sovereignty created a framework for peaceful coexistence—at least in theory.

The sovereign state became the **unit of legal identity**, the basis for diplomacy, and the container within which rights, duties, and justice were defined.

Sovereignty as Culture: *The Birth of National Identity*

But law alone does not create loyalty. What truly cemented sovereignty in the minds of people was the rise of **national identity**.

Think of the shift:

- From subjects to citizens.
- From fealty to flags.
- From being ruled to belonging.

This wasn't just a political shift. It was a **cultural transformation**. Governments and intellectuals began to cultivate **national stories**—myths of shared language, shared ancestry, shared struggle. Some were rooted in history; others were invented whole cloth. (We see you, Romantic poets of the 19th century.)

With the help of public education, national holidays, national anthems, and eventually **national television**, people came to feel that they were **part of a larger "we"**—not just residents of a state, but members of a nation.

In some cases, nationalism was used for liberation:

- In Latin America, independence leaders like **Simón Bolívar** and **José de San Martín** inspired national movements to break from Spanish rule.
- In Italy and Germany, disparate regions were united by national pride in the 19th century.
- In colonized Africa and Asia, nationalism became the cry of freedom against foreign domination.

But in other cases, nationalism was turned inward—used to exclude minorities, justify conquest, and enforce conformity. It became a powerful tool for both **liberation and oppression**, depending on who wielded it.

Still, the common thread remained: **sovereignty**

became deeply tied to identity. People didn't just want a functioning government. They wanted one that spoke their language, shared their history, and honored their customs.

Sovereignty as Morality: The Post-Colonial Ideal

The moral weight of sovereignty hit its peak in the **post-World War II and post-colonial eras.** After two devastating world wars, followed by a cascade of independence movements in Asia, Africa, and the Caribbean, the idea of national sovereignty became a **moral imperative.**

For formerly colonized peoples, sovereignty was more than a legal status—it was a **symbol of dignity.**

To be sovereign was to be:

- Recognized.
- Equal.
- No longer under the boot of an empire or the thumb of a foreign bureaucrat.

The formation of the **United Nations in 1945** enshrined this new moral order. The UN Charter begins with the stirring phrase: "We the peoples of the United Nations, determined to save succeeding generations from the scourge of war..." and then proceeds to outline a world of **equal, sovereign nations** acting in concert for peace and prosperity.

The principle of **non-interference in domestic affairs** became sacred in international relations. Even today, it's invoked like a talisman every time the international community tries to pressure a government over human rights, military aggression, or environmental destruction.

And while this principle was designed to protect the weak from the powerful, it also **grants enormous latitude to governments that abuse power** behind their own borders.

The paradox? **Sovereignty defends both freedom and tyranny**—depending on whose hands it's in.

SOVEREIGNTY AS POLITICAL CAPITAL: *The Populist Resurgence*

Fast-forward to today, and sovereignty is no longer just a principle of diplomacy or a badge of independence—it's a **political rallying cry**.

- In Europe, populist parties campaign on "taking back control" from Brussels.
- In the U.S., the phrase "America First" became shorthand for resisting globalization.
- In India, Turkey, Brazil, and elsewhere, leaders invoke sovereignty to deflect criticism of domestic crackdowns, press restrictions, or minority repression.

It turns out sovereignty is the political equivalent of duct tape: **it can be used to fix anything—or silence anything.** Whether it's EU regulations, international climate treaties, trade agreements, or war crimes tribunals, sovereignty is the go-to excuse for non-compliance.

And here's the thing: it works. People rally around it. Why?

Because in a world of complexity, sovereignty offers **clarity**. In a world of economic precarity, it promises **control**. In a world of cultural change, it offers **familiarity**. It's not just about borders—it's about **psychological reassurance**.

So while globalists may deride it as outdated, and international institutions may find it frustrating, **sovereignty continues to resonate**.

How Sovereignty Protects Diversity, Local Governance, and Autonomy

In today's era of global streaming platforms, multinational corporations, and borderless data flows, you might assume that national borders would be passé—relics of a less enlightened time. Yet sovereignty not only persists; it's fiercely defended. Why?

Because for all its imperfections and occasional abuses, **sovereignty has been one of humanity's most effective tools for preserving diversity, local governance, and autonomy**. It's the firewall between cultural annihilation and survival, between governance tailored to local needs and rule by faceless consensus.

If globalization is the tide that seeks to smooth the surface of the world, **sovereignty is the rock that gives identity shape and friction**. And to dismiss sovereignty as an obstacle to progress is to **underestimate its role in safeguarding the very pluralism that progress requires**.

Let's examine how this plays out—politically, culturally, and practically.

Diversity *and the Sovereign Shield*

Take a moment to consider what we mean by "diversity." It's not just demographic variety—it's **cultural autonomy, linguistic preservation, spiritual tradition,** and **indigenous self-determination.**

Without sovereignty, these forms of diversity are *vulnerable to homogenization*—whether by dominant empires, global corporations, or international norms designed with one-size-fits-all logic. Sovereignty offers marginalized and minority communities a shield: **a defined space to maintain their language, religion, and customs without external imposition.**

Examples abound:

- **Bhutan**, a small Himalayan kingdom, has used its sovereign status to enforce environmental protections and cultural policies aimed at preserving its Buddhist identity—even while resisting modern mass tourism and economic dependence.
- **Tunisia**, after the Arab Spring, used its national sovereignty to draft a **unique secular-democratic constitution**blending Islamic principles with liberal human rights, on its own terms.
- **Bolivia**, under President Evo Morales, became one of the first nations to **codify indigenous cosmology into national law**, recognizing the rights of nature (Pachamama) and granting autonomy to indigenous communities.
- In **Canada**, sovereignty enables constitutional protections for Quebec's **French-speaking identity**, and land claims agreements with First

Nations offer **regional self-governance** within a federal framework.

None of this would be possible under a centralized world government—or even an overly aggressive global treaty regime. Sovereignty, for all its flaws, gives space for experimentation, preservation, and resistance.

It's the reason a mosque in Morocco doesn't look like a cathedral in Spain. It's why a street market in Thailand doesn't sell the same goods as one in Estonia. It's why the world, despite Netflix's best efforts, still has hundreds of cuisines, dialects, dance forms, and legal systems.

Diversity thrives in sovereign soil.

Local Governance: *The Case for Decentralized Solutions*

There's another practical reason sovereignty matters: **most effective governance is local.**

Your national government might handle defense or macroeconomics, but when it comes to:

- fixing potholes,
- managing water resources,
- regulating education,
- or responding to a wildfire,

it's your **state, province, or municipality** that takes the lead.

This is true within sovereign states—but also true **between** them. What works for flood-prone Bangladesh won't work for drought-scorched Namibia. What suits the Netherlands' zoning laws won't match the rural sprawl of Montana.

Sovereignty allows nations to craft **contextual policy solutions**—designed for their ecosystems, economies, and societies. It enables **trial and error**, where innovations can emerge locally and then spread by example, not coercion.

Think about:

- **Costa Rica's environmental protections**—setting aside nearly 30% of its land as protected forest, powered by local tourism and conservation policy.
- **Finland's education system**, which departs from standardized testing in favor of teacher autonomy—and consistently outperforms global averages.
- **Singapore's urban planning**, marrying strict governance with infrastructural innovation to create one of the most livable cities on Earth.

Would any of these models have been possible under a global government that demanded uniformity? Probably not. Sovereignty enables **policy pluralism**, which in turn fosters innovation, competition, and resilience.

It's not about isolation—it's about **adaptation**.

Autonomy and the Right to Self-Determination

At its most basic level, sovereignty is about **agency**—the right of a people to **determine their own future**.

This is not just a political concept—it's an existential one.

When we say that a people deserve sovereignty, we are affirming that:

- Their **choices matter.**
- Their **voice counts.**
- Their **destiny is not for sale or subjugation.**

That's why sovereignty is invoked so passionately in contexts like:

- **Scotland's independence referendum**, where voters debated whether their identity and political values were best served inside or outside the UK.
- **Palestinian statehood**, where the desire for recognition is inseparable from the cry for dignity.
- **Hong Kong's autonomy**, where sovereignty has become the frontline between democracy and authoritarian control.

And it's not just the oppressed who seek sovereignty. Even powerful countries like the United States or China invoke it constantly—not because they lack agency, but because they fear **losing it** to multilateral bodies, foreign interference, or supranational institutions.

That's why sovereignty must be understood not just as a legal structure, but as a **spiritual demand**—for ownership of history, responsibility for the present, and authorship of the future.

The Fragile Balance

Yet here's the paradox. The more sovereignty is **used to shield against responsibility**, the more it becomes a **barrier to cooperation.**

Consider this:

- If every country insists on its absolute right to pollute, **climate action stalls.**
- If every regime claims "non-interference" while committing atrocities, **human rights become aspirational slogans.**
- If each nation resists collective economic reform, **inequality widens**—and instability follows.

We're left with a sobering truth: **sovereignty without solidarity can kill.** It can suffocate action, enable injustice, and fragment efforts that require unity.

The answer is not to abolish sovereignty, but to **redefine it for the 21st century.**

That means:

- Keeping the right to self-rule, while embracing shared obligations.
- Defending culture, while curbing carbon.
- Protecting borders, while welcoming global cooperation.

It's not an either/or. It's a **both/and.** That is the foundation of the **hybrid model** this book proposes.

A Bridge to Chapter 3: When Nations Dream Together

In our next chapter, we'll explore how this balance began to tilt toward cooperation in the aftermath of World War II—when leaders stared into the abyss of destruction and chose a new path: **multilateralism.**

We'll meet the architects of the **United Nations, the IMF, the WHO,** and other institutions that sought to build a world governed not by conquest, but by **consensus.**

It was a bold experiment. One born not out of utopian fantasy—but **from the ashes of failure.**

But did it work? And what happens when consensus fades and cooperation breaks down?

3

THE BIRTH OF GLOBAL INSTITUTIONS

From Ashes to Architecture – Post–World War II and the Origins of Multilateral Cooperation

PICTURE THE WORLD IN 1945. Entire cities had been flattened. Economies shattered. Tens of millions dead. The Holocaust had revealed unimaginable cruelty. Hiroshima and Nagasaki had introduced a technology capable of vaporizing civilizations in seconds.

If ever there was a moment for rethinking how humans govern themselves, this was it.

And for a brief, extraordinary moment, the nations of the world did just that.

Out of the blood and rubble of World War II emerged a vision: that peace could not be sustained by alliances alone, or by temporary treaties between victors and vanquished. Instead, peace required **global institutions**—forums for negotiation, mechanisms for cooperation, and shared rules for engagement.

The world didn't need another empire. It needed **architecture**—a system that could handle the pressure of modern interdependence without collapsing into another global conflagration.

This moment gave birth to the **United Nations**, the **International Monetary Fund (IMF)**, the **World Bank**, and later, the **World Health Organization (WHO)** and the **General Agreement on Tariffs and Trade (GATT)** (which evolved into the **World Trade Organization**).

These weren't abstract ideas—they were designed with a very real purpose: **to prevent another world war.**

The United Nations: Hope with a Headquarters

On October 24, 1945, in the wake of unimaginable destruction, the **United Nations Charter** was ratified by 51 countries. Its preamble reads like a declaration of moral realignment:

"We the peoples of the United Nations determined to save succeeding generations from the scourge of war... and to reaffirm faith in fundamental human rights..."

It was an ambitious document. It envisioned a world where:

- **Nations resolved disputes peacefully.**
- **Human rights were protected universally.**
- **Military aggression was condemned and punished.**
- **Cooperation replaced conquest.**

The UN was not intended to replace nations. It was designed to help them **work together without sacrificing** their independence. In other words, the UN was the **prototype of hybrid global governance**—an institution where sovereign nations could act collectively.

Its structure reflected this balancing act:

- The **General Assembly**, where every country had a vote (democratic in spirit).
- The **Security Council**, with five permanent members holding veto power (pragmatic in politics).
- A range of specialized agencies— from **UNESCO** to **UNHCR**—tasked with tackling education, refugees, hunger, and more.

And where was it headquartered? **New York City**—a symbol of American power and a nod to the idea that the U.S., despite its sovereign might, was willing to host and support a **global institution for peace**.

The UN was the beating heart of a new vision: *a world that could disagree without destroying itself.*

The Bretton Woods System: Rebuilding the Economy

While the UN tackled diplomacy and peace, the economic side of the postwar order needed just as much rebuilding.

Enter the **Bretton Woods Conference**, held in New Hampshire in 1944—yes, before the war had even ended. Delegates from 44 countries gathered to redesign the global economy, hoping to avoid the disastrous mistakes of the 1930s: competitive devaluations, protectionism, and economic collapse that helped fuel fascism.

Out of that conference came two of the most important institutions in global economic history:

- **The International Monetary Fund (IMF)**
- Created to stabilize currencies, prevent financial crises, and serve as a lender of last resort for nations in economic trouble.
- **The World Bank**
- Designed to fund infrastructure and development in war-torn or impoverished nations, helping them get back on their feet.

Together, these institutions provided not just loans, but **rules, guidelines, and a framework for financial cooperation.**

Think of them as the **financial scaffolding of the new world order**—ensuring that no nation had to go it alone, and that the global economy had at least some safeguards against another depression or trade war.

THE WORLD HEALTH ORGANIZATION: A Global Immune System

In 1948, the world went a step further, launching the **World Health Organization (WHO)** to coordinate international public health efforts.

Why? Because war, displacement, and poverty had left billions vulnerable to disease. And because leaders finally recognized that **viruses don't need visas.**

The WHO represented another piece of the puzzle: **if nations were going to survive together, they needed to treat public health as a shared responsibility.** Vaccination campaigns, disease surveillance, and emergency response planning were no longer the domain of single states—they required **global coordination.**

Decades later, the WHO would be instrumental in eradicating smallpox, fighting polio, and coordinating responses to pandemics like Ebola, SARS, and COVID-19.

Again, we see the same hybrid logic: **nations retain control over their health systems, but share data, resources, and protocols** through an international body. Sovereignty respected, but cooperation empowered.

The GATT and the Evolution of Trade Governance

Let's not forget the realm of trade, which had been a key contributor to both world wars. In 1947, the **General Agreement on Tariffs and Trade (GATT)** was signed to **reduce trade barriers, prevent protectionism, and increase economic interdependence.**

The logic was simple: countries that trade with each other are less likely to go to war.

GATT laid the foundation for what would eventually become the **World Trade Organization (WTO)** in 1995—a rules-based institution for resolving disputes, setting trade standards, and enforcing agreements.

And again, the model is familiar: **nations join voluntarily, maintain their own trade policies, but agree to a shared set of dispute mechanisms and obligations.** It's not a surrender of sovereignty—it's a **contractual sharing of authority**, with mutual benefits.

The Vision of a New World Order

In the years following World War II, something extraordinary happened: **the most powerful countries in**

the world voluntarily limited their own unilateral authority to create structures that empowered collective action.

This was not an act of altruism. It was a **pragmatic reckoning**—an admission that in a world where nuclear weapons, global finance, and pandemics existed, no single nation could thrive in isolation.

It was the birth of **modern multilateralism**—a network of institutions designed to:

- Reduce the risk of war,
- Share the burden of development,
- Promote peace, health, and prosperity.

Was it perfect? Far from it. The institutions reflected the power dynamics of their time. The UN Security Council gave veto power to the victors of World War II. The IMF and World Bank have been criticized for favoring wealthy nations and imposing harsh conditions on the Global South.

But the **underlying idea was revolutionary**: that sovereignty and cooperation **were not mutually exclusive**. That nations could act **together** without giving up the right to act **independently**.

That idea is the precursor to the hybrid model this book is building toward.

Goals and Ideals Put to the Test – Trials of the Multilateral Experiment

THE INK WAS BARELY dry on the UN Charter when the realities of geopolitics came crashing in.

On paper, the postwar order was a marvel of moral clarity. The world had said "never again" to war, genocide, and conquest. The newly created global institutions were armed with mandates to foster peace, development, and human rights. Global cooperation had a flag, a building, and a vision.

But realpolitik doesn't read manifestos.

The same year the United Nations was officially founded, the United States dropped atomic bombs on Japan. Within two years, former allies in the fight against Nazism—America and the Soviet Union—were engaged in **a cold but ferocious struggle for global influence**. And so began the **Cold War**—an era that would put the institutions of multilateralism through fire and friction.

Let's explore what happened when those postwar dreams had to survive **the harsh weather of power, conflict, and nationalism**.

The Cold War: Frozen Cooperation

The Cold War presented a unique challenge to global institutions. On one hand, the **threat of nuclear annihilation** made cooperation seem not just virtuous, but necessary. On the other hand, the ideological chasm between East and West often **paralyzed the very institutions meant to mediate conflict**.

Nowhere was this more evident than in the **UN Security Council**, where the five permanent members (the U.S., U.K., France, the Soviet Union, and China) each held veto power. This design, meant to prevent future great power wars, became a chokepoint for progress.

Between 1946 and 1989, the Soviet Union alone cast **over 120 vetoes**, blocking action on everything from peacekeeping to sanctions. The U.S. joined the veto party later, particularly on resolutions concerning Israel.

This gridlock rendered the UN **powerless during some of the most intense crises** of the 20th century:

- The Soviet invasion of Hungary (1956),
- The U.S. intervention in Vietnam (1964–75),
- The Soviet invasion of Afghanistan (1979),
- And countless proxy wars in Africa, Asia, and Latin America.

Meanwhile, the **IMF and World Bank** focused heavily on **reconstruction in Europe and the containment of communism**. Loans, investments, and trade rules were often shaped not by neutral economics, but by strategic alignment with the West.

Multilateralism, in this context, often became **a polite façade over a competitive world**. Institutions built to elevate cooperation were **repurposed for rivalry**.

Still, even amidst the tensions, global cooperation didn't die. It adapted. And occasionally, it delivered remarkable results.

Moments of Triumph: Cooperation That Worked

Despite the dysfunction, the postwar institutions managed **a number of quiet revolutions**—areas where global coordination produced lasting benefits.

1. Peacekeeping Operations

While the UN couldn't prevent wars between major powers, it became instrumental in managing **post-conflict environments** and **preventing smaller conflicts from escalating**.

UN peacekeepers (the "Blue Helmets") were deployed in:

- The Suez Crisis (1956),
- Cyprus (1964–present),
- The Balkans (1990s),
- Rwanda (albeit tragically too late),
- And many more regions.

Although often underfunded and hamstrung by vague mandates, peacekeeping missions provided a **framework for international presence without occupation**, allowing for **de-escalation, civilian protection, and elections**.

2. Public Health

The **World Health Organization (WHO)** helped **eradicate smallpox**—a feat that required a global vaccination campaign across ideological lines. This wasn't just cooperation; it was **collaboration among enemies** during the Cold War.

Later, WHO coordinated major efforts against malaria, polio, and Ebola, showing that **science-based multilateralism can save millions of lives**—when allowed to function.

3. Trade and Development

The **GATT framework**, and later the **World Trade Organization (WTO)**, helped expand global trade, contributing to **economic growth in developing countries** and reducing the chances of trade-based conflict.

Though controversial in its impact on inequality, global trade governance helped standardize rules, arbitrate disputes, and promote **economic interdependence**—a key pillar of peace theory.

These moments showed the potential of the global

architecture: not perfect, but powerful in moments of crisis or moral clarity.

Failures and Frustrations: When Multilateralism Stumbled

But for every success, there were **deep failures** that eroded the legitimacy and trust in these institutions.

1. Genocide and Inaction

Perhaps no failure haunts the UN like **Rwanda in 1994**, where over 800,000 people were slaughtered while the world watched. Despite clear warnings, UN forces were withdrawn, and the Security Council dithered.

The same occurred in **Srebrenica** (1995), where Dutch UN troops failed to protect Bosnian Muslims from massacre by Serbian forces.

These were not failures of information or logistics. They were **failures of political will**, hamstrung by sovereignty concerns and bureaucratic paralysis.

2. The Iraq War (2003)

When the United States, along with a "coalition of the willing," invaded Iraq without explicit Security Council authorization, it exposed **the limits of UN authority**.

The war fractured global consensus and **highlighted how powerful states can bypass multilateral mechanisms** when it suits their interests—undermining the very principle of collective security.

To critics, this proved that **multilateralism was optional for the powerful** and **irrelevant for the weak**.

3. Debt and Structural Adjustment

The **IMF and World Bank**, while promoting development, were also accused of imposing **rigid neoliberal policies** on poorer nations.

Through **structural adjustment programs,** they demanded:

- Austerity,
- Privatization,
- Deregulation, as conditions for loans—policies that often **devastated local economies, gutted public services, and increased inequality.**

This legacy, especially in Latin America and sub-Saharan Africa, fueled deep skepticism toward global institutions. To many, the IMF became shorthand for **external economic control,** not empowerment.

THE GROWING IMBALANCE: *Whose Globalism?*

By the late 20th century, global institutions had become victims of their own design.

- They claimed **universal membership,** but often reflected **Western priorities.**
- They promised **shared governance,** but decisions were often made by the **wealthiest or most powerful.**
- They touted **sovereign equality,** but in practice, sovereignty was **selectively respected.**

Emerging powers like China, India, and Brazil began to demand **a seat at the table**—not just as participants, but as **shapers of policy.**

This led to the rise of new institutions:

- **The BRICS Development Bank,**

- **China's Belt and Road Initiative,**
- Regional blocs like **ASEAN, MERCOSUR,** and the **African Union**—as alternative centers of influence.

The world wasn't rejecting multilateralism—but it was **demanding reform.**

THE HYBRID PARADOX Emerges

And here we arrive at the core dilemma: global institutions are **too weak to enforce cooperation,** but **too strong to ignore.** They operate in a space where **sovereignty is sacred,** but **cooperation is essential.**

This is the beginning of what this book calls **the hybrid paradox:**

- We need institutions with enough power to act—but not so much that they erase national autonomy.
- We need rules that apply equally—but flexibility to allow for local context.
- We need cooperation that doesn't feel like coercion.

And yet... **the current system was not built for that balance.** It was built for a world with clearer lines between "us" and "them," war and peace, developed and developing.

Today's world is messier, faster, more integrated, and more fragile. The architecture is outdated—even as the ideals remain urgent.

International Law, Global Governance, and the Challenge of Collective Action

The United States of the World vs. The United Nations

. . .

Let's begin with a simple truth that international relations professors love to repeat at parties (right before someone changes the subject): **there is no world government.**

There is no global police force. No binding legislature. No sovereign parliament of the Earth. And yet, nations still manage to create, sign, and sometimes follow **international law**. So what gives?

How does a world with nearly 200 fiercely independent countries—each with its own constitution, culture, and historical baggage—come together to agree on anything at all?

The answer lies in a delicate, often frustrating, yet surprisingly persistent invention: **global governance**.

Global governance is not the same as global government. It's a loose patchwork of **institutions, treaties, norms, and informal agreements** that create **rules without rulers**, and coordination without compulsion.

At its best, it's diplomacy elevated to policy. At its worst, it's a series of vague aspirations held hostage by sovereignty. But make no mistake—**this system is the scaffolding of international order**, and it plays a critical role in everything from war crimes tribunals to pandemic response to the regulation of space and cyberspace.

Let's take a closer look at how it works—and where it breaks down.

The Rise of International Law

International law might sound like a contradiction in terms. How can law exist in a system with no global sovereign to enforce it?

The answer is that **international law is rooted in voluntary consent.** Nations agree to be bound by rules through:

- **Treaties** (like the Geneva Conventions),
- **Conventions** (like the Convention on the Rights of the Child),
- **Protocols** (like the Kyoto Protocol or Paris Climate Agreement),
- **Customary law** (practices that become accepted as legally binding over time).

When a country signs a treaty, it's not surrendering sovereignty—it's **exercising it**. It's choosing to be bound by a rule for the sake of mutual benefit. Think of it as **contractual cooperation**.

The problem, of course, is what happens **when countries violate these agreements.** Who enforces the rules? And what are the consequences?

That's where global governance becomes more art than science.

The Enforcement Problem

Let's say a country launches a war of aggression, in violation of the UN Charter. Or violates international human rights law. Or breaches climate pledges.

What happens?

The answer is: **it depends.**

- Sometimes, there are **sanctions** imposed by other countries or international bodies.
- Sometimes, there are **legal proceedings**, as in

the case of war criminals brought before the **International Criminal Court (ICC).**
- Sometimes, there's **diplomatic isolation** or public shaming.
- And sometimes... **nothing at all.**

The enforcement of international law is **highly selective**, heavily dependent on **politics, power, and public pressure.**

If you're a small country, you might face real consequences. If you're a major power—say, the U.S., Russia, or China—you may **ignore rulings, veto resolutions,** or simply **withdraw from agreements altogether.**

This double standard erodes trust. It fuels nationalist critiques of globalism as hypocritical and toothless. And it leads to a pattern where **the weak are disciplined, the strong are indulged, and the system loses legitimacy.**

Why Countries Still Participate

Given all this, you might ask: Why do countries even bother?

Why sign treaties, join institutions, or submit to multilateral review?

Because—imperfect as the system is—**global governance still creates value:**

- It provides **predictability** in trade, diplomacy, and law.
- It allows for **shared resources** in emergencies (think: vaccine distribution, humanitarian aid).
- It enhances **global reputation**, which matters for foreign investment and alliances.

- It helps prevent **misunderstandings** that could escalate into conflict.

More than that, participation in global governance is often **a form of strategic self-interest.** Countries realize that:

- **Climate disasters cross borders.**
- **Terrorism is transnational.**
- **Financial contagion spreads rapidly.**
- **Public health depends on surveillance and cooperation.**

In short: **nobody wants a world without rules—they just want rules they can live with.**

The Challenge of Collective Action

Despite these benefits, global governance suffers from a classic problem: **the tragedy of the commons.**

Everyone benefits when all nations cooperate. But each individual nation has an incentive to:

- **Free ride** (enjoy benefits without contributing),
- **Defect** (violate rules to gain advantage),
- **Delay** (avoid painful reforms).

This is especially clear in climate negotiations:

- Every country wants to avoid global warming.
- But each fears that if they reduce emissions unilaterally, they'll suffer economically while others cheat.

- So they negotiate endlessly, set modest targets, and often **fail to meet them.**

The same applies to:

- Disarmament treaties,
- Refugee resettlement,
- Corporate taxation,
- Ocean conservation,
- Even pandemic preparedness.

Without strong enforcement or mutual trust, **collective action fails**, and the weakest suffer most.

The Need for Reform: Toward a Hybrid Model
So what do we do?
We don't scrap the system. We **renovate it.**
We build a **hybrid model of global governance**—one that:

- **Respects sovereignty** but creates **binding rules for global issues,**
- **Retains national identity** but develops **universal standards for human dignity,**
- **Empowers local governance** but coordinates through **regional blocs and global institutions.**

This model doesn't require a global parliament or an Earth Constitution. It requires **functional cooperation on shared threats**, combined with **flexibility and representation** to make sure no culture, region, or people feels steamrolled by distant elites.

Imagine:

- A reformed UN Security Council with rotating representation from major world regions.
- A **Global Environmental Authority** that enforces climate goals the way the WTO enforces trade rules.
- A **Universal Basic Rights Treaty** that includes mechanisms to pressure governments committing atrocities—without requiring tanks at their doorstep.
- A **Global Innovation Charter** that governs artificial intelligence, biotechnology, and digital privacy across jurisdictions.

In this model, the goal is not to centralize power—but to **network it** more intelligently.

The Moral Case for Global Governance

At the core of all this lies a moral truth: **the rights of humans should not depend on the happenstance of birth.**

A child born in a refugee camp is no less deserving of food, education, or safety than one born in Zurich or Seattle. A worker exploited in a sweatshop is no less entitled to dignity than an executive in London. A river polluted in Indonesia damages the same oceans that feed families in Japan and Kenya.

Global governance is not about bureaucracy. It's about **acknowledging that we live on one planet—and must live together or not at all.**

It's not about weakening nations. It's about **strength-**

ening their ability to solve problems they cannot solve alone.

That's why, despite its flaws, the global institutional experiment matters. And that's why the next chapters of this book will explore how to make that experiment more **just, inclusive, and effective.**

*A BRIDGE TO CHAPTER 4: **When Globalism Works***

The final part of this first act turns from theory to practice. In **Chapter 4**, we'll explore **case studies where multilateral cooperation has succeeded**—in tackling disease, regulating the ozone layer, preventing war, and sharing knowledge.

We'll ask: What made those successes possible? And can we replicate them in the challenges of today—before the window for meaningful cooperation slams shut?

4

WHEN GLOBALISM WORKS
CASE STUDIES OF SUCCESSFUL MULTILATERAL COOPERATION

If you listen to some corners of political commentary, you'd think that international cooperation is about as useful as a screen door on a submarine. They say the United Nations is all talk, that global agreements are just paper promises, and that the only thing more bloated than the IMF's bureaucracy is the conference buffet table.

And yes, we've seen failure. We've seen inaction, gridlock, hypocrisy. But what gets lost in all the finger-pointing is a much quieter story—a story of **when globalism actually works**.

Because here's the truth: **multilateral cooperation has achieved remarkable things**. Some of them so seamlessly that we've forgotten how extraordinary they are. Others were hard-fought, against political headwinds and bureaucratic inertia, but still succeeded. They didn't end nationalism. They didn't eliminate borders. But they proved, beyond doubt, that **sovereign nations can solve global problems when they choose to do so.**

Let's take a tour through some of those victories.

. . .

1. The Eradication of Smallpox: A Victory for Planetary Public Health

Imagine this: In 1967, smallpox was killing **2 million people a year**, scarring millions more, and spreading in poor and war-torn regions with little access to medical care. It had existed for centuries—decimating indigenous populations during colonization and killing emperors, queens, and peasants alike.

Then, in one of the most under-celebrated miracles of the modern age, the **World Health Organization (WHO)** launched an ambitious, globally coordinated vaccination campaign.

What made this effort unique wasn't just the scope—it was the **collaboration between bitter rivals during the Cold War.** The United States and Soviet Union, despite glaring ideological divisions, **worked together** to distribute vaccines, share medical research, and provide funding.

Health workers in the field, often under dangerous conditions, tracked outbreaks, trained local providers, and **built trust in communities that had little faith in outsiders.** It took more than a decade, but in 1980, smallpox became the first disease in human history to be **eradicated worldwide.**

No single country could have done this alone. This was a **purely global achievement**—a hybrid of sovereignty and solidarity.

The lesson? When the stakes are high enough, and the strategy clear enough, even ideological enemies can become partners in progress.

2. The Montreal Protocol: Healing the Ozone Layer

Remember the hole in the ozone layer?

In the 1980s, scientists discovered that man-made chemicals—**chlorofluorocarbons (CFCs)** used in refrigerants, air conditioners, and aerosol sprays—were depleting the ozone, the Earth's natural sunscreen. If left unchecked, this would increase skin cancer rates, disrupt ecosystems, and damage crops.

The science was clear. The risk was global. But the **solution required coordinated action**, because the chemical industry was massive, and CFCs were used everywhere.

In 1987, the world agreed to the **Montreal Protocol**, a binding international treaty to phase out ozone-depleting substances. What made it successful?

- It had clear scientific consensus.
- It included **funding mechanisms** to help poorer countries transition.
- It **adapted over time**, tightening its targets as alternatives became available.

Every country signed it. Every country complied.

Fast forward to today: the ozone layer is **healing**. Scientists predict a near-full recovery by 2065. It is perhaps the **greatest environmental success story of our time**.

Why did it work? Because it had **specific targets, financial incentives, a timeline, and universal buy-in**—hallmarks of effective globalism.

3. The Paris Agreement: A Work in Progress, But a Historic Shift

Let's shift to climate change, where the stakes are higher, the politics messier, and the science even more urgent.

The **Paris Climate Agreement**, adopted in 2015, brought together 196 countries in a commitment to:

- Limit global warming to well below 2°C,
- Pursue efforts to cap it at 1.5°C,
- And submit national plans (NDCs) to reduce emissions over time.

Unlike the earlier **Kyoto Protocol**, which imposed binding targets only on developed countries, Paris used a **"bottom-up" approach**. Countries set their own targets and pledged to revise them every five years.

Critics point out that Paris lacks enforcement teeth—and they're right. But what it achieved was something different: **universal consensus on climate action**, including buy-in from China, India, the U.S., and the EU.

Since Paris:

- Renewables have boomed globally,
- Green finance has exploded,
- Net-zero pledges have become the norm (if not yet the reality),
- And climate has become a **central issue in international relations**, from the G7 to the UN General Assembly.

Is it enough? Not yet. But Paris proved that **global climate cooperation is possible**, even among vastly different economies and political systems.

It's a fragile, slow, imperfect process—but the alternative is global chaos. And most nations know it.

. . .

4. CERN and the Large Hadron Collider: Science Without Borders

Not all global cooperation is about crises. Sometimes, it's about **curiosity**.

The **European Organization for Nuclear Research (CERN)**, home of the **Large Hadron Collider**, is one of the most extraordinary examples of peaceful international scientific collaboration.

Over **23 member states** and dozens of partner countries work together to probe the secrets of the universe. The 2012 discovery of the **Higgs boson particle**—a keystone of the Standard Model of particle physics—was not the result of national ambition, but of **collective investment in knowledge.**

CERN shows what's possible when scientists are given the resources, autonomy, and global framework to work **across borders and beyond politics.**

More importantly, it sets a precedent for future challenges in areas like:

- Artificial intelligence,
- Quantum computing,
- Genetic engineering,
- And space governance.

In an era where technology moves faster than law, **scientific cooperation needs a global home.** CERN is that home —and a model for future hybrid institutions.

5. The International Space Station: A Cold War Dream Realized

Speaking of science fiction turned fact: how

about **Russia, the United States, and Europe building a house together—in space?**

The **International Space Station (ISS)** is a marvel of engineering and diplomacy. Launched in 1998, it brought together **five space agencies** (NASA, Roscosmos, ESA, JAXA, and CSA) to build, fund, and operate a shared laboratory orbiting Earth.

Despite geopolitical tensions, the ISS has remained a zone of **continuous peaceful collaboration** for over two decades.

It's done more than scientific research. It's served as:

- A testbed for international cooperation,
- A reminder that rivalry can coexist with partnership,
- And a symbol of what a **truly global project looks like.**

It wasn't driven by profit. It wasn't imposed by a single power. It was built by consensus—one module at a time.

THE COMMON DENOMINATORS *of Success*

These case studies span health, environment, science, and technology. But they all share common traits:

- **Clear and present danger** or opportunity,
- **Scientific consensus** or shared knowledge base,
- **Institutional trust**—even among rivals,
- **Financial support** for the least advantaged,
- **Adaptive design**—allowing treaties and agreements to evolve,
- **Mutual benefit**—not zero-sum thinking.

Most importantly, they show that **sovereignty and cooperation can coexist**. Each country acted in its own interest—but also in concert with others.

That's the essence of the hybrid model we're building toward.

The Limits of Cooperation – When Globalism Stalls

EVERY ORCHESTRA HAS its off nights. But when the orchestra includes 193 sovereign nations with their own tempo, language, and sheet music—and half of them brought drums to a violin concerto—the chances of disharmony increase exponentially.

In the world of global cooperation, **failure is not a surprise—it's the norm**. The miracle isn't that international agreements succeed. The miracle is that they work at all.

And yet, for every smallpox eradication or ozone treaty, there's a shadow—a cautionary tale of treaties abandoned, institutions ignored, and collective efforts undercut by national politics, pride, or profit.

Let's explore several of these cautionary tales, each illustrating **a specific type of breakdown in the global order**—from institutional paralysis to trust deficits, to political backlash, to outright withdrawal.

1. The Doha Round: Global Trade Talks Gone Stale

In 2001, with hopes high for expanding the benefits of globalization, the **World Trade Organization (WTO)** launched the **Doha Development Round**—a multilateral negotiation process aimed at reforming global trade rules.

Its mission?

The United States of the World vs. The United Nations 69

- Reduce tariffs,
- Address agricultural subsidies,
- Boost trade for developing countries.

Sounds like a win-win, right?

Instead, it became a textbook case of gridlock. Countries couldn't agree on:

- How fast to open their markets,
- What concessions to make,
- And how to balance rich-world protections with poor-world development goals.

Years dragged on. Talks sputtered. By 2015, the Doha Round was essentially **declared dead**—an 18-year negotiation with **no final agreement**.

Why did it fail?

- **Mistrust between the Global North and South.**
- Fear of domestic backlash (especially among farmers and labor unions).
- The rise of **bilateral and regional trade deals**, which undermined the WTO's authority.

This failure highlighted a fundamental flaw in multilateralism: **global consensus becomes impossible when national interests diverge too widely.**

The irony? The very institution designed to facilitate cooperation—**the WTO**—was sidelined by nations eager to cut deals on their own terms.

. . .

2. *The Kyoto Protocol: Climate Commitments Without Commitment*

Before the Paris Agreement, there was **Kyoto**—a landmark climate treaty signed in 1997 that committed industrialized countries to reduce greenhouse gas emissions.

It was a bold move. But it came with flaws:

- Developing nations, including China and India, were exempt from binding limits.
- The United States signed, then refused to ratify it.
- Canada withdrew in 2011.
- Many countries failed to meet their targets, and there were **no meaningful penalties**.

The result? Between 1997 and 2012 (the end of Kyoto's first commitment period), **global emissions rose**, not fell.

Kyoto's collapse taught the world a hard lesson: **binding targets without universal participation = political suicide.** And universal participation without accountability = **policy theater.**

Hence, the shift in Paris toward a **"pledge and review"** model—less enforceable, but more politically palatable.

3. *The Migrant Crisis: A Borderless Problem Meets Barbed Wire Politics*

In 2015, civil war in Syria and unrest in parts of North Africa triggered a **massive wave of migration into Europe.** More than one million refugees crossed borders seeking asylum. Many died at sea. Others were turned away, detained, or stranded.

The European Union, a model of regional integration, found itself **bitterly divided:**

- Germany opened its doors. Hungary built fences.
- Greece and Italy were overwhelmed. Northern countries hesitated to share the burden.
- The **Dublin Regulation**, which required asylum seekers to remain in the country of first arrival, collapsed under pressure.

What began as a humanitarian emergency quickly became a **political crisis,** fueling the rise of nationalist parties and the erosion of **public support for multilateralism.**

Despite calls from the UN and the EU for a coordinated response, the refugee system fractured—**a clear case of national priorities trumping global responsibility.**

Even today, the world lacks a **comprehensive international framework for refugee resettlement**—one that balances human rights with sovereign control.

4. COVID-19: The Great Global Disconnect

If ever there was a moment for international cooperation, it was 2020. A novel coronavirus was spreading across the globe, disrupting supply chains, overwhelming hospitals, and upending economies.

And yet, what did we see?

- **Nations closing borders,** even to neighbors.
- **Medical equipment hoarding.**
- **Vaccine nationalism,** with rich countries

securing supplies for their populations while poorer ones waited.
- The U.S. **withdrew from the World Health Organization** under the Trump administration, accusing it of bias.
- China was **accused of early information suppression**, which undermined global trust.

While organizations like **COVAX** tried to ensure equitable vaccine distribution, the result was still lopsided:

- By mid-2021, over **80% of vaccines had gone to high-income countries**.
- Some low-income nations had vaccinated less than **2% of their populations**.

COVID revealed the **limits of trust, speed, and solidarity in global health governance**. Even though the WHO provided essential coordination and information, it lacked enforcement authority—and was **subject to political attacks**.

In essence, **sovereignty won the pandemic**—not science, not solidarity.

5. *The Ukraine War and the Limits of Collective Security*

In 2022, Russia invaded Ukraine in a flagrant violation of international law, sovereignty, and multiple treaties. The global response was swift:

- The **UN General Assembly** condemned the invasion.

- The **International Criminal Court** issued an arrest warrant for Vladimir Putin.
- The **West imposed sanctions**, sent military aid, and coordinated financial penalties.

But—and it's a big but—**Russia is a permanent member of the UN Security Council.** It vetoed all attempts at collective action. The same institution built to prevent wars was **powerless to stop one by its own member.**

What's more, the war exposed deeper fractures:

- Many countries in the Global South refused to take sides, citing double standards by the West.
- China positioned itself as a **neutral mediator** while still partnering economically with Russia.
- NATO, not the UN, became the de facto coordinator of the West's response.

The Ukraine war shattered illusions that the **postwar security architecture is still fit for purpose.** When a major power decides to act outside the system, the system struggles to respond.

This isn't just a security crisis. It's a **governance crisis.**

Patterns of Breakdown

What do these failures have in common?

1. **Lack of Enforcement**
2. Treaties and agreements often have no meaningful consequences for defection or delay.
3. **Asymmetric Participation**

4. Powerful nations can bend or bypass the rules; weaker nations face stricter scrutiny.
5. **Short-Term Politics Over Long-Term Solutions**
6. Governments prioritize domestic popularity over global cooperation.
7. **Institutional Fragmentation**
8. Multiple bodies with overlapping mandates and no coordination lead to redundancy and confusion.
9. **Trust Deficit**
10. Past betrayals and present power imbalances lead to suspicion, not solidarity.

These are not minor bugs in the system. They are **foundational flaws**—ones that any new hybrid model must acknowledge and address.

Global Interdependence—Learning from Successes and Failures

LET'S step back and take a breath—not just because we've covered ozone holes, vaccine nationalism, and agricultural subsidies, but because we're standing on the edge of a critical turning point.

The age of globalism is not over. It's evolving. And the question that confronts us now isn't whether we should cooperate—but *how* we can do so in a way that is **equitable, enforceable, and enduring.**

Because if there's one consistent lesson across all the global case studies we've examined, it's this: **interdependence is inevitable—but solidarity is a choice.**

So let's ask: What made the good work? What doomed the bad? And what kind of system might bridge the gap between sovereignty and cooperation, between the local and the planetary?

To do this, we'll review five core dimensions of global interdependence and how they play out across success and failure.

1. Legitimacy and Trust: The Fuel of Cooperation

Success Stories like the Montreal Protocol, the WHO's smallpox campaign, and the Paris Agreement didn't succeed solely because of science or resources. They succeeded because countries **trusted the process and believed in the outcome**.

That trust was built on:

- Inclusive negotiation,
- Respect for national differences,
- Transparent reporting,
- A balance between leadership and listening.

Contrast that with failures like the Doha Round or the Iraq War, where **perceived hypocrisy, exclusion, or bad faith negotiations** undermined global legitimacy.

Lesson: Legitimacy in global cooperation depends on perceived **fairness, transparency,** and **respect for sovereignty**. Countries comply when they feel heard, not coerced.

In a hybrid model, this means building institutions that have **democratic representation, regional input,** and **mechanisms for accountability** that aren't dominated by any one power or ideology.

. . .

2. Power and Participation: Who Sits at the Table?

One of the glaring patterns across failed global efforts is **asymmetry**.

- Kyoto failed because developing countries were excluded from meaningful targets.
- The WTO is gridlocked because emerging economies feel the rules favor the West.
- The UN Security Council is paralyzed because its power structure is frozen in 1945.

On the other hand:

- The Paris Agreement worked better because **everyone participated.**
- GAVI (the global vaccine alliance) succeeded because **funding and vaccine distribution** included voices from the Global South.
- The ISS continues because **every partner has ownership and pride in the mission.**

Lesson: Sustainable cooperation must be **shared, not dictated.** Countries will resist top-down mandates from unrepresentative institutions.

A hybrid system must be **decentralized yet coordinated,** allowing for input from **regional blocs, indigenous nations, small island states, and civil society,** not just the usual suspects with big militaries or economies.

3. Enforcement and Incentives: The Teeth Behind the Talk

Most people think the problem with global governance is lack of will. But more often, it's a lack of **tools**.

Global agreements often fail because they:

- Lack **penalties for non-compliance**,
- Fail to **reward leadership or over-performance**,
- Or don't include **binding mechanisms** to ensure follow-through.

The Montreal Protocol worked because **there were legal consequences** for noncompliance and **funding to help poorer countries transition**. The WTO, when functioning, enforced rulings that compelled countries to change policies.

Meanwhile, the Paris Agreement's voluntary model—though politically viable—remains weak on enforcement.

Lesson: Global systems need **carrots and sticks**. They need **graduated consequences**, like trade access, financial support, or legal action—not just strongly worded press releases.

In a hybrid model, **national courts**, **regional compacts**, and **global bodies** should share enforcement duties. Sovereignty isn't violated—it's activated in service of collective responsibility.

4. Clarity of Mission: Do We Know What Success Looks Like?

Treaties like the **Montreal Protocol** succeeded because they had:

- A **narrow scope** (ozone-depleting substances),
- **Clear metrics** (measurable reductions),
- And a **specific timeline**.

In contrast, the Doha Round aimed to reform the entire global trade regime—a Herculean task with vague endpoints. It collapsed under its own weight.

The same is true of refugee compacts, cyber agreements, and AI treaties: too broad, too fuzzy, too slow.

Lesson: Global cooperation must be **goal-driven and tightly scoped**. Success must be **measurable**, not mystical.

A hybrid model could break global challenges into **modular, mission-focused campaigns:**

- One institution to manage global water,
- Another for climate transition,
- Another for AI ethics.

Each would be **agile, accountable, and tightly defined**—more like task forces than empires.

5. Cultural Respect and Narrative Power: Why People Need to Feel Seen

Finally, the emotional dimension. People don't resist globalism because they hate the planet. They resist it because they fear being **erased, ignored, or assimilated** into a culture not their own.

Successful global initiatives allow people to **see themselves in the story:**

- The WHO empowered local health workers, not just foreign experts.
- The Paris Agreement lets countries design their own climate plans.
- The ISS includes scientific missions reflecting the priorities of its diverse partners.

Meanwhile, many failures come from **the perception that globalism is a form of moral imperialism**—that someone else is writing the rules.

Lesson: Global cooperation must be **culturally intelligent**. It must speak many languages, reflect many histories, and **honor many ways of knowing**.

The hybrid model must allow for **cultural pluralism** within shared norms—what some scholars call "**unity in diversity**."

THE HYBRID FUTURE: What Comes Next

So where does this leave us?

It leaves us with a clear choice:

- Either we continue to **rely on outdated, overly centralized, and underenforced global institutions**, or...
- We move toward a **hybrid system**, one that blends **the strength of sovereignty with the wisdom of cooperation.**

That system would be:

- **Flexible**, not rigid.
- **Networked**, not hierarchical.
- **Grounded in trust**, not just treaties.
- And **built to solve problems**, not just preserve process.

It would allow nations to act independently **without acting irresponsibly**. And it would give global institutions the **teeth to matter**, without the fangs to dominate.

Because at the end of the day, we aren't choosing between **independence and** interdependence. We're choosing whether we want to design systems that **make interdependence work**—or let it overwhelm us.

*A Bridge to Chapter 5: **When Sovereignty Resists***

Of course, not everyone agrees. As we'll see in Chapter 5, there are powerful movements—and legitimate reasons—why some nations, communities, and leaders **resist globalism outright**.

From Brexit to border walls, from trade disputes to vaccine nationalism, the appeal of **sovereignty-first politics** remains potent. It promises control, clarity, and cultural preservation.

And while it can be protective, it can also be **paralyzing**.

In **Chapter 5,** we'll explore this resistance—its roots, its power, and its implications for the hybrid future.

5

WHEN SOVEREIGNTY RESISTS
REJECTING THE GLOBAL—MOMENTS OF DEFIANCE

In a world teetering between interconnected crises and cooperative breakthroughs, sovereignty has become **both shield and sword**. And when the winds of globalism pick up too quickly—when treaties seem too intrusive or institutions too ambitious—nations often retreat to the one political refuge they trust most: **their own borders.**

This isn't a glitch in the global system. It's a feature. Because global governance, no matter how well designed, will always contend with an immovable truth: **sovereign nations don't like being told what to do**—especially by people they didn't elect, institutions they don't control, or norms they don't believe in.

This part of the chapter explores the moments when **sovereignty pushed back**—when national interests, identities, or ideologies drove states to **defy, depart from, or dismantle** global frameworks.

Whether you call it realism, resistance, or rebellion, it's a recurring rhythm in international affairs. And it offers a cautionary lesson for any hybrid model of cooperation: **ignore sovereignty at your peril**.

1. *Brexit: The Political Earthquake Heard Round the World*

Let's start with the most dramatic—and arguably most consequential—example of sovereignty reasserting itself in the 21st century: **Brexit**.

In 2016, the United Kingdom voted—narrowly but definitively—to leave the **European Union**, the most advanced experiment in supranational governance the world has ever known.

The EU was founded on the idea that nations could **pool sovereignty** to prevent war, promote prosperity, and wield collective global power. Over decades, it built a **single market, shared laws, free movement**, and even a **common currency** (which the U.K. had always kept at arm's length).

And yet, for millions of Britons, the EU had become **a symbol of lost control**—over immigration, over regulation, over national identity.

"Take back control" wasn't just a slogan. It was a primal scream—against bureaucracy in Brussels, economic insecurity, and a rapidly changing multicultural society.

The Brexit vote sent shockwaves through the global order. It revealed:

- That even in stable democracies, **supranationalism has limits.**
- That sovereignty remains **an emotionally resonant force.**
- And that, for many, **global integration feels like alienation.**

Whether Brexit ultimately helps or hurts the U.K. economically is still debated. But politically, it was a reassertion of **national primacy over internationalism**—and a warning shot to other global institutions.

2. *U.S. Treaty Withdrawals: The Exceptional Nation Opts Out*

The United States has long held a contradictory position in global affairs: it is both **the architect of multilateralism** and its most frequent **absentee member**.

Over the last several decades, the U.S. has **signed but not ratified**, or **withdrawn from**, a long list of international treaties and agreements, including:

- The **Kyoto Protocol** (climate),
- The **International Criminal Court** (war crimes jurisdiction),
- The **Paris Climate Agreement** (rejoined under Biden),
- The **Trans-Pacific Partnership** (trade),
- The **UN Human Rights Council**,
- UNESCO,
- The **Iran nuclear deal (JCPOA)**.

Each of these decisions had different motivations—some partisan, some strategic—but they shared a common thread: **a deep national discomfort with external constraints on American policy.**

The reasons vary:

- Fears that **international law could override U.S. law.**
- Worries about **sovereignty dilution.**

- Distrust of global institutions being "biased" or "ineffective."
- A political culture that values **independence over integration.**

To some observers, this behavior reflects hypocrisy: the U.S. wants global leadership **without global accountability.** To others, it reflects realism: **don't sign up for clubs where you can't set the rules.**

Either way, it sends a message: **even the world's most powerful country resists globalism when it feels boxed in.**

3. *The Rise of "Strongmen Sovereignty"*

Across the globe, a new generation of populist and authoritarian leaders has embraced the language of sovereignty—not as a defense of democracy, but as a **shield against scrutiny.**

- **Viktor Orbán in Hungary** has used "national sovereignty" to justify media crackdowns, judicial reforms, and anti-immigrant policies that clash with EU norms.
- **Recep Tayyip Erdoğan in Turkey** claims sovereignty as justification for silencing dissent, curbing academic freedom, and purging civil servants.
- **Jair Bolsonaro in Brazil** defied global environmental agreements, arguing that Amazon deforestation was a matter of "national development."
- **Rodrigo Duterte in the Philippines** withdrew from the **International Criminal Court**, refusing

to submit to its jurisdiction over alleged extrajudicial killings.

This new brand of "sovereignty-first" leadership is not about isolationism. These leaders often remain active in global trade and diplomacy. But they resist **normative obligations**—on human rights, transparency, and legal accountability.

They use sovereignty as **a nationalist trump card**—not to reject internationalism entirely, but to **cherry-pick which parts of it they'll tolerate**.

In this context, globalism isn't defeated by nationalism—it's **fragmented by selective participation**.

4. Vaccine Nationalism: The Pandemic Stress Test

If COVID-19 taught the world anything, it's that when the chips are down, **sovereignty surges**.

In the early days of the pandemic:

- Countries **closed borders** and **restricted exports** of medical equipment.
- Wealthier nations made **bilateral deals** with pharmaceutical companies—securing vaccines before they were even approved.
- The COVAX program, backed by the WHO and designed for equitable vaccine distribution, was **undermined by side-deals and national stockpiling**.

The result? While countries like the U.S., U.K., and Israel vaccinated their populations rapidly, large parts of Africa and Southeast Asia were left behind.

This wasn't a lack of compassion. It was the **reassertion of sovereign responsibility**—"my citizens first."

It also revealed a hard truth: even when the threat is global, **the instinct of national self-preservation can overpower the logic of cooperation.**

5. Digital Sovereignty: The Internet Gets Bordered

One of the great promises of the internet was a **borderless world**—a free flow of information, ideas, and connections.

But in recent years, countries have begun to **reassert sovereignty in cyberspace:**

- **China's Great Firewall** is perhaps the most extreme example—an entirely curated internet experience governed by the state.
- **The European Union's GDPR** asserts strict data sovereignty—forcing tech giants to comply with EU privacy rules, even when operating abroad.
- **Russia and Iran** are building **sovereign internet infrastructure**, capable of disconnecting from the global web during crises or uprisings.
- **India has pushed for "data localization,"** requiring companies to store user data within national borders.

This trend reflects a growing belief that **even in the digital realm, sovereignty matters.** And it marks a retreat from the early vision of cyberspace as an open, global commons.

Instead, we're seeing **a Balkanization of the internet,**

where digital borders mirror—and reinforce—political ones.

THE EMOTIONAL CORE of Resistance

Beyond policy and power, sovereignty has a **deep psychological pull:**

- It speaks to **control in a chaotic world.**
- It affirms **identity in the face of change.**
- It evokes **dignity for those who have been ruled from outside.**

That's why it persists—even when cooperation seems more rational. It's not just about tariffs or treaties. It's about **who we are, who decides,** and **what it means to belong.**

That's why any hybrid system of global cooperation must **respect this emotional terrain.** It can't be imposed. It must be **invited, incentivized, and co-authored.**

Cultural, Religious, and Political Arguments for National Independence

IF SOVEREIGNTY WERE MERELY about borders and bureaucracy, it probably would've disappeared long ago—swept aside by faster trade, shared technologies, and international institutions.

But sovereignty persists, even strengthens, because it is **not just structural—it's sacred.**

It is how communities preserve their **way of life,** how believers defend their **spiritual autonomy,** and how nations shield their **values and traditions** from homogenization.

For all the technocratic logic of global cooperation, there is a beating heart at the center of sovereignty: the desire for people to **govern themselves in their own voice, by their own lights, with their own story.**

In this section, we explore the **non-economic, non-strategic reasons** sovereignty remains a powerful idea—and why any hybrid global model must accommodate them if it hopes to succeed.

1. Cultural Identity: Sovereignty as a Vessel of Tradition

Language. Dress. Ritual. Memory. Cuisine. Dance. Architecture. Ancestral lands. None of these show up in IMF balance sheets or WTO trade agreements. But they are the very **soul of a people**—and often, the first to be endangered by cultural imperialism.

For many societies, sovereignty is the **only shield strong enough to protect cultural integrity** from the dissolving force of globalization.

Consider:

- **France,** where resistance to "Anglo-American cultural dominance" has led to strict laws mandating the use of French in advertisements and public signage.
- **Bhutan,** which measures progress using "Gross National Happiness" and mandates cultural education to preserve Buddhist traditions.
- **The Sámi people** of northern Scandinavia, who assert indigenous sovereignty through language preservation, land rights, and traditional governance.

- **Hawaiian sovereignty movements**, which seek not secession, but recognition of their right to maintain cultural and land-based traditions within a U.S. framework.

These are not expressions of isolationism. They are attempts to **control the pace and shape of change**, to retain what is meaningful in a rapidly globalizing world.

Globalism, when untethered from respect, often feels like cultural erosion. Sovereignty becomes the dam.

2. Religious Autonomy: Faith, Law, and the Politics of Pluralism

Religion and sovereignty have always had a complicated relationship. From theocracy to secular republics, how a society governs itself is often tied to **how it interprets the divine.**

For many nations, sovereignty ensures the **freedom to embed religious principles into legal and political structures**—or, conversely, to guard against religious dominance.

Examples include:

- **Iran**, a theocratic republic governed by Shi'a Islamic jurisprudence, which often resists international human rights frameworks as incompatible with Islamic law.
- **India**, officially secular, but home to deep tensions over whether Hindu values should shape national identity and law.
- **Saudi Arabia**, which has resisted signing many UN conventions on gender and family rights, citing conflict with Sharia-based legal codes.

- **Israel**, where Jewish law and democratic norms coexist in delicate legal balance, particularly in issues of family law and religious courts.

Even within the West, **religious exceptions to international standards**—on abortion, euthanasia, gender identity, or education—often shape national policy and provoke debate about **whose morality global norms should reflect**.

Sovereignty, in this context, is not just about laws—it's about **spiritual survival**. And for many, submitting to external moral frameworks feels like apostasy in disguise.

Global governance that ignores religious identity becomes illegitimate in the eyes of those who live by it.

3. Political Systems: The Right to Choose a Different Path

Not every country wants to be a liberal democracy. Not every people believes in capitalism. And not every society agrees on what constitutes "freedom," "development," or "justice."

Sovereignty allows nations to **choose different political and economic models**, even if they contradict Western norms.

Consider:

- **Vietnam** and **China**, both one-party states with strong state-led economic systems that challenge the assumption that free markets must be married to liberal democracy.
- **Cuba**, with its socialist governance and deep resistance to market liberalization, even under economic sanctions.

- **Venezuela**, whose political model has become a battleground between national sovereignty and international humanitarian pressure.

To globalists, these are examples of authoritarianism. To others, they are **expressions of resistance against imposed political orthodoxy**.

And yes, sovereignty can be abused to shield corruption, repression, or propaganda. But it can also be the space where **experimentation, reform, or non-Western political traditions** flourish.

A hybrid model must make room for **multiple paths to progress**—without demanding uniformity under the banner of "global standards."

4. Post-Colonial Trauma: Sovereignty as Reparative Justice

Perhaps no argument for sovereignty is more emotionally grounded than that of **formerly colonized nations**.

For centuries, millions were governed by **foreign flags, foreign laws, foreign languages**, and **foreign gods**. Decolonization was not just a political process—it was a **psychological, cultural, and existential reclamation**.

Sovereignty, in this context, is not a luxury. It is **redemption**.

That's why nations like:

- **Kenya** resist external critiques of their judicial reforms,
- **Indonesia** asserts its "non-aligned" foreign policy doctrine,
- **South Africa** champions local development models over IMF prescriptions,

- **Zimbabwe** rejected Western-led land reform frameworks (however controversial) in the name of post-colonial justice,

These decisions may be flawed, but they are rooted in a historical memory: **when outside powers ruled, the outcomes were often violent, racist, and extractive.**

Global institutions, still largely headquartered and funded by former colonial powers, must understand that **sovereignty is the currency of dignity in the post-colonial world.**

Without meaningful reform and representation, **globalism risks replaying imperial dynamics with new terminology.**

5. *Decentralization and Federalism: Sovereignty Within Nations*

Finally, sovereignty doesn't just operate between nations —it operates **within them.**

Federal systems like those in:

- **The United States**, where states assert rights on issues like abortion, education, and climate.
- **Germany**, where Länder control cultural and religious policy.
- **India**, where linguistic and religious diversity is protected through state-level governance.
- **Nigeria**, where power is balanced across ethnic regions and oil-rich states.

These sub-national sovereignties allow **experimenta-**

tion, pluralism, and representation—and often buffer against authoritarianism.

If sovereignty can thrive within a nation, why not within a **global system that respects decentralized autonomy?**

This is the core design principle of a hybrid model: **govern globally only where necessary; govern locally wherever possible.**

Toward a Philosophy of Sovereignty-In-Relationship

So what's the takeaway?

Sovereignty isn't the enemy of cooperation. It's the **precondition for meaningful participation.**

People will not engage globally if it means erasing themselves. They will not cooperate if it means **being governed by strangers** in languages they don't speak. They will not submit to institutions that see them only as data points, markets, or "populations."

But they will join systems that **listen, adapt, and respect.**

The hybrid path forward requires a new kind of sovereignty—not one of isolation or supremacy, but **sovereignty-in-relationship:**

- Where national identity is preserved, but not weaponized.
- Where autonomy is honored, but not absolute.
- Where cooperation is conditional, but not optional.

Because in the world we've built—a world of shared air, shared data, shared threats—**sovereignty alone is insufficient. But without it, nothing else is possible.**

The Nationalist Appeal in a Fractured World

IF SOVEREIGNTY IS THE PRINCIPLE, then **nationalism is the passion**. And like all great passions, it is capable of **building cathedrals—or starting fires**.

In the modern world, nationalism has become **the dominant language of resistance**—against globalization, migration, economic uncertainty, and cultural change. It doesn't just say, "Let us govern ourselves." It says, "We are under threat—and only *we* can protect *us*."

Nationalism doesn't need facts. It doesn't rely on policy briefs. It doesn't wait for multilateral approval. It **connects viscerally**—to identity, history, grievance, and pride.

And in a fractured world where millions feel **unseen, unheard, and unprotected**, nationalism offers something that abstract global institutions often cannot: **a sense of belonging, clarity, and mission**.

To build a hybrid system that works, we must understand the **emotional architecture of nationalism**—and why people reach for the flag before the treaty.

1. *The Psychology of "Us" and "Them"*

Humans are tribal by nature. This isn't an insult—it's a survival trait. Our brains evolved to distinguish friend from foe, in-group from out-group, insider from outsider.

Nationalism taps directly into this evolutionary hardware. It tells people:

- Who they are,
- Who they're not,
- And who's to blame for their struggles.

When globalization brings dislocation—when factories close, dialects disappear, jobs migrate overseas—people don't just lose income. They lose **identity**. And nationalism offers it back.

This is why nationalist movements:

- Emphasize **shared culture**, not class,
- Focus on **immigration**, not automation,
- Blame **foreign elites**, not domestic policy failures.

It's not always rational. But it's **emotionally coherent**. And in politics, coherence often wins.

2. The Narratives That Nationalism Owns

Let's look at the **narratives nationalism deploys**, often with great rhetorical power:

- **The Betrayal Narrative:** "Our leaders sold us out to foreigners."
- Common in post-industrial regions where globalization is seen as a con.
- **The Revival Narrative:** "We must restore our former greatness."
- Used in slogans like *Make America Great Again* or *Take Back Control*.
- **The Siege Narrative:** "We are under attack—culturally, racially, economically."
- This fuels anti-immigration politics and religious nationalism.
- **The Purity Narrative:** "We must defend our values against corrupt outsiders."

- Common in ethno-nationalist and far-right ideologies.

These narratives are powerful because they are **simple, emotive,** and often **rooted in historical pain**. They work because they **offer meaning**, not just policy.

Contrast this with globalist narratives:

- "Complex problems require multilateral coordination."
- "We must strengthen international norms to ensure sustainability."
- "Open markets and free movement create net benefits over time."

True? Perhaps. Compelling in a crisis? Not quite.

Globalism has **the math**. Nationalism has **the myth**. And politics, more often than not, runs on myth.

3. Nationalism in Democracies: Populist Surge

In democracies, nationalism often takes the form of **populism**—a style of politics that claims to represent "the real people" against a corrupt elite.

Leaders like:

- **Donald Trump** in the U.S.,
- **Marine Le Pen** in France,
- **Matteo Salvini** in Italy,
- **Andrzej Duda** in Poland,
- **Narendra Modi** in India,

have successfully combined **nationalist rhetoric with**

The United States of the World vs. The United Nations 97

populist grievance, turning complex problems into **binary choices**:

- Globalism = loss of control.
- Sovereignty = reclaiming power.

They promise to:

- Protect "our" jobs,
- Defend "our" borders,
- Revive "our" culture,
- And reject "globalist" interference.

These appeals often **cut across class and ideology**, creating new coalitions of urban-rural, secular-religious, rich-poor—all bound by a common fear: **losing identity in a global tide.**

And because global institutions often lack democratic legitimacy or visibility, it's easy to paint them as **faceless, elite, and unaccountable.**

4. Nationalism in Autocracies: Control and Coercion

In authoritarian regimes, nationalism plays a different—but no less potent—role. It becomes a **tool of state power**, used to:

- Rally public support without democratic consent,
- Justify censorship, surveillance, and repression,
- Redirect domestic anger outward.

In places like Russia, China, Iran, and Turkey, nationalism is not just rhetoric—it's **state doctrine**.

- Russia frames its war in Ukraine as a defense of "Russian civilization."
- China's "Wolf Warrior diplomacy" asserts national pride against Western criticism.
- Iran casts sanctions and protests as foreign conspiracies.
- Turkey blends Ottoman nostalgia with Islamic identity to bolster Erdoğan's rule.

In these contexts, nationalism fills the void left by democracy. It replaces public debate with **patriotic obligation**. Dissent becomes treason. Globalism becomes foreign meddling.

The result? **Nationalism becomes a firewall against reform**, not a path to renewal.

5. Why Nationalism Is So Hard to Counter

So why is it so hard to push back against nationalism—even when it turns toxic?

Because nationalism doesn't just solve problems—it **satisfies yearnings:**

- The yearning for **belonging** in a fragmented world.
- The yearning for **control** in an uncertain economy.
- The yearning for **meaning** in a postmodern culture.

- The yearning for **home**, when home no longer feels safe.

Until globalism can speak to these yearnings—**in human, not technocratic terms**—it will always feel like a threat to those who see themselves slipping through the cracks.

And until reformers acknowledge nationalism's legitimate roots—not just its dangerous extremes—they'll keep losing the political narrative.

Can Nationalism Be Reclaimed?

Not all nationalism is toxic. In fact, some of the most inspiring movements in history were **nationalist at their core:**

- Anti-colonial revolutions,
- Indigenous sovereignty movements,
- Democratic uprisings against empires.

The key is to distinguish between **inclusive nationalism** —which seeks dignity and self-rule—and **exclusive nationalism**, which thrives on scapegoats and fear.

In a hybrid global model, there's room for:

- **Civic pride without xenophobia,**
- **Cultural preservation without isolationism,**
- **Local control without international neglect.**

The future will not be won by erasing nationalism, but by **reimagining it**—as something that coexists with interdependence, rather than fighting against it.

Sovereignty as a Double-Edged Sword

Sovereignty has been called the cornerstone of international law. The protector of peace. The guarantor of dignity. And it is all of those things.

But let's be honest: **it's also a get-out-of-jail-free card.**

Sovereignty defends the oppressed—and shelters the oppressor. It empowers cultures to flourish—and allows tyrannies to endure. It enables self-rule—and often resists self-critique.

In the hands of a visionary leader, sovereignty is a shield. In the hands of a despot, it becomes a mask.

And in our current global system, we often **can't tell the difference—because the doctrine of sovereignty treats them as legally identical.**

This is the paradox we face: sovereignty is both **essential and insufficient**, both a foundation and a trap. And if we are to build a global system that works, we must understand **how to preserve its virtues while mitigating its vices.**

The Good Sword: When Sovereignty Liberates

First, let's acknowledge sovereignty's **liberating power**. It is the political expression of **self-determination**—the idea that people should not be ruled by external powers, but by their own laws, cultures, and institutions.

Sovereignty gave birth to:

- **Anti-colonial revolutions,**
- **Indigenous land reclamation,**

- **Democratic transitions,**
- **Constitutional autonomy.**

It protects small nations from being steamrolled by larger ones. It defends cultural minorities from assimilation. It guarantees linguistic, spiritual, and legal diversity in a world that otherwise pushes toward homogenization.

Sovereignty also gives nations the space to **experiment:**

- Bhutan with Gross National Happiness,
- Costa Rica with demilitarization,
- Finland with education reform,
- Rwanda with hybrid legal systems that mix customary and modern justice.

Without sovereignty, all of these would require international permission—or would be subject to external veto.

Sovereignty is what lets the plural flourish.

THE BAD BLADE: When Sovereignty Hides Injustice
But now for the other edge.

Sovereignty is too often invoked not to **liberate people**, but to **evade accountability**. It is the phrase leaders use when:

- Refusing international observers during elections,
- Dismissing war crime allegations,
- Rejecting human rights treaties,
- And silencing journalists as "foreign agents."

Let's look at a few recent examples:

- **Myanmar's military junta** justifies its crackdown on dissent as "an internal matter."
- **Syria's government**, during the civil war, invoked sovereignty to block humanitarian access—even as it bombed its own cities.
- **Saudi Arabia**, facing global outrage over the murder of journalist Jamal Khashoggi, reminded the world it was "an independent kingdom" with its own laws.
- **North Korea**, perhaps the most extreme case, uses sovereignty to rationalize decades of isolation, famine, nuclear threats, and repression.

International institutions—out of respect for sovereignty—often **stand by helplessly**, issuing statements, urging peace, offering aid, but unable to **intervene meaningfully**.

In such moments, sovereignty becomes **a shield for the powerful**, not a sword for the people.

The Legal Dilemma: Equal Recognition, Unequal Reality

International law is built on a beautiful idea: **sovereign equality**. Every country, big or small, gets one vote in the UN General Assembly. Every flag flies at the same height.

But in practice, the system reinforces inequality:

- The **UN Security Council** gives veto power to five countries.
- The **IMF and World Bank** allocate voting shares based on financial contributions.

- International courts pursue **small-country warlords**, while **major powers refuse jurisdiction.**

Meanwhile, sovereignty gives nations the right to:

- Ignore climate targets,
- Reject refugee quotas,
- Evade transnational taxation,
- Or build surveillance regimes that defy international norms.

This is sovereignty **without shared obligation.** It's not cooperation. It's **mutual tolerance of dysfunction.**

THE GOVERNANCE GRIDLOCK: Problems Without Borders, Solutions Without Teeth

Nowhere is this more dangerous than in **borderless crises:**

- **Pandemics** don't care about visa stamps.
- **Climate change** ignores maritime boundaries.
- **Cyberattacks** leap from one nation's server farms to another's power grid.
- **Human trafficking, money laundering, terrorism,** and **AI development** are transnational by nature.

Yet when the world tries to respond—through the WHO, the UN, or climate summits—it is often **blocked by national vetoes, weak compliance mechanisms,** or **refusals to share data** in the name of sovereignty.

The result? Delayed action. Fragmented response. **Preventable damage.**

Sovereignty was designed for a world where threats came from outside the border. Today, **the biggest threats seep through the seams**—and sovereignty, as currently understood, **isn't equipped to stitch them together.**

A New Definition: Sovereignty as Stewardship

So what do we do?

We don't abolish sovereignty. That would be both politically impossible and philosophically unwise.

Instead, we **redefine it**—from a rigid wall into a **relational contract.**

What if sovereignty were understood not just as the **right to rule within borders**, but as the **responsibility to act within a shared world?**

What if sovereignty came with:

- **Duties,** not just rights?
- **Transparency,** not just autonomy?
- **Accountability,** not just freedom from oversight?

We could imagine a world where:

- Nations must **report data transparently during pandemics.**
- Countries lose access to trade privileges if they **ignore environmental treaties.**
- Regional courts can **review digital rights violations**, regardless of where the servers are.
- Sovereignty is **earned and sustained through**

The United States of the World vs. The United Nations 105

responsible membership, not just declared by fiat.

This isn't utopianism. It's **the next stage of sovereignty,** fit for a world of entangled fates.

The Moral Argument: From Power to Responsibility

The old idea of sovereignty was forged in the shadow of empire and conquest. It was a cry for freedom, a wall against domination.

But the next version must be forged in the shadow of climate change, data empires, and pandemics.

It must ask not just:

- "What can I do within my borders?" But also:
- "What impact do my actions have beyond them?"
- "Who pays the price for my negligence?"
- "What do I owe the world in exchange for what I take from it?"

This moral shift is already underway—in grassroots movements, in youth climate activism, in indigenous governance models that see land and community as **shared responsibilities,** not private property.

Sovereignty, at its best, is not the right to ignore the world. It is the platform from which to serve it.

A Bridge to The American Approach to Power and Principle

This concludes the philosophical and historical groundwork for understanding the tension between globalism and nationalism.

Now, we turn our focus to the United States—a nation uniquely positioned and deeply conflicted. A country that helped invent modern global institutions, yet often undermines them. A superpower torn between exceptionalism and entanglement.

6

THE AMERICAN APPROACH TO POWER AND PRINCIPLE

POSTWAR MULTILATERALISM AND THE ARCHITECTURE AMERICA BUILT

America's Dual Identity—Global Leader and Sovereignty Guardian

To understand America's place in the global order, you have to accept two things at once.

First: The United States was the **primary architect of modern multilateralism**. It provided the vision, the money, the military protection, and often the moral language that launched and sustained institutions like the United Nations, the World Bank, the IMF, NATO, and the WTO.

Second: The United States has also been **one of the world's most vocal and consistent critics of global constraints**—frequently refusing to ratify treaties, ignoring international rulings, and invoking sovereignty whenever cooperation became inconvenient.

In short: **America built the system—but never fully moved in.**

This duality isn't just hypocrisy. It's identity. The U.S. sees itself as a **global leader**, but also as a **sovereign exception**—a country meant to shape the world, not be shaped by it.

This tension is woven into every chapter of postwar history. And to grasp how global governance functions (or fails), we must begin by examining how **the most powerful nation on Earth simultaneously supports and undermines the very institutions it helped create.**

The Aftermath of War: From Isolation to Engagement

When World War II ended in 1945, the U.S. stood atop the ashes of Europe and Asia—its industrial base untouched, its economy booming, its military unmatched. But it also carried **the memory of its own isolationism**, a policy that had kept it out of World War I until late, and had failed to prevent the rise of fascism.

Franklin D. Roosevelt and his administration were determined not to repeat that mistake.

Their vision was bold: a postwar world defined not by imperial empires, but by **rules, institutions, and cooperation**—a system that could manage economic recovery, prevent future wars, and create stability through interdependence.

At the center of this vision stood the United States—not as conqueror, but as **benevolent hegemon**.

Thus began the American-led construction of the **liberal international order**.

The UN: Designed in San Francisco, Funded in Washington

The **United Nations Charter**, signed in 1945, bears the unmistakable imprint of American ideals:

- Peace through dialogue,
- Sovereign equality,

- Human rights,
- Collective security.

But it also bore the strategic fingerprints of American realists. The U.S. ensured that the **Security Council would include a veto for the five permanent powers**, effectively giving itself and its WWII allies **a lock on military decisions**.

The General Assembly could debate. The Security Council could act. But only with Washington's consent.

The U.S. located the UN headquarters in **New York City**, hosted its first major meetings, and became its largest financial contributor. Even today, the U.S. provides roughly **22% of the UN's regular budget**.

But this investment came with strings: **influence, leadership, and leverage**. The U.S. helped build the UN not as a surrender of sovereignty, but as an **instrument of global stewardship aligned with American interests**.

The IMF and World Bank: Bretton Woods and the Dollar Order

In 1944, even before the war had ended, delegates from 44 countries met in **Bretton Woods, New Hampshire** to design the postwar economic order. The U.S. dominated the proceedings.

From that summit emerged the **International Monetary Fund (IMF)** and the **World Bank**:

- The IMF would provide short-term balance-of-payment loans to stabilize currencies and promote trade.

- The World Bank would fund long-term development projects to rebuild Europe and, eventually, the Global South.

The **U.S. dollar became the global reserve currency**, pegged to gold (until 1971), and the U.S. held the largest share of votes in both institutions—effectively giving it **veto power** over major decisions.

These weren't neutral global institutions. They were **engineered to reflect U.S. leadership**.

This created a system in which:

- America exported capital and imported influence,
- Allied countries gained stability,
- And developing nations entered into relationships that often came with **Washington-approved conditions**.

It was a **Pax Americana in financial form**.

NATO: Multilateral Security, American Command

In 1949, as Cold War tensions solidified, the U.S. spearheaded the formation of **NATO**—a military alliance binding Western Europe and North America in a mutual defense pact.

The message was clear: if the Soviet Union attacked one member, it would face all. But let's be real—"all" meant **primarily the United States**.

NATO was (and remains) a **multilateral alliance with a unilateral backbone**. The U.S. provides the majority of funding, maintains command of key forces, and hosts most of the nuclear umbrella.

Europe gets protection. The U.S. gets **strategic bases, influence, and political alignment.**

Once again, America designed the institution. But unlike the UN, which tries to speak for the world, NATO was **built to serve the West**—and to **project American power through multilateral legitimacy.**

THE GENERAL AGREEMENT on Tariffs and Trade (GATT): Globalization, American-Style

On the trade front, the U.S. helped launch the **GATT** in 1947, the precursor to the **World Trade Organization (WTO).**

The goal was to reduce tariffs, eliminate trade barriers, and promote **open markets.** For the U.S., this meant:

- A world open to American goods,
- A platform to promote capitalism over communism,
- And a framework that tied other countries' economic fortunes to U.S. consumer demand.

Through GATT and later the WTO, the U.S. used trade policy as **a tool of both diplomacy and deterrence.** Trade with America became the carrot; loss of access became the stick.

Again, sovereignty was preserved on paper. But in practice, the system worked best when **nations aligned with U.S. rules, norms, and market principles.**

. . .

Global Leadership, American Exception

By the 1960s, the pattern was clear: the U.S. was leading a world it helped build—but not always **following the rules it had set.**

It supported international law, but refused to join the International Criminal Court.

It promoted human rights, but backed dictators when convenient.

It preached open markets, but protected its own industries with subsidies and tariffs.

And crucially, it never ceded an inch of its **sovereign decision-making.**

This wasn't a betrayal of the system. It was **part of the design.**

American multilateralism has always been **strategic, selective, and self-protective.** It seeks a world shaped by shared rules—but written in **an American accent.**

The Roots of the Dual Identity

Why this contradiction? Why build a system that you only half trust?

There are several reasons:

1. **American Exceptionalism:** The belief that the U.S. is not just another country, but a unique force for good—entitled to lead without being constrained.
2. **Constitutional Sovereignty:** Deep skepticism of any external body influencing U.S. law or undermining the primacy of the Constitution.
3. **Domestic Politics:** U.S. senators and voters often

resist treaties that limit national action—even when presidents support them.
4. **Strategic Hedging:** The U.S. supports global institutions that advance its interests—and distances itself when those interests are threatened.

This dual identity—**global architect and reluctant participant**—has defined America's role for nearly 80 years.

It's part of why the liberal world order still exists. It's also part of why that order is fraying.

The Contradictions of Selective Sovereignty

To borrow a phrase from constitutional law, the United States treats international cooperation the way it treats federalism: **it's great—when it agrees with the outcome.**

Nowhere is this clearer than in America's approach to sovereignty. The U.S. champions rules-based order, human rights, and international law... so long as those rules don't get in the way of U.S. interests. When they do? Sovereignty becomes the ultimate trump card.

This selective sovereignty isn't just strategic—it's institutionalized. And it helps explain why America's relationship with the international system it helped build has been **complex, conditional, and often contradictory.**

Let's walk through some of the key domains where **America's globalism meets its nationalism head-on.**

1. The Treaty Trap: Ratify, Sign... Then Stall

Let's start with treaties. The U.S. has signed dozens of major international agreements—on human rights, environmental protection, disarmament, and global justice. But when it comes to ratification?

Cue the brakes.

Notable examples:

- **The Convention on the Rights of the Child**
- Ratified by every UN member state—except the United States.
- **The Convention on the Elimination of All Forms of Discrimination Against Women (CEDAW)**
- Signed by the U.S. in 1980. Still not ratified.
- **The Rome Statute establishing the International Criminal Court (ICC)**
- Signed by President Clinton in 2000, "unsigned" by President Bush in 2002.
- **The Kyoto Protocol on Climate Change**
- Signed by the U.S. in 1998. Never submitted for Senate ratification. Eventually rejected outright.

Why the hesitation?

The answer lies in America's **constitutional structure** and **political culture:**

- **Treaties require a two-thirds majority in the Senate**—a steep hurdle in polarized times.
- Many U.S. lawmakers are **skeptical of ceding legal authority to international bodies.**
- And there's a deep-rooted belief in **American exceptionalism**—the idea that the U.S. doesn't need to be bound by others' rules.

In effect, the U.S. often **champions global norms from the outside**, encouraging other countries to comply with treaties it won't ratify itself.

2. Military Might Without Mandate: Unilateral Intervention

Nowhere is selective sovereignty more dramatic than in **military policy**.

The United States frequently acts as the **world's self-appointed sheriff**—intervening in conflicts, conducting drone strikes, enforcing no-fly zones, and engaging in regime change operations **without UN authorization**.

Key examples:

- **Kosovo (1999):** NATO airstrikes led by the U.S. took place without UN Security Council approval.
- **Iraq (2003):** The U.S. invaded based on claims of weapons of mass destruction—against the wishes of the UN and many allies.
- **Libya (2011):** Initially approved by the UN, the U.S.-led NATO operation expanded into regime change territory.
- **Syria (2017–2018):** U.S. airstrikes on chemical weapons facilities occurred without UN approval or a formal congressional declaration of war.

Each of these actions was framed as defending **international norms** (human rights, non-proliferation, protection of civilians). But they were executed through **national sovereignty**, not global consensus.

The result is a doctrine of **"multilateralism when possible, unilateralism when necessary"—a philosophy that has made allies nervous and adversaries cynical.

3. The Sanctions Regime: Economic Pressure Without Global Approval

Beyond military action, the U.S. wields enormous **economic power**—and it uses that power through **unilateral sanctions** that often sidestep international law.

Examples include:

- **Iran:** Sanctions were reimposed in 2018 after the U.S. withdrew from the JCPOA (nuclear deal), despite Iran's compliance with the agreement and opposition from other signatories.
- **Cuba:** Subject to one of the longest embargoes in history—opposed annually by a near-unanimous vote at the UN General Assembly.
- **Venezuela:** The U.S. sanctioned officials and state companies, aiming to pressure regime change.
- **Russia:** U.S.-led sanctions have targeted Russian oligarchs, banks, and industries in response to the Ukraine invasion—often in coordination with allies, but also through national law.

Sanctions allow the U.S. to **project power globally without boots on the ground.** But they also create resentment—especially when applied extraterritorially, affecting third countries and companies not under U.S. jurisdiction.

This is **sovereignty as economic enforcement**, where

the U.S. acts as both judge and enforcer—often beyond the reach of international courts or consensus.

4. Withdrawing When It's Inconvenient

Another hallmark of U.S. selective sovereignty is its **willingness to withdraw** from international agreements when they become politically or economically burdensome.

A short list:

- **UNESCO:** Left in 1984 (rejoined), then left again in 2017. Cited anti-Israel bias.
- **Paris Climate Agreement:** Withdrew under President Trump in 2017. Rejoined under Biden in 2021.
- **UN Human Rights Council:** Withdrew in 2018. Rejoined in 2021.
- **Iran Nuclear Deal:** Abandoned in 2018, despite international verification of Iran's compliance.

These moves send a clear message: **no global agreement is binding if it conflicts with America's domestic politics.**

This has led to a trust deficit: allies grow hesitant to invest politically in deals the U.S. might abandon after the next election. Adversaries see inconsistency as vulnerability. And global institutions find themselves **struggling to function without American participation.**

5. Domestic Courts and International Law: Not Always Compatible

Even within U.S. borders, **international law is treated as advisory, not authoritative.**

The U.S. Constitution is the supreme law of the land. And while treaties are part of federal law, they are **interpreted through American courts,** not international tribunals.

This has led to several clashes:

- **The International Court of Justice (ICJ)** ruled in 2004 that the U.S. had violated the Vienna Convention by denying consular access to foreign nationals on death row. The U.S. Supreme Court disagreed.
- **The U.S. refuses to join the International Criminal Court (ICC)** and has even passed laws authorizing military action to rescue any American tried at The Hague (the so-called "Hague Invasion Act").

This legal insulation reflects a deep skepticism of **global judicial authority.** For American lawmakers, sovereignty means **no judge beyond the Constitution.**

The Consequences of Selective Sovereignty

America's approach has shaped the world. But it has also:

- Undermined the legitimacy of global institutions,
- Empowered other nations to ignore international norms,

- Created **a world of rules—but no consistent rule-maker.**

Countries like China and Russia often cite U.S. unilateralism to justify their own. And developing nations grow skeptical of a system where **the sheriff doesn't wear the badge full-time.**

Even allies complain that U.S. leadership feels more like **conditional cooperation than committed partnership.**

Yet despite these contradictions, many still look to the U.S. to lead—precisely because it built the system, funds the institutions, and commands influence across trade, finance, tech, and military alliances.

Can the U.S. Evolve Its Model?

To move toward a hybrid global model, the U.S. will need to:

- **Embrace international law not just as a tool— but as a commitment.**
- **Balance national autonomy with global responsibility.**
- **Lead by example**, not just by exception.

This doesn't mean giving up sovereignty. It means understanding that **true leadership requires reciprocity.**

Because the world America helped build is still waiting for America to **fully inhabit it**—not just when it's convenient, but when it counts.

. . .

Global Leadership or Global Retreat?

If the 20th century was the "American Century," the 21st might be the "American Question." Not just *what* the United States will do abroad—but *whether* it still wants to lead at all.

In recent years, the debate over America's role in the world has gone from **think tank white papers to kitchen table conversations**, from Senate Foreign Relations hearings to rally chants. "America First," once the slogan of 1930s isolationists, returned to mainstream politics—and stayed.

The result? A fractured consensus. Where once there was broad bipartisan support for U.S. global leadership, now there is **division, fatigue, and uncertainty**. Foreign policy has become **a domestic battlefield**, where global treaties are litmus tests, trade deals are culture wars, and international cooperation is painted alternately as necessary or treasonous.

Let's explore what's driving this tension—and how the debate over globalism versus nationalism plays out **inside America itself.**

1. Polarization on Global Engagement

In the mid-20th century, Democrats and Republicans broadly agreed on America's international role. The Cold War created a shared sense of mission: **defend democracy, contain communism, lead the free world.**

But with the fall of the Berlin Wall and the rise of a multipolar world, **the old consensus cracked.** And by the 21st century, U.S. foreign policy became increasingly **partisan.**

Today:

- **Democrats** generally support multilateralism, climate agreements, human rights treaties, and engagement with global institutions.
- **Republicans**, particularly under the influence of populist movements, have become more skeptical of international law, trade liberalization, and foreign aid.

This polarization shows up in:

- **Debates over the United Nations** (is it a global force for peace—or a corrupt, anti-American bureaucracy?),
- **Funding for WHO or NATO** (investment in global stability—or burden on taxpayers?),
- **Climate treaties** (saving the planet—or kneecapping American jobs?),
- **Trade agreements** (economic growth—or offshoring and cultural dilution?).

In short, foreign policy has become **domestically tribalized.** You can often guess someone's stance on global governance based on **their cable news preferences and Twitter algorithm.**

2. *Populist Reframing of Foreign Policy*

One of the biggest shifts in American political culture has been the **populist reframing of global engagement**—from elite responsibility to elite betrayal.

In this new narrative:

- **Global institutions** = unaccountable bureaucrats who erode national sovereignty.
- **Free trade** = job loss and wage suppression.
- **Climate agreements** = liberal plots to control the economy.
- **Immigration** = porous borders and cultural erosion.
- **Military alliances** = rich countries free-riding on U.S. defense spending.

This view is not new—but it's now **mainstream** in much of American politics.

It was articulated most clearly by former President Donald Trump, who declared at the UN General Assembly in 2019:

"The future does not belong to globalists. The future belongs to patriots."

Whether you agree or not, that line captured the **emotional tenor of the nationalist turn**: The world is dangerous. The system is rigged. The elites don't care about you. It's time to take care of our own.

This message resonated—not just with conservatives, but with working-class Americans across party lines who **feel left behind by globalization**.

3. War Fatigue and the Cost of Empire

Another major force behind the retreat from globalism is **war fatigue**.

After 20 years in Afghanistan, and a controversial war in Iraq, many Americans—across the political spectrum—began to question the idea that **military engagement abroad makes Americans safer at home**.

Poll after poll shows a growing **skepticism of foreign interventions**, particularly when they seem:

- Unending,
- Unclear in mission,
- Or disconnected from core national interests.

This weariness extends beyond military matters. Americans are also questioning:

- **Why the U.S. funds global health programs** when its own healthcare system is fractured.
- **Why it negotiates trade agreements** when factories close and wages stagnate.
- **Why it upholds international norms** when adversaries like China or Russia ignore them.

There is a growing sense that **global leadership is costly —and unrewarded.**

This has fueled calls for a **"foreign policy for the middle class"**, a phrase coined under the Biden administration to signal a pivot toward domestic benefit.

The implication is clear: **global engagement must serve American prosperity**, or it will lose American support.

4. *The Rise of Progressive Internationalism*

At the same time, another current is emerging—especially among younger Americans: **progressive internationalism.**

This worldview seeks a **global order that is more equitable, inclusive, and democratic—but one that also **holds the U.S. accountable.**

It prioritizes:

- Climate justice,
- Racial and gender equity,
- Global labor rights,
- Demilitarization,
- And **reforming global institutions to reflect post-colonial realities.**

Progressive internationalists are often critical of both:

- Traditional liberal interventionism (seen as arrogant or imperial),
- And nationalist retrenchment (seen as xenophobic or regressive).

They want a new globalism—**rooted in solidarity, not dominance.** And they argue that America's moral leadership must come from **example, not exceptionalism.**

This movement remains politically marginal—but its influence is growing in **NGOs, youth activism, and global climate negotiations.**

5. *The Electoral Whiplash Effect*

One of the biggest challenges for global institutions is **America's inconsistency.**

Because the U.S. political system swings so drastically between administrations, its global commitments are often **reversible, unpredictable, and short-term.**

The United States of the World vs. The United Nations   125

- **Climate Policy:** Join Paris (Obama) → Leave Paris (Trump) → Rejoin Paris (Biden).
- **Iran Nuclear Deal:** Negotiate (Obama) → Withdraw (Trump) → Attempt renegotiation (Biden).
- **WHO:** Fund and support (Bush/Obama) → Defund and withdraw (Trump) → Rejoin and fund (Biden).
- **NATO:** Central pillar of foreign policy → "Obsolete" → Renewed commitment.

This inconsistency has weakened America's credibility. Allies now ask:

- Will the U.S. uphold its commitments?
- Will the next president tear them up?
- Can global agreements survive four-year electoral cycles?

This is not a partisan problem. It is a **systemic challenge** for a hybrid global model that depends on **stable leadership and policy continuity.**

6. What Does the American Public Want?

Surveys reveal a nuanced picture:

- A majority of Americans support **international cooperation** in principle.
- Most favor **alliances like NATO.**
- Many believe **the U.S. should play a leading or major role in world affairs.**

- But there is deep skepticism of **military interventions, economic globalization,** and **outsourcing sovereignty.**

In other words: Americans want to lead, but not bleed. They want influence, but not interference. They want cooperation, but not submission.

This ambivalence lies at the heart of **America's hybrid identity**—and it will shape the next era of global governance.

The Way Forward—Balancing Sovereignty and Leadership

Let's be clear: the United States cannot—and should not—abandon its sovereignty. But neither can it afford to treat the global system as a buffet, picking the dishes it likes and ignoring the bill at the end.

The world America helped build is entering a new phase: multipolar, digital, ecological, and fragile. In this moment, **American leadership matters more than ever—not as dominance, but as stewardship.**

To lead in this era, the United States must evolve from a **hegemon reluctant to share rules** into a **partner committed to co-creating them.**

This doesn't mean yielding to every international institution or submitting to unchecked global authority. It means **investing in a principled, adaptive hybrid model**—one that harmonizes sovereignty with solidarity, and leadership with legitimacy.

Let's explore how that future might look.

1. Embrace Sovereignty as Responsibility, Not Immunity

The first shift is philosophical: **sovereignty should be understood as a responsibility, not a shield.**

That means:

- **Participating in international courts and legal frameworks**, not ignoring them when inconvenient.
- **Accepting peer review**, especially on human rights, environmental standards, and democratic processes.
- **Complying with treaties the U.S. signs**, and working to ratify those it morally endorses.

Just as the Constitution binds states within the U.S., so too should **the international order bind nations—not absolutely, but meaningfully.**

This would signal that the U.S. respects law not only as a domestic virtue, but as a global good.

2. Make Multilateralism a Strategic Priority

For too long, multilateralism has been treated as a **secondary tool**, useful only when bilateral deals fall short.

That needs to change.

The U.S. should:

- **Strengthen the United Nations** by advocating Security Council reform, increasing funding for

peacekeeping and development, and supporting the institutional independence of bodies like the WHO and the International Criminal Court.
- **Lead in climate diplomacy** not only through pledges, but through enforcement mechanisms that reward compliance and penalize backsliding.
- **Invest in regional partnerships,** such as the African Union, ASEAN, and Latin American coalitions, ensuring the Global South has real agency in shaping global norms.

Strategic multilateralism is not weakness—it's how influence becomes durable and cooperative power becomes **a force multiplier.**

3. Prioritize Domestic Renewal as Foreign Policy

Global leadership begins at home. The hybrid model depends on credibility. And credibility depends on consistency between **what a country does abroad and how it functions within.**

The U.S. must:

- **Invest in infrastructure, education, and democratic resilience**—showing that liberal democracy can still deliver.
- **Fight corruption and disinformation domestically,** rather than just condemning it abroad.
- **Rebuild civic trust,** so that Americans once again see international cooperation as serving their values and interests—not eroding them.

This is the heart of a "foreign policy for the middle class": not isolationism, but **integration that uplifts domestic well-being.**

Because a nation fractured within cannot lead beyond.

4. Reimagine Trade and Technology as Tools for Shared Prosperity

Global trade has lifted millions from poverty. But it has also devastated communities, hollowed out industries, and fueled political backlash in the U.S.

To move forward, the U.S. must lead on:

- **Ethical globalization:** Centering labor rights, environmental sustainability, and corporate accountability in trade agreements.
- **Data governance and digital sovereignty:** Creating frameworks that protect privacy, ensure platform transparency, and curb digital authoritarianism.
- **Tech diplomacy:** Coordinating AI standards, space policy, and biotechnology ethics through forums like the G7, the OECD, and new tech-focused international bodies.

In this space, the U.S. has both the innovation and the convening power to **shape norms that preserve sovereignty while encouraging interoperability.**

5. Co-Lead a New Global Compact on Governance Reform

Here is where America can show bold leadership: by

launching and co-leading an international effort to **rethink global governance for the 21st century.**

Call it a **Global Democracy and Cooperation Compact**, with three key goals:

- **Modernize global institutions** (UN, WTO, IMF) to reflect 21st-century demographics, economics, and geopolitics.
- **Define shared responsibilities**—on climate, pandemics, migration, and cybersecurity—through enforceable, flexible agreements.
- **Codify a universal framework of rights and representation** that protects cultures and communities while ensuring accountability.

The U.S. would lead **not as the boss**, but as the **initiator of a new social contract between nations**—modeled on pluralism, subsidiarity, and subsidiarity (local solutions first, global coordination when needed).

It would be the geopolitical equivalent of updating a constitution—not to erase the past, but to make the future livable.

6. Model Humility as Strength

Perhaps the most transformative shift would be cultural: **modeling humility as a form of power.**

This means acknowledging past mistakes:

- Support for dictators during the Cold War.
- The invasion of Iraq.
- The destabilizing effects of economic policy in the Global South.

It means listening more, dictating less. Collaborating more, exceptionalizing less. And admitting that **even the most powerful democracy can learn from others**—from New Zealand's pandemic response to Costa Rica's environmental policy.

True leadership doesn't pretend to be perfect. It **invites others into a process of shared growth.**

The Hybrid Role America Must Play

America doesn't need to choose between globalism and sovereignty.

Instead, it can become the **prototype of a hybrid power:**

- Big enough to lead,
- Wise enough to collaborate,
- Humble enough to reform,
- And principled enough to follow the rules it helped write.

In doing so, the U.S. could set the standard for a new kind of world order—not post-American, but **post-imperial.** One where strength is measured not by dominance, but by **how many nations rise with you.**

A Bridge to Chapter 7: Unilateral Action and Selective Engagement

In the next chapter, we dive deeper into the **darker side of U.S. foreign policy**—how its pattern of unilateral military action, economic coercion, and exceptionalist ideology has undermined the very multilateral order it claims to uphold.

Because to build a better future, we must confront the past—not as guilt, but as **an honest reckoning with the costs of leading alone.**

7

UNILATERAL ACTION AND SELECTIVE ENGAGEMENT

The History of U.S. Interventions Without Global Consensus

IF GLOBAL COOPERATION is the promise of peace through partnership, then unilateral action is **the backdoor key America often uses when the front door of diplomacy won't open fast enough.**

Throughout modern history, the United States has acted alone—or with a coalition it assembled independently—more often than it has waited for full international approval. Whether driven by national security, moral outrage, or strategic opportunism, the U.S. has consistently demonstrated that while it values multilateralism, it is **not constrained by it.**

This habit has consequences: for international law, global trust, and the legitimacy of institutions like the United Nations. And yet, these actions have also been defended as **necessary, decisive, and in some cases, effective**.

This part of the chapter explores the most consequential examples of **unilateral U.S. interventions**, the justifications behind them, and the patterns they reveal about **America's approach to global engagement when consensus fails or is too slow to matter.**

1. Korea, 1950: Multilateral Mandate—But U.S. Command

Let's begin with a semi-exception: the Korean War. In 1950, when North Korea invaded the South, the United Nations **did authorize military intervention**—but only because the Soviet Union was boycotting the Security Council at the time.

The result was technically a **UN-led mission**, but in practice, it was a **U.S.-led war**:

- The United States contributed the vast majority of troops.
- General Douglas MacArthur, an American, led the coalition.
- Strategic decisions were largely made in Washington.

This set a precedent: even when multilateral approval is secured, the U.S. often remains **the primary executor and decision-maker**, blurring the line between **collective action and American command**.

2. Vietnam, 1960s–70s: No Mandate, No Apology

The Vietnam War was a textbook case of **unilateral escalation in the absence of international consensus**.

- No global institution approved America's deepening involvement.
- The war expanded into Cambodia and Laos without international authorization.
- Domestic opposition grew, as did global condemnation.

The rationale? **Containment of communism**, framed as a global good. But the process bypassed international norms—and the aftermath severely damaged America's moral standing abroad.

Vietnam taught a hard lesson: **acting without allies or mandates can win battles, but lose legitimacy.**

3. Grenada, 1983: A Quick Strike with Lasting Doubts

In 1983, President Ronald Reagan ordered the invasion of Grenada—a tiny Caribbean nation—after a Marxist coup raised fears of Soviet expansion and the safety of American medical students.

The operation was swift. The U.S. claimed success. But the United Nations and several key allies (including the U.K.) criticized the move as a **violation of sovereignty** and **an unnecessary escalation**.

This was a clear case of **preemptive action without global endorsement**. It also signaled that **the U.S. was willing to act in its immediate sphere of influence** with or without international blessing.

Grenada may have been small. But it demonstrated **the asymmetry of U.S. power—and its readiness to act unilaterally when time, trust, or treaty obligations felt like obstacles.**

. . .

4. Iraq, 2003: The Hinge Point of Global Trust

Perhaps no U.S. intervention better illustrates the pitfalls of unilateralism than the 2003 invasion of Iraq.

- The Bush administration claimed Saddam Hussein possessed weapons of mass destruction.
- Despite months of UN weapons inspections, no such weapons were found.
- The U.S. pressed for a second UN Security Council resolution to authorize military action—but when it became clear that France, Russia, and others would oppose it, the U.S. led a **"coalition of the willing"** and invaded anyway.

The consequences were immense:

- Over 4,000 U.S. troops and hundreds of thousands of Iraqis died.
- The war destabilized the region, arguably contributing to the rise of ISIS.
- Global protests erupted.
- U.S. credibility—particularly in Europe and the Global South—**collapsed**.

The Iraq War marked a turning point: many nations began to see **multilateral institutions as tools to be used or discarded based on U.S. interests**, rather than forums for genuine global consensus.

It wasn't just the war—it was the **method** that shook the world.

5. Libya, 2011: A Multilateral Cover for a Unilateral Pivot

Initially framed as a **UN-backed humanitarian mission**, the 2011 intervention in Libya quickly expanded into **regime change**.

- The UN authorized a no-fly zone to protect civilians during the Libyan civil war.
- NATO, with heavy U.S. support, carried out the mission.
- But the campaign escalated, leading to the death of Muammar Gaddafi and the collapse of state institutions.

Though not a purely unilateral action, Libya highlighted how **the U.S. and its allies could reinterpret a limited mandate into an expansive military goal.**

Critics accused Washington of:

- Overstepping the UN resolution,
- Failing to plan for postwar stabilization,
- Creating a power vacuum filled by militias and chaos.

Libya reinforced global skepticism: **even when the U.S. enters multilaterally, it may act unilaterally within the mission.**

6. Syria: Red Lines and Shadow Wars

Syria represents a different kind of unilateralism—**covert, selective, and ambiguous.**

- In 2013, President Obama declared a "red line" on Assad's use of chemical weapons.

- When Assad crossed it, the U.S. did not secure UN action—partly due to Russian veto power.
- Covert operations, drone strikes, and targeted air raids followed—without congressional approval and without a broader legal mandate.

Meanwhile, the U.S. supported rebel groups, clashed with ISIS, and navigated a battlefield crowded with Russian, Iranian, Turkish, and Kurdish forces.

Syria illustrates a new model of U.S. engagement:

- **Low visibility,**
- **High stakes,**
- **Minimal legal oversight.**

Unilateralism in the age of drones and special operations isn't about grand declarations. It's about **unannounced realities.**

7. Economic Warfare: Sanctions Without Borders

Beyond the battlefield, the U.S. increasingly relies on **economic unilateralism:**

- **Sanctions on Iran**, even when European allies object.
- **Export bans** on Huawei and Chinese tech companies.
- **Tariffs on allies and adversaries alike,** with or without WTO approval.

These tools are deployed through:

- The **Office of Foreign Assets Control (OFAC)**,
- Presidential executive orders,
- And emergency economic powers.

Unlike military action, economic warfare can be **prolonged, politically invisible, and devastating**.

Yet it also erodes multilateral trade norms, encourages **de-dollarization**, and fuels **anti-American resentment** —even among nominal partners.

WHY DOES the U.S. Act Unilaterally?
There are several motivations:

1. **Speed:** Multilateralism is slow. Crises are fast.
2. **Control:** Partnerships dilute decision-making.
3. **Strategic Clarity:** Acting alone avoids compromise.
4. **Domestic Politics:** Congress often blocks treaties but permits unilateral executive action.
5. **Global Distrust:** If others won't act, the U.S. feels forced to.

But these come at a price:

- Loss of **international legitimacy**,
- Institutional erosion,
- Blowback and instability,
- Isolation in future crises,
- And **diminished moral authority**.

The Paradox of Power

The paradox is this: the U.S. has the power to act alone—but its interests are best served when **others follow**. Yet unilateral action **reduces the willingness of others to follow**, creating a feedback loop of **declining trust and increased burden**.

To sustain leadership, the U.S. must learn the art of **coercive cooperation**—leading decisively while still honoring **multilateral process and institutional integrity**.

In other words: be the first mover, not the only one moving.

Economic Power as a Tool of Sovereignty

Military might may turn heads, but economic might **moves the world**—sometimes with a handshake, sometimes with a chokehold.

The United States has long understood this. As the center of the global financial system, the U.S. doesn't just play by the rules—it often **writes them, enforces them, and updates them without asking**. And while military action draws headlines, it's economic policy that shapes long-term behavior—by punishing adversaries, incentivizing allies, and projecting sovereignty **through spreadsheets instead of soldiers**.

In this part of the chapter, we examine how America has turned **economic infrastructure into geopolitical leverage**, how it balances cooperation with coercion, and what this strategy reveals about **the new frontier of unilateral action in a globalized economy**.

. . .

1. The Dollar: Global Currency, American Control

Let's start with the keystone: the U.S. dollar.

- Roughly **60% of global foreign exchange reserves** are held in dollars.
- Most international trade, including **nearly all oil sales,** is denominated in dollars.
- The **SWIFT system** for international bank transfers depends on U.S.-based correspondent banking.
- American financial institutions are deeply embedded in **cross-border transactions**, giving the U.S. government **unmatched visibility into global money flows.**

This dominance gives the U.S. a **powerful lever**: the ability to **cut off individuals, companies, and even entire nations from the global economy** by denying them access to U.S. banking infrastructure.

No tanks. No troops. Just a Treasury Department keyboard.

This is **economic sovereignty writ large**—a sovereignty so powerful that it can impose legal consequences **on non-U.S. actors operating outside U.S. borders.**

2. Sanctions: The New Foreign Policy Default

Over the last three decades, **sanctions have become Washington's go-to policy tool:**

- Iran, North Korea, Venezuela, Cuba, Russia, China—the list grows longer each year.

- Sanctions can target **governments, companies, individuals, banks, and sectors.**
- They can be **comprehensive** (embargoes) or **targeted** ("smart sanctions" on elites).
- They can be **unilateral, bilateral,** or **multilateral** —but most often start with the U.S. acting **alone.**

Why are sanctions so attractive?

- **Low domestic cost** (no troops, no political bloodshed).
- **High symbolic value** (they "do something").
- **Rapid deployment** through executive authority.
- **Scalable pressure**—sanctions can be escalated or lifted flexibly.

But they also come with **significant downsides:**

- **Civilian suffering** in target countries,
- **Rally-around-the-flag effects** that strengthen authoritarian regimes,
- **Sanctions fatigue,** where overuse diminishes impact,
- And the creation of **alternative financial systems** to bypass U.S. control.

In the long run, excessive sanctions risk **undermining the very centrality of the dollar** they rely on.

3. Extraterritorial Reach: America's Legal Sovereignty Without Borders

What makes U.S. sanctions particularly controversial is

their **extraterritoriality**.

Take the case of:

- **European companies fined for doing business with Iran** after the U.S. reimposed sanctions.
- **Banks in France, Germany, and Japan punished for violating U.S. export controls**—even when their actions were legal in their home countries.
- **Huawei's CFO arrested in Canada** at the request of U.S. authorities, sparking a geopolitical standoff with China.

The message is clear: if you want to do business in U.S. dollars—or through U.S. financial institutions—you're bound by U.S. law, **even if you're not American.**

This raises profound questions:

- Where does sovereignty end?
- Can one country's domestic law govern the world?
- And if so, who decides the rules?

For critics, this is **"weaponized interdependence"**—using the very systems of globalization to enforce national will.

4. Trade Policy as Geostrategy

Trade is often described as a win-win engine of growth. But for the U.S., it's increasingly **a tool of selective engagement:**

- The **Trans-Pacific Partnership (TPP)** was abandoned in 2017, despite years of multilateral negotiation, because it was seen as a threat to U.S. workers.
- The **U.S.–China trade war** introduced sweeping tariffs under the guise of national security.
- The U.S. has used **Section 301 and Section 232** laws to impose unilateral tariffs, often bypassing WTO procedures.
- Export controls on **semiconductors, AI chips, and critical tech** are used to contain Chinese innovation.

Trade has become less about comparative advantage, and more about **strategic advantage**:

- Who controls the supply chain?
- Who writes the standards?
- Who benefits from economic dependencies?

This is **economic nationalism in action**—not through autarky, but through **selective decoupling and re-shoring**.

5. Foreign Aid: Strategic Altruism

Even America's most cooperative economic tool—**foreign aid**—comes with strings.

Yes, the U.S. supports development, health, and humanitarian relief around the world. But much of its aid:

- Advances **strategic goals** (e.g., supporting allies in conflict zones),

- Comes with **political conditions** (e.g., promoting democracy or restricting abortion services),
- Or is tied to **purchases from U.S. companies.**

Aid becomes a **carrot**—just as sanctions are the stick.

While aid can be deeply impactful (think PEPFAR's role in fighting AIDS), it also reinforces **America's position as both patron and gatekeeper** in the global system.

This dual role—**helper and enforcer**—complicates perceptions of U.S. intent.

6. The Digital Dollar and Future Frontiers

Looking forward, the next arena of economic power will be **digital**.

- The U.S. is exploring a **central bank digital currency (CBDC)**—a programmable, trackable dollar.
- Cryptocurrencies challenge the centrality of state currencies—and U.S. control.
- China's **digital yuan** is being tested as a competitor to dollar dominance.
- Decentralized finance (DeFi) threatens to create parallel systems outside regulatory reach.

How the U.S. manages this transition will shape:

- **Global financial inclusion,**
- **Anti-corruption efforts,**
- **Privacy and surveillance norms,**
- And the balance between **economic sovereignty and interoperability.**

The key challenge? Designing systems that protect **national interests** while allowing **shared governance of digital infrastructure**.

7. Repercussions and Backlash

As the U.S. continues to exercise economic power unilaterally, it risks:

- **Pushing allies to develop alternative systems** (e.g., INSTEX in Europe),
- **Fueling efforts to de-dollarize global trade** (led by China and Russia),
- **Triggering retaliatory sanctions** or legal frameworks (EU's Digital Markets Act, for example),
- And deepening perceptions that America uses globalization as **a weapon, not a commons**.

Ironically, the more the U.S. flexes economic power, the more it **undermines the global system it relies on**.

This is the sovereignty trap: **overreach invites resistance, and resistance fragments cooperation**.

Toward Cooperative Economic *Power*

To move forward, the U.S. must:

- Use economic leverage **judiciously**, not reflexively.
- Support **multilateral financial institutions** with greater inclusion for emerging economies.

- Collaborate on **digital currency standards, anti-money laundering**, and **tax transparency** through democratic forums.
- Balance **national control with shared stewardship** of global economic infrastructure.

This is not weakness. It's wisdom. Because true economic leadership isn't about domination. It's about **building systems others want to belong to**.

Selective Humanitarianism and the Morality of Engagement

For a country that proudly champions human rights, liberty, and the defense of the oppressed, the United States has an uncanny habit of **helping some and ignoring others**—sometimes in the same breath.

This is the uncomfortable reality of American humanitarianism: it is often **selective, strategic, and asymmetrical**. Not because the people involved are unworthy of help, but because **sovereignty, domestic politics, media visibility, and geostrategic value** tend to dictate who receives aid, intervention, or attention—and who doesn't.

This section explores how the U.S. makes these decisions, what narratives it uses to justify them, and what this selectivity reveals about the **moral calculus of foreign policy in a sovereign world**.

1. Rwanda vs. Bosnia: Who Gets the Marines?

Let's rewind to the 1990s.

- In **Bosnia**, a European conflict that erupted after the collapse of Yugoslavia, the U.S. eventually intervened militarily under NATO, helping end ethnic cleansing and broker the **Dayton Accords**.
- In **Rwanda**, a genocide unfolded in 1994, killing 800,000 people in just 100 days—mostly ethnic Tutsis—while the U.S. and other powers largely stood by.

Why the difference?

- Bosnia was in **Europe**, near NATO territory, with implications for European stability.
- Rwanda was in **central Africa**, with minimal strategic impact on U.S. interests.
- Bosnia featured **white, Christian populations**, which (uncomfortably) shaped media and political attention.
- Rwanda's crisis was harder to explain, harder to access, and easier to dismiss as "tribal violence."

The U.S. has since apologized for inaction in Rwanda. But the lesson remains: **the value of lives abroad is often filtered through strategic lenses.**

2. *Syria vs. Yemen: Whose Suffering Counts?*
Fast-forward to the 2010s.

- In **Syria**, the U.S. funneled billions in humanitarian aid, supported rebel groups, launched airstrikes against Assad, and debated regime change.

- In **Yemen**, where a Saudi-led coalition (with U.S. support) contributed to what the UN calls the **worst humanitarian crisis in the world**, America's role was more muted.

The U.S.:

- Provided intelligence and logistical support to the Saudi military,
- Approved arms sales,
- Hesitated to confront Riyadh, a close energy and counterterrorism ally.

Meanwhile, millions of Yemenis faced famine, cholera, and displacement.

Syria's humanitarian appeal aligned (to a point) with U.S. geopolitical objectives: containing Iran and Russia, and checking Assad's brutality. Yemen's crisis was **inconveniently tied to an ally.**

Once again, **morality was tempered by allegiance.**

3. Ukraine vs. Palestine: Whose Resistance is Supported?

In 2022, when Russia invaded Ukraine, the U.S. and its allies:

- Rallied to Ukraine's defense,
- Imposed sweeping sanctions on Russia,
- Sent weapons, aid, and diplomatic support.

Ukrainians were rightly celebrated for their resistance. And the humanitarian response was swift: refugees welcomed, aid pledged, solidarity expressed.

In contrast:

- **Palestinian suffering**—under decades of occupation, blockade, and cyclical violence—has not received the same consistency of U.S. empathy or intervention.
- The U.S. continues to provide **unconditional aid to Israel,** including military assistance.
- Calls for Palestinian statehood or accountability for human rights violations are **often blocked or vetoed in international forums**—frequently by the U.S.

Why the discrepancy?

- Ukraine was attacked by a clear aggressor (Russia), seen as a systemic rival.
- Palestinians are stateless, and their struggle is entangled in U.S. domestic politics, pro-Israel lobbies, and post-9/11 security narratives.
- The U.S. views Israel as a critical regional partner; Palestine is seen (by some) as a diplomatic risk.

The result: **a selective moral lens,** where resistance in one place is freedom, and in another, extremism.

4. Refugee Policies: Who Is Welcomed?

The U.S. has long seen itself as a beacon for the "huddled masses yearning to breathe free." But not all masses are treated equally.

- **Ukrainian refugees** in 2022 were granted rapid entry, with bipartisan support and expedited legal pathways.
- **Afghan refugees**, after America's withdrawal in 2021, faced bureaucratic delays, vetting backlogs, and political backlash.
- **Syrian, Central American, and African migrants** have often been detained, deported, or denied entry under strict asylum policies.

Public sympathy varies based on:

- **Race and religion**,
- **Perceived alignment with U.S. interests**,
- **Media coverage and visibility**,
- And **domestic political narratives** about crime, terrorism, or economic strain.

In short, **humanitarianism is filtered through the lens of perceived familiarity and strategic value.**

5. Foreign Aid: Who Gets the Check?

The U.S. provides **more foreign aid in absolute terms than any other nation**. But where does it go?

Top recipients include:

- Israel,
- Egypt,
- Jordan,
- Afghanistan (prior to 2021),
- Ukraine.

These are not necessarily the poorest nations—but they are **strategically important:**

- Israel and Egypt help maintain regional stability.
- Jordan manages refugee flows and borders conflict zones.
- Ukraine is now the front line of Western resistance to Russia.

Meanwhile, countries facing **massive humanitarian crises**—like Haiti, South Sudan, or Congo—receive less sustained aid and fewer political visits.

This is not to question the value of U.S. aid—but to note its **strategic selectivity.**

6. Narratives of Moral Exceptionalism

To understand how this selectivity is justified, we must look at **the stories America tells itself:**

- That it is the **"indispensable nation"**, with a unique moral calling.
- That it **stands for freedom, democracy, and dignity**—but must act wisely, not sentimentally.
- That **realism sometimes requires hard choices**, and that **imperfection doesn't negate intention.**

These narratives allow America to **embrace moral action when it aligns with interest**, and to **justify inaction when it does not.**

This is the essence of **selective humanitarianism:** not the absence of compassion, but the **ranking of compassion beneath strategy.**

7. Toward a Coherent Humanitarian Ethic

So, what would it mean for the U.S. to embrace a more **consistent, principled humanitarian posture**?

It might look like:

- **Universal standards** for intervention, aid, and asylum—tied to human need, not geopolitical benefit.
- **Increased funding for under-resourced crises**, even when cameras aren't rolling.
- **Decoupling foreign aid from military priorities**, allowing development and diplomacy to stand on their own.
- **Reforming domestic asylum systems** to reflect global responsibility, not partisan volatility.

It would also require reexamining the idea that **sovereignty always trumps suffering**. Because if humanitarianism is always contingent on borders, then its very purpose is undermined.

The Limits of Exceptionalism

EXCEPTIONALISM IS, at its best, an invitation to lead by example. At its worst, it becomes a reason to **refuse accountability**. In the foreign policy lexicon of the United States, "exceptionalism" has functioned like a well-worn passport: granting access to praise, power, and occasionally, **a free pass on the global stage**.

But in a world where **global threats demand cooperative action**, the concept of American exceptionalism is increasingly under strain. As nations rise, institutions groan under the weight of 20th-century assumptions, and climate, pandemics, and AI disregard national borders, we are forced to confront a fundamental tension: **How long can the United States remain both rule-maker and rule-breaker before the rules no longer matter?**

Let's examine the origins, expressions, contradictions, and consequences of this idea.

1. The Origins of American Exceptionalism

The term "American exceptionalism" dates back at least to **Alexis de Tocqueville,** who in the 1830s observed that the U.S. was a "distinctive" democracy—without a feudal past, with a frontier spirit, and with a civic religiosity all its own.

Over time, this uniqueness hardened into ideology:

- The belief that **America was not only different, but better.**
- That it had a **special role to play in history**—to defend liberty, oppose tyranny, and promote democracy.

During the Cold War, this identity was sharpened into a **global mission:** to lead the "free world" against communism. American leadership became both **a moral obligation and a strategic imperative.**

And post–Cold War, it evolved again—into the assumption that **globalization itself bore an American accent.**

2. The Language of Superiority

You'll hear exceptionalism in every corner of the U.S.

political spectrum:

- **"The city on a hill"** – Ronald Reagan quoting John Winthrop.
- **"The indispensable nation"** – Madeleine Albright.
- **"The leader of the free world"** – a title every U.S. president assumes by default.

These phrases are aspirational, but they also carry baggage:

- They imply **moral clarity** in a morally ambiguous world.
- They conflate **capacity with virtue**—as though power automatically implies wisdom.
- And they create **resistance among allies** who see American leadership as **preachy, hypocritical, or self-serving**.

As a result, exceptionalism often **undermines the very partnerships it seeks to inspire.**

3. Exceptionalism and the Double Standard
Exceptionalism permits the U.S. to do things it criticizes in others:

- Oppose the **International Criminal Court**, while demanding justice for war crimes elsewhere.
- Promote **free trade**, while subsidizing domestic agriculture and imposing tariffs.

- Champion **democracy**, while supporting autocratic allies.
- Demand **UN compliance**, while ignoring its resolutions.
- Frame interventions as humanitarian, while condemning others for the same.

The rationale is always familiar: **we're different.** Our motives are purer. Our history is exceptional. But over time, that logic **frays the legitimacy of global governance.**

Other countries notice. And they begin to ask: If the most powerful country doesn't follow the rules, **why should we?**

4. Domestic Exceptionalism Shapes Foreign Policy

The problem isn't just international. American exceptionalism is deeply domestic:

- The Constitution is often treated as **not only a foundational document, but a perfect one.**
- Courts are wary of accepting international law as precedent.
- Politicians fear **being seen as surrendering sovereignty** to foreign bodies.

This shapes public attitudes:

- Most Americans believe the U.S. **has a unique moral role** in the world.
- But they also **resist joining global institutions**, particularly those with enforcement powers.

So the U.S. becomes a **reluctant globalist**—wanting to lead, but not be led.

This contradiction is unsustainable in a system that increasingly depends on **shared governance, shared standards, and shared sacrifice.**

5. When Exceptionalism Backfires

There are moments when exceptionalism does real damage.

Iraq (2003):

The U.S. believed it could remake a nation through force —because **its values were inherently superior.** The result: destabilization, distrust, and decades of blowback.

Climate Change:

For years, the U.S. delayed action, arguing that its economy was unique, its energy needs different. This **justified inaction**, while global emissions soared.

The Global Pandemic:

America's refusal to coordinate early COVID responses, its withdrawal from WHO, and its **vaccine nationalism** all revealed the downside of **self-centric crisis management.**

Each time, exceptionalism made it harder for the U.S. to **work collaboratively**, to **listen**, and to **build trust.**

6. Can There Be Ethical Exceptionalism?

Not all exceptionalism is toxic.

It can serve as a source of:

- **Inspiration** ("If we led the way on civil rights, can we lead on climate?"),

- **Innovation** ("Can we model a post-carbon economy?"),
- **Democratic renewal** ("Can our institutions evolve and still inspire?").

But to be healthy, exceptionalism must be **earned, not assumed**. It must be:

- **Reflective**, not arrogant.
- **Self-critical**, not self-congratulatory.
- **A standard to live up to**, not an excuse to opt out.

A humble exceptionalism—a **principled leadership** based not on moral superiority, but **moral commitment**—could be the key to America's future role in the world.

7. *Letting Go of the Myth—Without Losing the Mission*

The real challenge isn't abolishing exceptionalism. It's **transforming it**.

Instead of claiming that America is "better," we could say:

- We are **learning faster**.
- We are **listening harder**.
- We are **more willing to take responsibility** for the system we built.

This would mean:

- **Joining and strengthening** international courts and agreements,
- **Supporting institutional reform** to reflect new global realities,
- **Leading by constraint,** not just capability,
- And embracing **a leadership role within a network, not above it.**

That's not surrender. That's maturity.

That's what leadership will look like in the next era: not a singular "American century," but a **shared global chapter**, authored together.

A Bridge to Chapter 8: Global Engagement on U.S. Terms

In the next chapter, we'll examine how the United States has still managed to **shape multilateral institutions to its liking**—leading not by relinquishing power, but by **structuring systems that reflect its interests and norms**, even when it participates.

This is the other side of selective engagement: not avoidance, but **conditional cooperation.**

8

GLOBAL ENGAGEMENT ON U.S. TERMS

Leading the Table—How the U.S. Shapes Multilateral Institutions

LET'S BE HONEST: while some countries struggle to get a seat at the global table, the United States often **builds the table, sets the menu, and reserves the right to send the waiter home if the service isn't fast enough.**

This is not a critique. It's an acknowledgment of fact. For over 75 years, the United States has been the **chief architect, financier, and guardian** of the postwar international order. But what's equally true is that America has consistently **designed that order to reflect its own values, institutions, and geostrategic calculus.**

Global engagement for the U.S. is rarely an exercise in compromise. It's an exercise in **alignment**—bringing others into a framework that largely mirrors American constitutional principles, market norms, and legal procedures.

This is the story of how the U.S. has led **not from within**

The United States of the World vs. The United Nations 161

the crowd, but **from the front of the room,** and why that model—while powerful—faces increasing challenges in a multipolar world.

1. Institutional Design: The Postwar Blueprint

The post–World War II era offered the U.S. a rare moment of **uncontested authority**. With Europe in ruins, Asia rebuilding, and colonial empires unraveling, America had the credibility, capital, and vision to **redesign the global architecture**.

What emerged was a system based on:

- **Liberal economics** (Bretton Woods institutions: IMF, World Bank),
- **Collective security** (United Nations, NATO),
- **Rule of law** (UN Charter, international conventions),
- And **moral universalism** (human rights frameworks).

But let's be clear: these systems **reflected American ideals**:

- Free enterprise over state planning,
- Republican democracy over monarchy or authoritarianism,
- English-language diplomacy over French, Arabic, or Mandarin norms,
- A bias for **federalism, checks and balances,** and **meritocratic governance**.

The U.S. wasn't just joining a new world—it was **writing**

the software for it.

2. NATO: The Most American Multilateral Alliance

NATO is often hailed as the most successful military alliance in history. But it is also, in structure and function, the most **U.S.-centric.**

- The Supreme Allied Commander Europe (SACEUR) is **always an American general.**
- The U.S. contributes the majority of NATO's budget and firepower.
- While NATO decisions require consensus, **U.S. preferences shape the agenda**—from expansion to intervention mandates.

NATO has allowed the U.S. to **project military power under a multilateral flag,** giving strategic operations a veneer of shared responsibility—even when **Washington is in the driver's seat.**

This has been effective. But it also means NATO's legitimacy is often tethered to American credibility. When the U.S. stumbles—as in Iraq or Afghanistan—**NATO's cohesion wobbles too.**

3. The Bretton Woods Twins: IMF and World Bank

The **International Monetary Fund** and the **World Bank** were designed to stabilize currencies and support reconstruction—but their deeper purpose was to ensure that **the postwar global economy aligned with American capitalism.**

Here's how:

- Voting shares are based on financial contributions—**the U.S. has the largest share**, and often effective veto power.
- Leadership follows an informal rule: **an American heads the World Bank, a European the IMF.**
- Policy advice often reflects the Washington Consensus: deregulation, privatization, fiscal discipline.

Critics argue this has led to:

- A one-size-fits-all approach to economic development,
- The prioritization of investor confidence over social spending,
- Conditional loans that echo **neocolonial leverage.**

Yet for all the criticism, **these institutions have endured**, in large part because the U.S. has **continued to underwrite and defend them**—sometimes even when domestic politics made that support unpopular.

4. The United Nations: Universal in Theory, Hierarchical in Practice

The UN was meant to be the great equalizer—one country, one vote in the General Assembly.

But the real power lies in the **Security Council**, where the U.S. holds one of five permanent vetoes. That veto power means:

- No intervention can occur without U.S. consent.
- No resolution can bind the U.S. without its approval.
- The Council often reflects **U.S.–Russia–China rivalries**, more than global consensus.

Beyond the veto:

- The UN headquarters is in **New York**,
- The U.S. is the largest contributor to its **regular budget** and **peacekeeping operations**,
- And many key agencies (e.g., the World Food Programme, UNICEF) rely heavily on **U.S. funding and political support**.

This creates a paradox:

- The UN is **globally symbolic**, but **functionally dependent on U.S. goodwill**.
- It's a forum for universalism, but **bounded by strategic realpolitik**.

5. *The WTO and Trade Regimes: Rules-Based Order, America-First Rules*

The **World Trade Organization (WTO)**—which evolved from GATT—is meant to regulate global trade, arbitrate disputes, and ensure fairness. But:

- The U.S. helped write the rules, especially on intellectual property and service liberalization.

- The dispute resolution body has been **undermined by U.S. intransigence,** especially since 2017, when it began blocking the appointment of new judges.
- America often **uses tariffs and trade remedies** outside of WTO mechanisms—especially through Section 301 and Section 232 of U.S. law.

This is **engagement on American terms:**

- Join the rules-based system,
- But **reserve the right to act unilaterally when domestic priorities demand.**

It's not illegal. But it's not inspiring either.

6. The Human Rights System: Champion and Challenger

The U.S. has been a global leader in human rights advocacy:

- It helped draft the **Universal Declaration of Human Rights,**
- Supports organizations like **USAID, Amnesty International,** and **Freedom House,**
- And routinely **criticizes abuses in China, Iran, Venezuela, and others.**

But it also:

- **Refuses to ratify key treaties,** like the CRC and CEDAW,

- Has left and rejoined the **UN Human Rights Council** multiple times,
- And frequently invokes sovereignty when international human rights bodies scrutinize its own practices (e.g., torture, police violence, prison conditions).

The message is mixed:

- We value rights—but **we define them**.
- We enforce accountability—but **we retain immunity**.

This undermines the moral clarity the U.S. often claims.

7. *Multilateralism, Lightly Salted*

What emerges from all this is a pattern of **multilateralism with caveats:**

- The U.S. prefers **coalitions of the willing** to universal consensus.
- It promotes institutions—so long as they **remain structurally compatible with U.S. law and strategy**.
- It funds global projects—but expects **leadership roles in return**.

This is **not isolationism**, and it's not imperialism either. It's **a hybrid form of leadership**, one that works well when the U.S. is trusted, but **falters when trust declines**.

. . .

The Problem **With Engagement on Your Own Terms**
Why does this matter?
Because in a changing world:

- **Rising powers** demand more say in global institutions,
- **Civil society** wants real accountability,
- And younger nations no longer accept **pre-written operating systems** from the postwar era.

If the U.S. only participates on its own terms, then other countries will eventually demand to **rewrite the terms themselves.**

Leadership by design only works if you keep **renovating the blueprint**—and making space for others at the drafting table.

STRATEGIC PARTICIPATION—WHEN Interests Align

ONE OF THE defining features of American foreign policy since the Cold War has been **strategic participation**—an approach that treats international institutions less like obligations, and more like opportunities. Think of it as a kind of foreign policy à la carte: the U.S. joins agreements when they align with its interests, withdraws when they become politically inconvenient, and builds alternatives when consensus proves elusive.

This isn't isolationism. It's **transactional globalism**: still outward-facing, still involved—but on **Washington's terms.** This part of the chapter explores how this approach has shaped American behavior on the global stage, and what its long-term consequences may be.

1. *In When It Works, Out When It Doesn't: The Toggling Habit*

The U.S. has developed a habit of **exiting and reentering global agreements** like a guest who leaves the dinner party, only to show up again with dessert when the mood improves.

Let's review a few key examples:

- **The Paris Climate Agreement:** Signed in 2015 (Obama), exited in 2017 (Trump), rejoined in 2021 (Biden).
    - *Why the exit?* Climate skepticism and sovereignty concerns.
    - *Why the return?* Global credibility, climate diplomacy, and domestic political shift.
- **UNESCO:** Left in 1984 (Reagan), rejoined in 2003 (Bush), left again in 2017 (Trump), rejoined in 2023 (Biden).
    - *Why leave?* Perceived anti-Israel bias and bureaucratic mismanagement.
    - *Why return?* Renewed emphasis on science, education, and cultural diplomacy.
- **Iran Nuclear Deal (JCPOA):** Negotiated in 2015, U.S. unilaterally withdrew in 2018, attempted renegotiation in 2021–2022.
    - *Why exit?* Distrust of Iranian compliance, domestic political opposition.
    - *Why reconsider?* Strategic interest in nuclear nonproliferation and regional stability.

This pattern suggests that multilateralism for the U.S. is **contingent on executive preferences and electoral outcomes**, not a sustained commitment.

2. Multilateral Forums with American Carve-Outs

Even when the U.S. joins international institutions, it often **negotiates exceptions** to ensure its autonomy:

- **The Law of the Sea Treaty:** Despite extensive U.S. involvement in drafting it, the U.S. never ratified the treaty—largely over concerns about ceding control of seabed mining and navigation rights.
- **The International Criminal Court (ICC):** The U.S. signed the Rome Statute but "unsigned" it under President George W. Bush. U.S. law prohibits cooperation with the court and even authorizes the use of force to free Americans tried at The Hague.
- **The World Health Organization (WHO):** The U.S. supports WHO funding and programs (e.g., polio eradication, disease surveillance), but has occasionally used funding as leverage—most notably in 2020, when the Trump administration began withdrawal proceedings before Biden reversed course.

These carve-outs reflect a persistent belief that **global institutions should serve U.S. power, not constrain it**—and when they do constrain it, the U.S. reserves the right to walk away.

. . .

3. Bilateralism and Regionalism Over Globalism

When global consensus proves too slow—or the rules seem too rigid—the U.S. increasingly prefers **bilateral or regional agreements**:

- **Trade:** After withdrawing from the Trans-Pacific Partnership (TPP), the U.S. pursued bilateral trade deals with countries like Japan, Canada, and Mexico (rebranded as USMCA).
- **Security:** While NATO remains central, the U.S. has expanded bilateral military partnerships with:
    - Israel (missile defense),
    - Japan and South Korea (containment of North Korea),
    - Australia and the U.K. (AUKUS submarine deal).
- **Tech and AI governance:** Instead of waiting for global frameworks, the U.S. has created **coalitions of like-minded democracies** (e.g., the Quad, the G7 AI principles) to shape norms around cybersecurity, data flow, and digital infrastructure.

Bilateralism offers **control, speed, and clarity**—but it also risks **fragmenting the global system** into spheres of influence.

4. The Problem of Inconsistency: Allies Take Note

Strategic participation may make short-term sense, but it creates **long-term trust deficits**:

The United States of the World vs. The United Nations 171

- **Europe** has grown increasingly wary of U.S. unpredictability, especially after the Trump years. The EU has begun discussing "strategic autonomy" and expanding defense and trade capabilities independent of the U.S.
- **The Global South** often sees U.S. participation as **conditional and self-serving**, particularly when international law is applied unevenly (e.g., support for Ukrainian sovereignty, silence on Palestine or Western Sahara).
- **Multilateral institutions** have become accustomed to hedging against U.S. disengagement—seeking **alternative funding** or **leadership from middle powers** when Washington retreats.

The result is a world where America is still at the head table—but **not always trusted to stay for the whole meal.**

5. When Participation Means Dominance

In some cases, U.S. "participation" effectively means **U.S. dominance**:

- **Internet governance** was long overseen by U.S.-based institutions (like ICANN), until pressure from other nations led to partial decentralization.
- **Standard-setting bodies** in aviation, telecom, and food safety have historically been shaped by **U.S. regulators, scientists, and industries.**
- Even in the **climate space**, U.S. leadership has dictated the pace and ambition of targets—often

watering down enforcement mechanisms to ensure domestic acceptability.

This kind of participation creates a conundrum:

- The U.S. wants to lead.
- Others want it to commit.
- But leadership without accountability **breeds resentment.**

6. *The Temptation of Parallel Structures*

When existing multilateralism becomes too unwieldy, the U.S. increasingly turns to **"minilateralism"**—coalitions of the willing, often informal, often exclusive:

- **The Quad (U.S., Japan, India, Australia)** for Indo-Pacific security.
- **The Five Eyes alliance** for intelligence sharing.
- **The G7** for economic coordination among advanced democracies.
- **AUKUS** for military tech cooperation.

These frameworks allow **faster action, tighter control, and shared values**—but they also:

- Bypass larger, more representative institutions,
- Exclude rising powers like Brazil, Nigeria, and Indonesia,
- And deepen the divide between **"rule makers" and "rule takers."**

If everyone copies this model, **global governance becomes a patchwork of gated communities.**

7. Can Strategic Engagement Be Redeemed?

Yes—but only if the U.S. embraces **strategic consistency**, not just strategic convenience.

This would involve:

- Clarifying its long-term institutional commitments—even across administrations.
- Reducing the temptation to exit treaties for short-term domestic gain.
- Supporting reforms that give other countries **a meaningful stake in shared rules.**
- Accepting **accountability mechanisms**, even when inconvenient.
- And viewing multilateralism not as a burden—but as **a stage for durable leadership.**

Strategic participation is not inherently cynical. But it must be backed by **principled endurance**, not just episodic alignment.

Bilateral Deals and the Rise of Ad Hoc Governance

In a world where complexity outpaces consensus, governance is evolving—not always toward more unity, but often toward **modular flexibility**. And no country has embraced this shift more energetically than the United States.

When international institutions stall, when universal frameworks fall short, and when vetoes or bureaucracy block collective action, the U.S. turns to its favorite diplomatic tool: **the bilateral deal.** Or increasingly, the **small-group ad hoc coalition.** These arrangements aren't about global equality. They're about **efficiency, trust, control, and speed.**

This part of the chapter explores how ad hoc governance is becoming the norm for U.S. foreign policy—and what that means for **transparency, equity, sovereignty, and global cooperation.**

1. The Bilateral Instinct: Simplicity, Control, and Reciprocity

There's a reason bilateral agreements appeal to Washington:

- **They're faster.** No need to herd 193 nations.
- **They're reciprocal.** You give something, you get something.
- **They preserve leverage.** The U.S. is almost always the stronger party.

From trade and military bases to cybersecurity and migration, the U.S. routinely prefers **custom agreements tailored to national partners.** Consider:

- The **U.S.–Japan security alliance,**
- **Bilateral investment treaties** with over 40 nations,
- The **U.S.–Mexico–Canada Agreement (USMCA),** replacing NAFTA with stricter labor and environmental clauses,

- Migration deals with Guatemala, El Salvador, and Honduras,
- U.S.–China negotiations that bypass WTO structures entirely.

Bilateralism also helps Washington **sidestep multilateral obligations** that might constrain U.S. policy.

But this comes at a cost: it **undermines common rules**, creates **asymmetric dependencies**, and leaves smaller nations **vulnerable to shifting political winds**.

2. Ad Hoc Coalitions: The Minilateral Moment

Where bilateral deals are one-on-one, **minilateralism** is the new buzzword for **coalitions of the capable and willing**:

- **The Quad** (U.S., Japan, India, Australia) coordinates on Indo-Pacific security.
- **AUKUS** (Australia, U.K., U.S.) facilitates submarine tech sharing and regional deterrence.
- **The Five Eyes** alliance (U.S., U.K., Canada, Australia, New Zealand) shares intelligence.
- **The Clean Network Initiative**—a U.S.-led alliance to exclude Chinese tech from 5G networks.
- **COVID Vaccine Diplomacy**: bilateral or trilateral deals to share surplus vaccines, bypassing the slower COVAX mechanism.

These are **functional clubs**, not formal institutions. They lack:

- Universal membership,
- Legal charters,
- Formal enforcement mechanisms.

But they deliver **speed, discretion, and focus**—which is increasingly what states value in a fragmented world.

3. The Appeal of "Gated Globalism"

The U.S. is not alone in this shift. Many powers now prefer **small, exclusive groupings**:

- The EU coordinates internally and acts externally through trade blocs.
- China builds partnerships through the **Belt and Road Initiative,** tailored country by country.
- Russia prefers **regional influence structures** like the Eurasian Economic Union.

What's new is that the **global commons**—once governed through inclusive institutions like the UN, WTO, or WHO—is now managed more like a **private club** with variable entry conditions.

Scholars call this "gated globalism": international engagement is no longer universal, but **curated**. You get in if you:

- Share values,
- Offer strategic assets,
- Or play by a dominant power's rules.

This model protects sovereignty—but at the cost of **equality and transparency.**

4. From Rule-Making to Rule-Stacking

In the traditional multilateral system, states negotiate rules and then adopt them across the board.

In the ad hoc model, **rules are stacked like apps**—layered agreements, overlapping standards, partial compliance.

Imagine the difference:

- A **universal climate treaty** vs. bilateral carbon trading pacts.
- A **global digital governance regime** vs. data flow agreements between the U.S. and EU (e.g., Privacy Shield, invalidated in 2020).
- A **universal AI ethics charter** vs. separate sets of principles emerging from OECD, G7, and Quad summits.

This patchwork approach creates:

- **Flexibility**, which states love.
- **Complexity**, which corporations navigate.
- **Opacity**, which citizens can't easily follow.
- **Loopholes**, which bad actors exploit.

The net effect is a **weakened global floor and a fragmented ceiling**—governance that is real, but hard to hold accountable.

5. Sovereignty Reinforced, But Only for Some

One irony of this model is that it **reinforces U.S. sovereignty while undermining others'**:

- The U.S. keeps its autonomy but can **shape others' behavior through conditional agreements.**
- Smaller nations gain access—but lose flexibility.
- Norms evolve based on **dominant power preferences,** not consensus.

For example:

- A country accepting U.S. cybersecurity standards may lose access to Chinese infrastructure funds.
- A government joining a U.S.-led climate compact may be required to **privatize utilities** or **cut subsidies** unpopular with domestic constituencies.
- A developing nation negotiating vaccine access or trade preferences might **accept U.S. terms in return for short-term relief**—at the expense of long-term policy autonomy.

In essence, ad hoc governance can become **bilateral empire**—without the military flags or formal hierarchies.

6. *When Ad Hoc Becomes the Norm*

The danger isn't that ad hoc governance exists. The danger is when **it becomes the default**, replacing institutions rather than supplementing them.

What's lost?

- **Transparency**: Deals are often negotiated behind closed doors.
- **Accountability**: No appeals process, no global tribunal, no meaningful review.
- **Democracy**: Citizens rarely get a voice in these arrangements.
- **Coherence**: Standards multiply, systems diverge, conflicts emerge.

Over time, this model can **erode trust in universal governance**, create overlapping obligations, and make global problem-solving harder—not easier.

7. The U.S. Role in Reforming the Fragmented Future

If the U.S. continues down this path, it risks **winning short-term influence but losing long-term legitimacy**.

But the U.S. could also lead a pivot:

- Use ad hoc success stories as **pilots** for formal global reform.
- Invite Global South partners into governance clubs as **equal architects.**
- Merge bilateral and multilateral tracks— **hybridizing flexibility with fairness.**
- Promote **modular international law** that scales from local to global participation.

In doing so, America can preserve its leadership **without rebuilding the Cold War's pyramids of power**. It can help create **governance for a networked world**, not a divided one.

. . .

The Global Trust Deficit

In diplomacy, as in personal relationships, consistency matters. You can't lead a partnership if your allies don't know whether you'll show up to the next meeting—or if you'll pull out halfway through the project. And yet, that is precisely the reputation the United States is acquiring in the 21st century: **powerful, principled, but increasingly unpredictable.**

Whether it's climate agreements, trade deals, peacekeeping support, or health partnerships, the U.S. has developed a pattern of **erratic engagement**. This isn't just about one administration. It's a structural issue: the fusion of foreign policy with domestic polarization has made **continuity a casualty of democracy.**

The result? A **global trust deficit**. Not in America's strength—but in its **staying power.**

1. Leadership on a Leash: The Perils of Partisan Foreign Policy

One of the foundational problems is that **foreign policy has become politicized**—deeply and permanently.

Historically, there was a "water's edge" norm: partisan disputes stopped when it came to international affairs. That norm is gone.

Now:

- Treaties are rarely ratified because the Senate is gridlocked.
- Agreements signed by one president are **reversed by the next.**

- Foreign aid is debated not on need, but on narrative.
- Multilateral institutions are alternately praised and vilified, depending on who's in power.

Examples:

- **Paris Agreement:** In–out–in again.
- **Iran Deal (JCPOA):** Negotiated, abandoned, then unrevived.
- **WHO membership:** Suspended, then reinstated.

Foreign leaders now **watch U.S. elections like referenda on international commitments.** Diplomats draft agreements with **escape clauses**, anticipating American whiplash.

This unpredictability **undermines long-term planning, discourages investment in partnerships, and weakens trust in U.S.-backed institutions.**

2. Allies Are Watching—and Hedging

For decades, American alliances functioned on a kind of autopilot: the U.S. leads, others follow.

But in recent years:

- **Germany has called for European "strategic autonomy."**
- **France has promoted defense initiatives independent of NATO.**
- **Canada and Mexico negotiated bilateral terms with the EU post-NAFTA upheaval.**

- Japan and Australia are deepening ties with Southeast Asia outside U.S. channels.

These aren't betrayals. They're **insurance policies**.

Allies are no longer betting on America always being "back." They're preparing for America possibly walking away. Again.

3. *The Global South: Between Disillusionment and Opportunity*

In much of the developing world, the trust deficit has been building for decades:

- Promises of aid that never materialized,
- Conditionality tied to Western economic models,
- Intervention in some crises, silence in others,
- Rhetoric of democracy, paired with **support for autocrats when convenient.**

During COVID-19:

- Vaccine hoarding by rich countries—including the U.S.—fueled anger.
- The delay in waiving IP rights for vaccine production was seen as **profit over lives.**
- The U.S. reasserted leadership late in the game—but the damage to its humanitarian credibility lingered.

The Global South sees U.S. engagement as **episodic and interest-driven**. As a result, many countries are **pivoting toward China, India, or regional partnerships**—not necessarily because they prefer them, but because **they feel neglected by Washington.**

4. The Institutional Fallout
International institutions are also suffering:

- The **WTO's appellate body remains paralyzed** because of U.S. obstruction.
- The **UN Security Council is routinely deadlocked**, often due to great power vetoes—including America's.
- The **ICC is under attack** not only from autocracies but also from the U.S., which has refused jurisdiction and imposed sanctions on ICC personnel.
- Climate forums, disarmament summits, and refugee conventions all **stall when the U.S. retreats or vacillates.**

When the world's most powerful nation can't—or won't—commit, institutions **lose momentum and moral clarity.**

5. The Rise of Trust Substitutes: Redundancy and Regionalism
In response, countries are turning to **trust substitutes:**

- **Redundant institutions:** multiple trade forums, parallel security pacts.
- **Regional solutions:** the African Continental Free Trade Area (AfCFTA), ASEAN-led climate dialogues, Latin American migration compacts.

- **Private diplomacy**: corporations and foundations filling in where states won't act (e.g., Gates Foundation during global health crises).
- **Issue-specific coalitions**: from tech standards to ocean treaties, modular groups are doing what global bodies can't.

This is functional—but fragile. **Redundancy is no substitute for universalism.** Without the U.S., many initiatives **lack enforcement, scale, or legitimacy**.

6. *The Trust Equation: Power + Predictability + Principle*

Trust isn't about perfection. It's about **reliability**.

For the U.S. to repair the trust deficit, it must demonstrate:

- **Power**: the capacity to lead, fund, and defend.
- **Predictability**: the ability to follow through, beyond one election cycle.
- **Principle**: the willingness to act based on values, not just interests.

This means:

- Institutionalizing foreign policy where possible—**ratifying treaties**, strengthening interagency coordination, empowering career diplomats.
- Supporting reforms to global bodies that **deepen representation and fairness**, even if it means **sharing influence**.
- Being honest about mistakes, consistent in enforcement, and **transparent in motives**.

Trust is slow to build and easy to lose. The U.S. has the toolkit. What it needs now is **political resolve**.

7. *The Cost of Lost Trust*
Without trust:

- Allies second-guess American leadership.
- Rivals exploit credibility gaps.
- Global problems go unaddressed—or are addressed by other powers with different values.
- The U.S. loses soft power, legitimacy, and **leverage**.

And in a crisis-prone century—defined by climate disruption, pandemics, cyberconflict, and mass migration—**we can't afford a world where no one trusts the sheriff.**

A Bridge to Chapter 9: The Domestic Debate Over Globalism

This concludes our exploration of how the U.S. shapes and often constrains multilateralism by insisting on participation **only on its terms**. But this posture doesn't emerge from nowhere.

In **Chapter 9**, we turn inward to explore the **domestic political debates** that fuel these global choices. From populist backlash to partisan polarization, we'll examine **how America's internal divisions shape its global posture—and what that means for the future of cooperative governance.**

9

THE DOMESTIC DEBATE OVER GLOBALISM

The Populist Backlash and the Politics of Sovereignty

BEFORE A COUNTRY WITHDRAWS from treaties or boycotts global summits, something happens at home: **the story of "us" versus "them" begins to shift**. And in the United States, that shift accelerated in the 21st century—transforming globalization from a bipartisan norm into a lightning rod for political grievance.

Where once foreign engagement was associated with leadership, prestige, and moral mission, it now often evokes suspicion, fatigue, and fury. Globalism, once considered a pragmatic inevitability, became synonymous with **elites, open borders, and lost control**. It became, in short, **a threat to sovereignty and identity**.

In this part of the chapter, we trace how **populist rhetoric reframed the global order as an enemy of the**

people, and how that reframing reshaped both American foreign policy and the global institutions that depend on U.S. participation.

1. Globalism as the Villain in a New Political Narrative

The backlash to globalization didn't happen overnight. It was a slow burn:

- **Trade agreements** were blamed for factory closures and job loss.
- **Immigration** became associated with insecurity, cultural dilution, and competition.
- **International institutions** were cast as unaccountable, unelected, and undemocratic.
- **Climate treaties** were portrayed as foreign constraints on domestic industry.

Enter the populist narrative: **the people vs. the global elite.**

- Globalists were cast as **cosmopolitan technocrats**, out of touch with American workers.
- International institutions were depicted as **bureaucratic overlords**, diluting U.S. sovereignty.
- Foreign aid and military alliances became **symbols of misplaced priorities**: "Why are we building roads in Afghanistan when ours are crumbling?"

This wasn't just rhetoric. It became **a political brand**, one with deep emotional resonance for communities dislocated by automation, deindustrialization, and cultural shifts.

2. *"America First": The Populist Foreign Policy Doctrine*

No phrase captured the populist transformation of foreign policy more than **"America First."** Popularized by President Donald Trump, the slogan became shorthand for:

- **Unilateralism** over multilateralism,
- **Tariffs** over trade liberalization,
- **Border walls** over open migration,
- **Domestic investment** over foreign aid,
- **Exit strategies** over nation-building.

It was more than a break from Obama-era internationalism. It was a **philosophical pivot:**

- From global cooperation to national primacy,
- From shared burdens to transactional demands,
- From universal values to **national self-interest as the highest good.**

Under this approach, global institutions were viewed with suspicion unless they served immediate U.S. goals. Long-term leadership was devalued. Short-term wins—renegotiated trade deals, troop withdrawals, budget cuts to the UN—were seen as victories for sovereignty.

. . .

3. The Cultural Politics of Globalism

Populist backlash wasn't only about economics. It was also about **cultural identity**.

Globalism was portrayed as:

- A threat to **traditional American values**,
- A facilitator of **mass immigration** and demographic change,
- A symbol of **elite detachment**—think Davos, not Dayton.

Right-wing media and political figures fused **cultural nostalgia** with geopolitical anxiety:

- "We don't make things anymore."
- "Our borders are broken."
- "They care more about Paris than Pittsburgh."

In this worldview, sovereignty became not just legal independence—it became **cultural defense**.

This reframing gave nationalism a **moral tone**: protecting the homeland from dilution, degradation, and dependency.

4. The Party Realignment Around Sovereignty

This populist shift transformed the political landscape:

- **Republicans**, once champions of free trade and NATO, became increasingly skeptical of international commitments.
- **Democrats**, traditionally more skeptical of war

and intervention, embraced global cooperation on climate, health, and human rights.

Sovereignty became **a partisan Rorschach test:**

- For conservatives: it meant **control, borders, and economic autonomy.**
- For progressives: it meant **resisting authoritarianism and corporate overreach**— often through **stronger international norms.**

As a result, foreign policy debates now mirror domestic polarization:

- The same distrust of federal institutions is projected onto global ones.
- The same populist disdain for experts is directed at diplomats and multilateral envoys.
- And the same tribal divisions define **which international partnerships are trusted or rejected.**

5. *Economic Displacement as Political Fuel*

Populist anti-globalism draws strength from real grievances:

- **Deindustrialization** devastated Midwestern and Southern towns.
- **Trade liberalization** exposed workers to foreign competition without adequate safety nets.

- **Automation and outsourcing** compounded the economic hollowing-out.

In this environment, **"Made in America"** became a battle cry—not just of pride, but of protest.

Foreign policy elites underestimated how deeply these changes affected American self-conception. To those left behind, globalization wasn't a rising tide—it was a **wave that washed away communities.**

Populist politicians didn't create this anger. They **channeled it**—and reframed foreign engagement as betrayal.

6. The Internet, Disinformation, and Global Paranoia

The digital age has amplified anti-globalist sentiment in three ways:

1. **Misinformation travels fast**—claims that the UN wants to confiscate guns, or that the WHO is plotting global lockdowns, spread quickly online.
2. **Conspiracy theories abound**—global institutions are painted as puppets of "deep state" actors or billionaire philanthropists with shadowy agendas.
3. **Algorithmic echo chambers** fuel polarization—users are fed content that affirms suspicion and demonizes nuance.

As a result, **global cooperation becomes harder to defend**, even when necessary. The very word "globalist" has become a slur in some corners of American discourse.

. . .

7. Can Populism and Global Engagement Coexist?

Oddly enough, yes—**if reframed wisely**.

Globalism doesn't have to mean elitism. Sovereignty doesn't have to mean isolation.

It's possible to:

- Promote **local industry** while still cooperating on climate.
- Defend **national security** while contributing to peacekeeping.
- Support **border enforcement** while honoring refugee obligations.
- Reject **corporate overreach** while embracing **cross-border labor protections**.

The key is to build a **foreign policy that speaks in the language of the people**, not the boardroom:

- Emphasize tangible benefits—jobs, safety, stability.
- Center values like **fairness, reciprocity, and dignity**.
- And restore trust through **transparency, accountability, and inclusion**.

Media, Messaging, and the Globalist Narrative Crisis

It used to be that international cooperation came with a halo. Think of JFK's Peace Corps, Reagan at the Berlin Wall, or Clinton signing NAFTA surrounded by bipartisan applause. For decades, American foreign policy—at least at the level of optics—was sold to the public as a sign of strength, leadership, and moral responsibility.

But something shifted.

Today, the word "globalism" doesn't conjure up idealism—it conjures up **conspiracy, loss, and elite capture**. The institutions of global governance are no longer seen as noble, but **remote**. Treaties are framed not as safeguards, but **surrenders**. And the media ecosystem has become both a mirror and a megaphone of this new public mood.

This part of the chapter examines how the **language of global engagement has failed**, and what might be done to **reclaim the narrative** in an age of fragmentation, misinformation, and rising distrust.

1. From Global Good to Global Threat

Globalism wasn't always a dirty word.

Throughout the Cold War and into the 1990s, it was common to see international engagement framed in terms of:

- **Peace** (arms control, diplomatic summits),
- **Prosperity** (trade agreements, economic development),
- **Progress** (human rights treaties, global health campaigns).

Media outlets showcased diplomats as heroes, humanitarian aid as a moral obligation, and summits as statesman-like rituals.

But by the early 2000s, several trends began to erode this framing:

- **Globalization's winners and losers** became starkly visible.
- The Iraq War undermined confidence in the "freedom agenda."
- The 2008 financial crisis exposed the **fragility of interconnected economies**.
- Mass migration and the rise of China sparked new fears about cultural identity and economic displacement.

Slowly, global engagement was reframed—from benevolent to **suspicious**, from stabilizing to **destabilizing**.

2. *The Rise of Populist Media and Anti-Globalist Framing*

Enter the echo chamber.

As cable news fragmented and digital media exploded, new voices emerged—many explicitly hostile to international institutions. These outlets didn't just report on global events. They **reframed them ideologically**.

For example:

- The **United Nations** was portrayed not as a peacekeeper, but as a "globalist plot" to impose foreign laws.
- **Climate treaties** were not solutions, but "jobs-killing regulations" written in Brussels or Beijing.
- **WHO advisories** were painted as infringements on American liberty.
- **Trade agreements** became shorthand for "outsourcing" and "open borders."

The United States of the World vs. The United Nations 195

In this environment, multilateralism was no longer the high road. It became **the elite's bypass around democracy**.

3. The Elite Messaging Gap: Technocrats vs. Storytellers

Meanwhile, the globalist camp made its own errors—**narrative ones**.

Supporters of international cooperation often relied on:

- **Technical language** ("tariff harmonization," "carbon offset markets"),
- **Statistical justifications** (GDP increases, multilateral funding pledges),
- **Institutional reverence** ("Rules-based international order").

But these messages **didn't speak to people's lived experiences**. They didn't address:

- The fear of job loss in rural America,
- The sense of cultural alienation in small towns,
- Or the erosion of trust in experts after economic promises went unmet.

In the battle of story vs. spreadsheet, the **story won**—even if it was misleading.

4. Conspiracy and Disinformation as Narrative Weapons

Anti-globalist narratives gained traction not just through news, but through **conspiratorial storytelling**:

- The "Great Replacement" theory linked migration with cultural extinction.
- The "Great Reset" was cast as a global elite plan to abolish private property.
- Vaccines were linked to population control.
- Climate change became a **Trojan horse for socialism.**

These weren't fringe views. They **broke into the mainstream**, fueled by viral content, political influencers, and a crisis of institutional credibility.

The problem wasn't just bad information—it was the **absence of a compelling counter-narrative.**

5. *Cultural Disconnects and Emotional Triggers*

Globalism also stumbled because it failed to connect emotionally. Its advocates too often assumed:

- People want to be "citizens of the world."
- Rational benefits will outweigh national pride.
- Multilateral institutions speak for everyone.

But most people still identify locally, nationally, culturally. They care more about their town, their job, their values than about **global norms.**

Anti-globalist narratives tapped into:

- **Pride in sovereignty,**
- **Anxiety over change,**
- **Mistrust of elite institutions,**
- **Desire for agency and self-determination.**

Globalist rhetoric failed to **meet people where they are.** It asked them to "buy in" without **telling them what they were buying**—and why it mattered to their daily lives.

6. *The Path to Narrative Recovery*

To restore public faith in international engagement, we don't need better facts. We need **better frames**—and **honest, relatable storytelling.**

That means:

- **Linking global engagement to local impact.** Don't just say "climate treaty." Say "cleaner air in your zip code."
- **Telling stories of success**: real people whose lives improved because of a treaty, a trade pact, or a peacekeeping mission.
- **Centering dignity and fairness**: show that global rules are about protecting workers, families, and the environment—not just markets and metrics.
- **Admitting past failures**: trust requires accountability. Globalism must own its blind spots (e.g., free trade without safety nets).

Most importantly, **reframe global cooperation as patriotic.** Not the opposite of sovereignty, but **the modern defense of it.**

7. *Who Tells the Story Matters*

This new narrative can't come from diplomats alone. It must include:

- Teachers explaining the UN in classrooms,
- Faith leaders connecting global justice with moral values,
- Mayors showing how global trade builds local jobs,
- Veterans sharing peacekeeping experiences,
- Farmers, nurses, engineers—**the human face of global engagement.**

We need to democratize the narrative, **de-elite the voice,** and make internationalism feel like something **Americans do**, not something **done to them.**

Sovereignty in the Age of Interdependence

Sovereignty was once a clear-cut concept. It meant **exclusive control over territory, people, and laws.** It was a fence around a nation-state's autonomy, built on centuries of blood and parchment. But in the 21st century, that fence is starting to look more like a speed bump—slowing, but no longer stopping, the forces that flow across borders.

From viral pathogens to carbon emissions, from cryptocurrency to refugee flows, sovereignty is under stress—not because of foreign invasions, but because of **shared vulnerabilities.**

In this part of the chapter, we explore how sovereignty must evolve—not as a surrender to globalism, but as **an adaptation to interdependence.** The question isn't whether sovereignty still matters. It's whether it can survive **unchanged** in a world that has changed fundamentally.

1. The Myth of the Sovereign Firewall

The United States of the World vs. The United Nations

For centuries, sovereign nations operated as if their borders were buffers. What happened inside was their business. What happened outside was only relevant if it crossed the line.

That logic no longer holds.

Examples:

- **COVID-19** showed that **a cough in Wuhan can shutter schools in Wisconsin.**
- **Climate change** makes wildfires in Australia a problem for air quality in South America.
- **Global financial crashes**, like in 2008, ricochet across continents in days.
- **AI tools and cyberattacks** can manipulate elections or sabotage infrastructure from thousands of miles away.

In each case, the source of disruption is **borderless**, but the consequences are deeply national. And yet, many national responses remain **inward-looking and reactive**, trying to restore autonomy in a world that no longer honors it as absolute.

2. The Rise of "Shared Sovereignty" *Models*

Some scholars and diplomats have proposed a new term: **shared sovereignty**.

This doesn't mean abandoning national identity or decision-making. It means:

- Pooling authority where problems are collective,
- Delegating powers to supranational bodies when effectiveness demands it,

- And creating **nested layers of governance** that allow **both local autonomy and global cooperation.**

Examples:

- The **European Union**, with its shared currency and court system, allows for mobility, trade, and law enforcement across 27 nations—while still preserving national governments and cultures.
- **Interpol** operates through national police agencies, offering global tools without replacing domestic control.
- **International health treaties** (like the International Health Regulations) set shared standards, but leave implementation to sovereign states.

These models are messy, iterative, and far from perfect. But they offer a **blueprint for balancing sovereignty with reality.**

3. Environmental Sovereignty: A Global Commons Paradox

Climate change is the ultimate test of sovereignty's limits.

Each country:

- Emits greenhouse gases,
- Experiences the consequences,
- But controls its own energy policies.

This creates a **classic prisoner's dilemma:**

- If everyone acts, all benefit.
- If some defect, others suffer.

Multilateral agreements like the **Paris Climate Accord** attempt to square this circle. They respect sovereignty by allowing **nationally determined contributions**, but also demand transparency, reporting, and peer pressure to raise ambition.

But without enforcement, these systems rely on **political will and moral suasion**—a weak currency in a world of short election cycles.

True climate sovereignty means **accepting that national emissions are a global act**, and therefore must be regulated, taxed, or offset in ways that go **beyond borders**.

4. Digital Sovereignty: Who Owns the Cloud?

In the digital domain, sovereignty is even murkier.

- Data is stored in one country, processed in another, and monetized in a third.
- Social media platforms shape national discourse, but are governed by corporate boards.
- Artificial intelligence learns from global inputs—but can manipulate domestic outcomes.

Who controls what?

- The **EU** has pushed forward with GDPR and the Digital Services Act.
- **China** has pursued cyber-sovereignty—strict control of internet infrastructure and content.

- The **U.S.** remains ambivalent, toggling between deregulation and national security panic.

The future of sovereignty may depend less on borders and more on **protocols**—who writes them, who enforces them, and who gets left out.

5. Health, Migration, and the New Borders of Care

COVID-19 exposed more than the limits of virus containment. It showed how **health itself is a shared security issue:**

- Vaccine nationalism delayed global recovery.
- Misinformation spread faster than containment policies.
- Supply chains for medical gear were clogged by export bans and panic.

Meanwhile, **migration flows driven by conflict, climate, and inequality** continue to challenge traditional sovereignty:

- Border walls don't stop desperation.
- Deportation does not solve demographic shifts.
- National immigration laws often lag behind international human rights obligations.

Sovereignty in these domains can no longer be zero-sum. It must become **cooperative**—sharing responsibility, burden, and solutions.

. . .

6. The Emotional Weight of Sovereignty

Despite these functional shifts, sovereignty remains **emotionally potent**.

It speaks to:

- Identity,
- Self-determination,
- Resistance to domination.

This is why sovereignty remains the **rhetorical center of populist politics**. It appeals not just to constitutionalists, but to cultural traditionalists, nationalists, and those who feel unmoored by global flows of goods, people, and ideas.

Therefore, any evolution of sovereignty must **honor these emotional truths**, even as it adapts its legal and operational frameworks.

7. Redefining Sovereignty for a Networked World

We don't need to abolish sovereignty. We need to **redefine it**.

Consider a new framing:

- Sovereignty as **a node in a network,** not an island.
- Sovereignty as **stewardship,** not just control.
- Sovereignty as **capacity to govern wisely in an interconnected world,** not merely the power to say "no."

This would mean:

- Investing in global institutions as extensions of national interest.
- Supporting international law as **a defense of sovereignty through order**, not a threat to independence.
- Embracing dual citizenship—of a nation and of humanity—not as contradiction, but as coherence.

REBUILDING a Shared National Vision of Global Purpose

AT ITS BEST, America's role in the world has been animated by a **sense of mission**: not domination, but **aspiration**. Think of the Marshall Plan, the moon landing, the Peace Corps. These weren't just foreign policy actions—they were **narratives**, stories that inspired, rallied, and united.

But in recent decades, that story has faltered. Global engagement became a bureaucratic task. Treaties became line items. Public diplomacy became press releases. And global institutions, no longer seen as symbols of freedom or progress, became faceless acronyms—**remote, rigid, suspect.**

Rebuilding a national vision of global purpose doesn't mean returning to Cold War propaganda or exporting democracy at gunpoint. It means crafting a new ethos of **shared fate and principled leadership**—one that is **local in language, pragmatic in delivery**, and **human in scale**.

Here's how.

. . .

1. Root Foreign Policy in American Civic Values

Rather than framing global cooperation as elite policy, we must **anchor it in American civic ideals:**

- **Liberty:** Promote freedom from want and oppression abroad, just as we strive for it at home.
- **Justice:** Support international law as an extension of our belief in due process and equality.
- **Opportunity:** Frame development aid and fair trade as ways to expand opportunity for all—not as charity, but as economic alignment.
- **Democracy:** Promote democratic resilience globally by first strengthening it domestically.

When international action is framed through shared values—not abstract interests—it becomes easier to explain, defend, and fund.

2. Reconnect Global Outcomes to Local Lives

People don't connect with foreign policy in the abstract. They connect when it **touches their zip code, their paycheck, their kitchen table.**

We must:

- Show how climate treaties **improve air quality and reduce disaster costs at home.**
- Link global health funding to **disease prevention in American cities.**
- Tie foreign infrastructure investment to **supply chain security and domestic job creation.**

- Connect educational exchanges to **local schools and community engagement**.

The question for every policy should be: *How does this serve the American people—and how can we show it?*

3. Engage Local Voices in Global Policy

Foreign policy is often top-down. That needs to change. Cities, states, and communities should be **actors in global diplomacy**, not just observers.

- Empower **mayors to participate in climate networks** like C40.
- Let **tribal nations engage in international conversations** on Indigenous rights and environmental stewardship.
- Involve **labor unions and small business associations** in trade negotiations.
- Give **youth councils and educators** a voice in shaping cultural diplomacy and student exchanges.

A national vision must be **plural**. It must reflect not only D.C., but **Detroit, Dallas, and Des Moines**.

4. Tell Better Stories, Not Bigger Ones

Foreign policy has suffered from a **storytelling failure**. Grand speeches about global order mean little to a voter worried about rising rent or disappearing jobs.

We must shift from:

- **Abstractions** to people: Not "development," but a nurse in Malawi with solar-powered tools.
- **Geopolitical chess games** to local heroes: Not "soft power," but a former Peace Corps volunteer running for office in Nebraska.
- **Buzzwords** to emotions: Not "multilateralism," but "we're in this together."

Stories move people. And right now, **globalists aren't telling enough of them.**

5. Depolarize the Global Engagement Debate

Foreign policy shouldn't be **left vs. right**. It should be **smart vs. short-sighted**. And we must work to build **cross-partisan narratives** that make room for:

- Conservative respect for sovereignty and national strength,
- Progressive emphasis on justice, sustainability, and inclusion,
- Independent focus on competence, realism, and cost-effectiveness.

This means:

- Reframing international cooperation as **constitutional, not conspiratorial**.
- Acknowledging legitimate concerns about elite capture and uneven globalization.
- Building messaging coalitions that unite veterans, farmers, students, scientists, and clergy around **shared moral and material interests**.

. . .

6. *Educate for Global Citizenship—Rooted in National Confidence*

Many Americans feel alienated by global conversations because they've **never been invited to participate in them meaningfully.**

A long-term vision requires investment in:

- **Civics and global literacy** in schools—taught not as binaries, but as coexisting frameworks.
- **Service programs** like AmeriCorps and Global Corps—domestic and international branches of the same mission.
- **Media literacy** to combat misinformation and polarization around international issues.

This is not about replacing patriotism. It's about **expanding it**—so that love of country includes **stewardship of the planet and solidarity with humanity.**

7. *Make Global Purpose a National Project*

We need a **moonshot for global cooperation**—a clear, public, participatory goal that symbolizes a new era of U.S. leadership.

What might that look like?

- A **Marshall Plan for climate resilience**—building green infrastructure from the Mississippi Delta to the Mekong.
- A **democracy data alliance**—safeguarding

elections from bots, billionaires, and authoritarian interference.
- A **Universal Public Health Compact**—to prepare for the next pandemic, with American cities as pilot sites.
- A **Trillionaire Club initiative**—requiring extreme wealth to contribute to global poverty and water eradication efforts.

Let this be our generational mission: not isolation in fear, but **integration with intention**.

.

10

AMERICA'S OPPORTUNITY—AND OBLIGATION

Why the U.S. Is Uniquely Positioned to Lead This Transition

AT EVERY CRITICAL juncture in global history, the United States has played a role—sometimes as architect, sometimes as saboteur, always as a pivot.

- After World War II, it helped design the United Nations and the Bretton Woods system.
- In the Cold War, it framed democracy and capitalism as the guardians of freedom.
- In the digital age, it produced the tools and companies that now shape global discourse.
- And in the 21st century, it has become a paradox—**a superpower in crisis, a divided democracy that still holds enormous global sway.**

This moment demands that America confront its legacy

The United States of the World vs. The United Nations 211

—not to apologize for it, but to **redeem and realign it** with the shared destiny of humanity.

Why the U.S.? Because it is uniquely positioned to lead the hybrid federation into being.

1. Structural Influence: The Power to Move Systems

No other single nation has the combination of:

A. Economic Reach

- The U.S. dollar is still the world's dominant reserve currency.
- U.S. corporations shape global labor markets, technology, and investment flows.

By endorsing hybrid economic reforms, such as:

- Global wealth redistribution,
- Tax justice frameworks,
- Climate reparations funds, …the U.S. can **accelerate system-wide change by flipping a single economic switch.**

B. Military Infrastructure

- With 750+ military bases in 80 countries, America's footprint is planetary.
- It spends more on defense than the next ten nations combined.

By repurposing its global infrastructure toward:

- Peacekeeping logistics,

- Climate response,
- Commons protection, …it can **redefine security as service, not domination.**

C. Cultural and Narrative Reach

- American media, music, and universities shape global imagination.
- U.S.-based movements (civil rights, feminism, tech innovation) ripple worldwide.

If America begins telling a new story—of **shared responsibility, of planetary democracy, of borderless belonging—the world listens.**

2. *Foundational Paradox: A Nation Born of Revolution and Empire*

The United States is not an innocent player. It carries:

- The burden of slavery and genocide,
- The shadow of interventionism,
- The scars of inequality and surveillance capitalism.

Yet it also carries:

- The DNA of revolutionary ideals,
- A written Constitution capable of amendment and reform,
- Generations of activists who have expanded democracy in the face of backlash.

This paradox is not a weakness. It is a mirror for the world.

The hybrid federation requires nations willing to say:

"We have erred, and we evolve. We are not perfect, but we are committed."

No nation better symbolizes **that ongoing struggle between ideal and reality** than the United States.

3. Constitutional Flexibility and Legal Precedent

The U.S. Constitution, though written in the 18th century, is:

- **Amendable,**
- **Interpretable by courts,**
- **Open to treaty commitments.**

It already recognizes:

- International law as binding via the Supremacy Clause (Article VI),
- Treaties as enforceable by courts,
- Executive agencies as instruments of transnational coordination.

This gives the U.S. an **internal legal framework compatible with global federation principles**—from ratifying new rights to implementing hybrid governance models domestically.

Where other nations may need revolutions, **America needs amendments, legislation, and interpretation.**

. . .

4. Democratic Traditions and the Crisis of Democracy

America's institutions are aging—but resilient:

- Local governance,
- Civic organizing,
- Independent media,
- State-federal balancing systems.

While these are under threat, they also provide **models for scaled governance:**

- National–state hybrid structures mirror federation–nation relationships.
- Civil rights law offers precedent for enforcing universal protections.
- Participatory budgeting, local ballot measures, and state-level experimentation make **American federalism a usable analogy for global hybrid governance.**

America does not need to invent new systems—it needs to **extend its best ones beyond borders.**

5. Youth, Multiculturalism, and Global Identity

The rising generation in the U.S. is:

- Majority non-white,
- Globally connected,
- Disillusioned by nationalism,
- Inspired by justice movements and digital pluralism.

They:

- Learn Korean pop and Nigerian film alongside English classics,
- Work remotely across continents,
- Mobilize for climate, racial justice, and democracy.

This generation **already lives a hybrid, federated identity.** U.S. leadership in a new global structure would **reflect its youth, not its institutions.**

6. Foreign Policy Realignment Opportunities

U.S. policy already includes the tools to support the hybrid vision:

- **State Department global democracy funds,**
- **USAID support for human rights**, health, and education,
- **Defense Department climate-readiness initiatives,**
- **National Science Foundation AI ethics research.**

All that's needed is **reframing and realigning** these tools toward federation goals:

- Ending food and water insecurity,
- Supporting digital commons and planetary infrastructure,
- Funding universal health, education, and ecological protection.

In short: **turning soft power into shared power.**

7. *Global Perception: Credibility Through Action*
The U.S. has often preached what it does not practice. To lead the federation, it must **do both:**

- **Implement domestic reforms** (see Part 2),
- **Model rights-based foreign engagement.**

Actions that would establish credibility:

- Join and strengthen the International Criminal Court,
- Lead in ratifying a Global Bill of Rights,
- Enforce carbon border adjustments that fund climate justice,
- Repurpose overseas bases for ecological stewardship and humanitarian aid.

Moral leadership must be visible, verifiable, and viral.

A Legacy Worth Leading Into the Future
America stands at a crossroads:

- One path leads deeper into isolation, nationalism, and decline.
- The other leads into **a new kind of leadership— not of dominance, but of dignity.**

The hybrid global federation will happen—with or without the United States.

But if the U.S. leads:

- It can **help design a system worthy of the Constitution's highest ideals**,
- It can **repair its reputation through reform, not rhetoric**,
- And it can become **not an empire in retreat— but a republic in rebirth.**

How Domestic Reform Strengthens Global Credibility

IN THE 20TH CENTURY, American leadership rested on two pillars:

- **Economic scale**, and
- **Moral narrative.**

It claimed:

- "We are the arsenal of democracy."
- "We are the land of opportunity."
- "We are the free world's protector."

But the 21st century has exposed contradictions:

- Skyrocketing inequality,
- Disinformation-fueled elections,
- Gun violence, mass incarceration, and voter suppression,
- A democratic system vulnerable to minority rule and corporate capture.

For the United States to lead the hybrid federation, it must **align its internal political practices with the external moral vision it promotes.** That means **rebuilding credibility from the inside out**—not with slogans, but with structural reform.

1. Campaign Finance Reform: Ending Legalized Corruption

No reform is more essential to restoring U.S. moral authority than **removing the grip of money on politics.**

Problem:

- Citizens United v. FEC (2010) opened the floodgates for unlimited corporate and dark money.
- Billionaires and special interests now dominate elections at every level.
- Policy outcomes often reflect donor interests, not voter will.

Federation Implications:

- A nation that cannot regulate its own democratic process **cannot design a legitimate global one.**

Required Reforms:

- Overturn Citizens United via constitutional amendment or new judicial precedent.
- Enact public financing of campaigns.
- Mandate real-time transparency of all contributions and expenditures.

- Ban lobbyist bundling and foreign-influenced corporate spending.

These reforms restore **the principle that governance flows from the people—not from wealth.**

2. *Electoral Integrity: Protecting the Voice of Every Citizen*
The U.S. electoral system faces:

- Gerrymandered districts,
- Outdated voter rolls,
- Disenfranchisement of formerly incarcerated individuals,
- Partisan voter suppression laws.

To be a model of democracy, the U.S. must ensure that **every person can vote, and every vote counts equally.**
Reform Actions:

- Enact automatic, universal voter registration.
- Establish independent redistricting commissions in every state.
- Guarantee voting access through early voting, mail-in ballots, and election holidays.
- Restore voting rights to incarcerated and formerly incarcerated citizens.

Federation credibility demands that **the U.S. model voting as a right, not a battleground.**

3. *Civic Education and Participation: Reviving the Public Mind*

Democracy is not just a procedure—it is a culture. The U.S. has suffered decades of:

- Declining civic education,
- Polarization,
- Public mistrust,
- And the erosion of shared facts.

A federation that depends on **informed planetary citizens** requires America to reawaken its **civic soul**.
Reform Actions:

- Mandate comprehensive, nonpartisan civic education in all K–12 curricula.
- Create public forums for deliberative democracy.
- Fund youth civic engagement programs and national service options.
- Support local media and fact-checking cooperatives.

Rebuilding civic trust at home is **preparation for fostering civic trust abroad.**

4. Racial Justice and Reparative Democracy
The moral leadership of the U.S. cannot rest on democracy alone—it must be founded in **justice**.

The U.S. bears unhealed wounds:

- Enslavement and structural racism,
- Indigenous displacement and genocide,
- Mass incarceration and economic exclusion.

These are not just domestic issues—they are **global symbols** of hypocrisy when unaddressed.

Federation Alignment Requires:

- Truth commissions on racial violence and systemic injustice,
- National reparations program for Black and Indigenous communities,
- Land return and tribal governance recognition,
- Dismantling of carceral systems built on racialized control.

A country that teaches the world about rights must **show how it repairs the denial of those rights.**

5. Reclaiming the Commons at Home

The U.S. must also **model the federation's economic and environmental vision** by reclaiming its domestic commons.

Examples:

- Transitioning water, energy, and broadband systems to public cooperative ownership.
- Enshrining clean air, water, and housing as constitutional rights.
- Protecting ancestral lands and biodiversity from extractive industries.
- Creating local food, transportation, and healthcare networks as **community rights**, not commodities.

This becomes the prototype for **planetary commons governance—grounded, tangible, and democratic.**

6. *Immigrant Justice and Border Reform*

America cannot lead a federation of borderless rights while:

- Jailing asylum seekers,
- Separating families,
- Militarizing its southern border,
- And denying refugees access to basic care.

Required Reforms:

- End detention of migrants and refugees.
- Provide pathways to legal residency and citizenship for undocumented residents.
- Restore and expand asylum protections.
- Create binational border commissions for human mobility and ecological protection.

Immigrant justice is not a wedge issue. It is a **litmus test of federation values.**

7. *Aligning Domestic Institutions with Federation Principles*

To truly lead, the U.S. must align its institutions with the federation charter:

- Congress must ratify global treaties on climate, migration, and human rights.

- The Supreme Court must recognize international obligations as part of constitutional interpretation.
- Federal agencies must integrate **federation scorecards and rights audits** into operations.
- Local governments must be empowered to implement federation-aligned programs with full funding and legal backing.

Governance becomes **an act of coherence**—domestic and global policies mutually reinforcing.

Repairing to Lead, Leading by Repair

The United States cannot export what it refuses to practice.

But neither must it be perfect to lead. It must be honest. It must be accountable. And it must be willing to **transform itself into the kind of democracy it believes the world deserves.**

Domestic reform is not a detour from global leadership.

It is the **only legitimate path toward it.**

America's opportunity is real.

Its obligation is clear.

Its future is still unwritten.

The Moral Responsibility of Global Leadership

When the future asks what role the United States played in humanity's defining century, the answer will not be measured in GDP or military budgets. It will be measured in **moral courage.**

- Did it lead when others hesitated?
- Did it repair when it could have denied?
- Did it make room for others at the table—or reinforce its throne?

Global leadership is not a birthright. It is a responsibility —one earned not by declaring values, but by **demonstrating them, at home and abroad.**

1. The Decline of Coercive Legitimacy

Historically, empires maintained global influence through:

- Colonization,
- Economic coercion,
- Military power,
- And control of trade routes and resources.

Today, that model is **unsustainable and morally bankrupt.**

- Military supremacy cannot solve climate breakdown.
- Corporate monopolies cannot rebuild ecological balance.
- Propaganda cannot generate trust.

The hybrid federation model **rejects coercive legitimacy.** It calls instead for:

- Voluntary alignment,
- Rights-based governance,

The United States of the World vs. The United Nations 225

- Participatory leadership.

For America to lead, it must renounce its status as hegemon and **redefine itself as a convenor of common cause.**

2. *What Leadership Looks Like in a Hybrid World*

In the hybrid federation, leadership is not dominance. It is service.

A leading nation:

- Shares technology without monopolizing it.
- Pays its fair share to planetary institutions.
- Accepts binding legal frameworks for accountability.
- Protects the commons rather than privatizing them.
- Models democratic participation in every sphere.

America's leadership potential lies in:

- Its ability to mobilize resources,
- Influence narratives,
- And coordinate systems rapidly and at scale.

But that power must be exercised **with humility, transparency, and solidarity.**

3. *Responsibility Scaled to Power*

The federation does not flatten responsibility— it **scales it.** The greater a nation's historical impact, emissions, military reach, and financial leverage, the greater its duty to:

- **Fund the transition** to regenerative systems,
- **Uphold universal rights** even when politically inconvenient,
- **Submit to enforcement mechanisms** that apply equally to all,
- And **make space for emergent voices**, especially from the Global South, Indigenous communities, youth movements, and marginalized populations.

Leadership means **carrying more—not commanding more.**

4. *Moral Repair as Foreign Policy*

The United States has a unique global footprint of:

- Military intervention,
- Cultural influence,
- Economic dominance.

It must also develop a **doctrine of moral repair**, which includes:

A. Acknowledgment

- Official recognition of historical harms (slavery, coups, land theft, etc.).
- Support for truth commissions and people's tribunals.

B. Restitution

- Reparations funds for nations and communities harmed by U.S. policy.
- Return of stolen cultural artifacts.
- Cancelation of unjust debts and unfair trade pacts.

C. Reinvestment

- Redirecting military aid toward climate adaptation.
- Funding public health, education, and infrastructure in post-conflict regions.
- Empowering civil society networks, not corrupt gatekeepers.

Moral repair becomes **foreign policy in practice—not just language in speeches.**

5. *The Opportunity to Model a New Social Contract*

The United States has the constitutional, institutional, and cultural tools to model what the hybrid federation aspires to become.

This includes:

- A **Bill of Rights** reinterpreted for the 21st century to include housing, climate, and digital access.
- **Local-federal relations** that resemble how nations might relate to the federation.
- A tradition of **civil resistance, legal reform, and pluralist debate** unmatched in scale and reach.

The U.S. doesn't need to invent the future from scratch. It needs to **align its past innovations with its future responsibilities.**

6. *From Fear-Based Exceptionalism to Purpose-Based Leadership*

American exceptionalism has long been a double-edged sword:

- A source of aspiration,
- And an excuse for avoiding accountability.

To lead the hybrid transition, the U.S. must **replace exceptionalism with example.**
Not "We're different, so we opt out,"
but **"We're responsible, so we step up."**
The shift is from:

- *Dominance to partnership,*
- *Immunity to alignment,*
- *Control to contribution.*

This is not weakness. It is **a new form of greatness.**

7. *The Call of History*

Future generations will not ask how the U.S. preserved its primacy.
They will ask:

- Did it prevent collapse?
- Did it protect the vulnerable?

- Did it build the scaffolding of planetary peace?

We are living through **a constitutional moment for the world.**

Just as 1776 marked the beginning of American democracy,

and 1945 marked the birth of international cooperation,

this century demands a new milestone:

The rise of a **just, participatory, enforceable global system—led not by power, but by principle.**

The United States can be a midwife to that future.

Or it can be a footnote in its origin story.

From Empire **to Earth Steward**

America has a choice:

- To cling to empire in decline,
- Or to lead **as Earth's steward—anchored in rights, powered by conscience, and guided by solidarity.**

The path forward begins not with domination, but with a new declaration:

"We hold these truths to be planetary:

that all people are created equal,

that dignity is indivisible,

and that the rights of the many shall be defended by the power of the willing."

America's opportunity is not to rule the future.

It is to help **build a world where no one has to.**

11

NEITHER EMPIRE NOR ISOLATION— THE HYBRID PATH

THE MIDDLE WAY BETWEEN GLOBALISM AND NATIONALISM

If the 20th century was a contest between empire and independence, and the early 21st has pitted globalization against nationalism, then the rest of this century must find a **new synthesis**—a hybrid approach that keeps the best of both worlds and **abandons the worst**.

The truth is this: neither unfettered globalism nor absolutist nationalism can address the scale and complexity of our modern challenges. One invites elite detachment and institutional overreach. The other leads to fragmentation, xenophobia, and paralysis in the face of interdependent crises.

The solution lies not in picking a side, but in **building a bridge.** A hybrid model of global governance rooted in:

- **National sovereignty** preserved,
- **Global cooperation** reimagined,
- And **shared values** operationalized through transparent, democratic institutions.

This part lays the intellectual and moral groundwork for

The United States of the World vs. The United Nations

that model—and argues that it is not only possible, but **urgently necessary**.

1. The Limits of Binary Thinking

For too long, political discourse has treated global engagement as **a zero-sum game:**

- You're either a nationalist or a globalist.
- You either support the UN or reject all multilateralism.
- You believe in national control or in world government.

But this binary is **a false choice**. Most Americans—like most people around the world—live in the **gray zone between extremes.**

They want:

- Strong borders and responsive government.
- Clean air, stable markets, and public health coordination.
- Economic opportunity at home and peaceful cooperation abroad.
- Accountability in international agreements and the ability to walk away when terms are unjust.

A hybrid model starts by acknowledging this **complexity as a strength**, not a contradiction.

2. What a Hybrid Model Is—and Is Not

A hybrid model does **not** mean:

- Replacing all nation-states with a global government.
- Giving unchecked power to supranational bodies.
- Diluting local cultures into a universal monoculture.

Nor does it mean:

- Fortress nationalism,
- Withdrawing from every global institution,
- Or refusing to share responsibility for shared problems.

Instead, a hybrid model means:

- **Governance layered by scale:** Local, national, regional, global—each doing what it does best.
- **Institutions that are flexible, inclusive, and enforceable**—neither toothless nor tyrannical.
- **National autonomy within shared frameworks**—a global floor for human rights, health, and climate; national ceilings for innovation and cultural preservation.
- **Responsive subsidiarity**—problems are solved at the level closest to the people they affect, unless coordination is clearly needed.

Think of it as federalism for the world, without pretending all countries are one country.

3. Historical Precedents for Hybrid Models

The idea of multi-layered governance is not new. Consider:

- **The United States itself:** A union of sovereign states with a central government. The Constitution defines shared powers and reserved powers. That balance has been contested, but it survives.
- **The European Union:** Countries retain sovereignty while participating in a shared market, currency (for some), legal system, and foreign policy coordination.
- **Indigenous governance frameworks:** Many tribal nations operate with a distinct political identity within larger federal systems—balancing autonomy with alliance.
- **Global federations of cities:** Networks like C40, ICLEI, and Mayors for Peace tackle climate, urbanization, and peace-building across borders.

These systems show that **sovereignty and shared decision-making can coexist**, even flourish, if designed with care.

4. Why the Hybrid Model Is Urgently Needed Now

Global problems are getting bigger, faster, and more interconnected:

- The next pandemic could spread in **hours**, not days.
- AI could rewrite laws, economies, and elections in real time.

- Climate feedback loops are speeding up—melting glaciers, displacing millions, destabilizing governments.
- Authoritarian regimes are learning from each other—**coordinating censorship, repression, and digital surveillance**.

At the same time, **public trust in global institutions is eroding**—thanks to bureaucracy, perceived elitism, and real policy failures.

The hybrid model is not just a third way—it's **a survival strategy**.

It says:

- Let nations retain their voices,
- Let people govern close to home,
- But let the world act together when it must—and enforce those actions with fairness and legitimacy.

5. *Core Principles of the Hybrid Approach*

The hybrid model rests on a few core principles:

1. Proportional Sovereignty

Not all powers belong at all levels. Health data sharing belongs at the global level. School curricula belong to communities. Immigration policy may be national—but refugee frameworks require coordination.

2. Responsive Accountability

Global institutions must be **democratically accountable**—through elected delegates, public referenda, or national parliamentary oversight.

3. Polycentric Leadership

Not one country in charge. Leadership rotates, is distributed, and reflects regional diversity. The U.S. can lead—but not **alone**.

4. Legal Integration with National Flexibility

Treaties must be binding, but adaptable. Global norms should **integrate with national legal systems**, not override them.

5. Inclusivity Without Homogenization

The model must **respect identity, religion, language, and local customs**—while enforcing universal human rights and basic standards of justice.

6. The U.S. Role in the Hybrid Future

America has a unique opportunity—**and obligation**—to help design this model.

Why?

- It has experience balancing local and federal power.
- It has a tradition of constitutionalism that can inform global legal innovation.
- It has resources and diplomatic infrastructure unmatched by any other nation.

But to lead credibly, the U.S. must:

- Reform how it engages: **no more whiplash between administrations.**
- Accept limits on unilateral action—**especially in conflict and sanctions.**

- Model humility: **acknowledge past mistakes**, invite shared leadership, and elevate voices from the Global South.

If the U.S. can **lead the transition to a hybrid model**, it can protect sovereignty at home and global stability abroad.
That's not weakness. That's wisdom.

Case Studies in Hybrid Thinking

If the hybrid model is the future, we don't have to build it from scratch—we can **learn from the present**. Around the world, governments, coalitions, and networks are already **testing hybrid approaches**: blending national control with global coordination, tailoring common rules to diverse realities, and seeking enforcement without empire.

In this section, we examine five case studies:

1. Climate Agreements (Paris Accord),
2. Global Tax Reform,
3. COVAX and Vaccine Diplomacy,
4. The Internet and Cyber Norms,
5. AI Governance and Digital Sovereignty.

Each reveals **a different facet of hybrid logic**: where it works, why it fails, and how it might evolve into **a stronger, more legitimate system of global problem-solving.**

1. *The Paris Climate Agreement: Cooperative Flexibility*

The **Paris Agreement**, signed in 2015 under the United

Nations Framework Convention on Climate Change (UNFCCC), is often cited as a **model of hybrid governance**.

Here's how it works:

- Each country submits a **Nationally Determined Contribution (NDC)**—a climate action plan tailored to its economy and capacity.
- There is **no legal penalty** for falling short, but there is a **mechanism for reporting, review, and global peer pressure**.
- The agreement sets a **shared global goal** (limit warming to 1.5–2°C), but lets countries **choose their path** toward it.

This is sovereignty **within a shared mission**.

Strengths:

- Universal participation—nearly 200 signatories.
- Flexibility respects national constraints.
- Morally binding, if not legally punitive.

Weaknesses:

- Voluntary compliance limits enforcement.
- Ambition gaps between countries create distrust.
- U.S. withdrawal in 2017 (and reentry in 2021) **exposed political fragility**.

Lesson: Hybrid governance works when nations feel **ownership of their commitments**—but it needs stronger compliance architecture to reach urgent goals.

. . .

2. *Global Tax Reform: Coordinated Sovereignty in Finance*

In 2021, over 130 countries agreed to a **global minimum corporate tax rate**—a historic deal brokered through the OECD.

The core idea:

- Set a **15% minimum tax** on multinational corporations to prevent "race to the bottom" tax competition.
- Enable countries to **tax profits where sales occur**, not just where a company is legally domiciled.
- Respect **national tax systems**, but **require minimum global standards**.

This is **shared sovereignty in fiscal policy**—one of the most jealously guarded domains.

Strengths:

- Stops corporate tax havens.
- Protects developing nations' tax bases.
- Built on **negotiated consensus**, not top-down imposition.

Weaknesses:

- Implementation is slow—some parliaments (including the U.S. Congress) may stall.
- No global enforcement body—compliance depends on peer pressure and reputational risk.

Lesson: Even on sacred sovereign turf like taxation, **a**

hybrid model can work—if structured as mutual protection, not punitive redistribution.

3. COVAX: Solidarity Meets Sovereignty in Vaccine Access

During the COVID-19 pandemic, the **COVAX initiative**, led by Gavi, CEPI, and the WHO, aimed to distribute vaccines equitably worldwide.

The logic:

- Pool global resources to buy vaccines in bulk.
- Prioritize delivery to health workers and high-risk groups in every country.
- Avoid "vaccine nationalism" by ensuring **minimum global coverage** before surplus bilateral deals.

This was a hybrid effort:

- Voluntary participation,
- National discretion on timelines and brands,
- But shared goals and logistics.

Strengths:

- Delivered over 2 billion doses to over 140 countries.
- Helped prevent catastrophic disparities in some low-income nations.

Weaknesses:

- Rich nations **hoarded doses early**, undermining trust.
- Funding shortfalls delayed shipments.
- Manufacturers prioritized high-paying countries first.

Lesson: Solidarity must be **backed by enforceable fairness**. Hybrid models need **incentives and limits** to prevent dominant players from undermining the collective.

4. The Internet: A Borderless Utility Meets National Firewalls

The global Internet is perhaps the most obvious case of interdependence—yet it is governed through **a tangled web of national, corporate, and transnational mechanisms**.

Consider:

- The **U.S. created the foundational infrastructure** (ARPA, ICANN), and still houses key nodes.
- The **EU leads on regulation** (GDPR, Digital Markets Act).
- **China controls domestic internet content and access**—a model of cyber-sovereignty.
- Global cybersecurity norms remain voluntary, fragmented, and often ignored.

Attempts at hybrid solutions:

- **Multi-stakeholder Internet Governance Forums,**
- Cyber norms discussions at the UN,

- Private sector–government partnerships on disinformation.

Strengths:

- Allows decentralized innovation.
- Prevents monopolization of control.

Weaknesses:

- Lacks clear jurisdiction.
- Vulnerable to disinformation, cyberattacks, and regulatory fragmentation.

Lesson: Digital space demands **sovereignty-sharing at protocol levels**, not just policy levels. A hybrid model must define **who governs the governors**—and how.

5. Artificial Intelligence: The Governance Race Ahead

AI is evolving faster than regulation. Its potential (and risks) are global—so hybrid frameworks are already forming.

Examples:

- **OECD Principles on AI** (adopted by 46 countries) emphasize human rights and transparency.
- **The U.S.–EU Trade and Technology Council** explores common standards.
- **China's AI laws** focus on social stability and government control.

- **The UN and G7** have called for global guardrails—but lack enforcement power.

Here, hybrid governance is not yet mature—but it's emerging:

- **Public-private coordination,**
- Cross-border academic networks,
- Early signals toward **AI ethics certification systems.**

Lesson: Hybrid governance must be **anticipatory**—setting norms before crises force action. It must also allow for **innovation, pluralism, and democratic oversight.**

What These Case Studies Tell Us

Across all five areas, we see the same pattern:

- **Hybrid models offer flexibility, inclusion, and shared purpose,**
- But they suffer from **weak enforcement, politicized participation, and institutional gaps.**

For the hybrid model to truly work, it must evolve from a **makeshift compromise** to a **coherent philosophy**:

- Built on clear rules and adaptive enforcement,
- Centered on democratic legitimacy,
- Designed to preserve sovereignty **without paralyzing collective action.**

From Philosophy to Policy—Building the Hybrid Infrastructure

Every political idea must, at some point, leave the ivory tower and enter the realm of **forms, charters, budgets, and ballots**. The hybrid model of global governance—balancing sovereignty with cooperation—is no exception.

The good news? Much of the raw material already exists: United Nations agencies, regional blocs, trade networks, court systems, digital protocols. The challenge is **coherently integrating them into a multi-layered framework** that is both democratic and functional.

In this part, we lay out the **practical tools** needed to turn the hybrid idea into a policy reality—including legal mechanisms, institutional design, and reform proposals across five key domains.

1. Strengthen Existing Institutions—Don't Abandon Them

Before inventing new bodies, we must reform the ones we already have. Hybrid governance doesn't require reinventing the wheel. It requires **aligning it to new terrain**.

Key steps:

- **United Nations:**
    - Expand Security Council membership to reflect today's geopolitical realities.
    - Create a **UN Parliamentary Assembly**—a democratic advisory body with public representation.
    - Grant independent investigative powers to

UN human rights offices with **enforcement triggers tied to treaty bodies.**
- **World Health Organization:**
  - Establish binding **pandemic response protocols.**
  - Require nations to share outbreak data in real time—linked to international inspections.
  - Create **a sovereign opt-in system** for temporary shared governance in global emergencies.
- **World Trade Organization:**
  - Revive the appellate body with term limits, diverse representation, and transparency mechanisms.
  - Add **climate and labor compliance clauses** to trade disputes.
  - Encourage regional "WTO-compatible" agreements with enforcement flexibility.

Lesson: A hybrid system builds **modular strength into legacy structures**—flexible where needed, binding where possible.

2. *Create Multi-Level Governance Networks*

Hybrid governance thrives on **networks**, not just hierarchies.

These networks should connect:

- **Local governments** (cities, provinces),
- **National ministries and parliaments,**
- **Regional blocs** (e.g., African Union, ASEAN),

- And **global forums** (UN, World Bank, IMF, IPCC).

Policy ideas:

- Institutionalize **city diplomacy** through a Global Municipal Council.
- Connect national legislatures to global forums via **observer delegations and advisory roles**.
- Create a "Global Subsidiarity Index" to determine **which level of governance is best suited** for various policy issues.

Imagine a world where a city's carbon plan automatically uploads to a global dashboard. Where Indigenous legal experts help draft international cultural rights protections. Where refugee policies are shaped by input from both border agents and displaced persons.

This is **networked governance with civic traction**.

3. Formalize Shared Enforcement Mechanisms

Shared rules require **shared tools of enforcement**—without surrendering sovereignty entirely.

Possible hybrid approaches:

- **Treaty-embedded arbitration panels** with rotating judges selected from member states, similar to NAFTA's dispute mechanisms.
- A **Global Accountability Office**: tracking compliance with climate targets, health regulations, and corporate taxation rules—

empowered to publish binding reports but not override domestic courts.
- **Sovereignty-sharing compacts** that are time-limited and task-specific (e.g., during pandemics, disasters, or cyberattacks).

These would not replace national enforcement, but **augment it**—especially where individual state capacity is weak.

Enforcement must be:

- **Proportional** (not one-size-fits-all),
- **Transparent** (public reporting and audit access),
- **Appealable** (a due process right for all members),
- And **collaboratively monitored**.

4. Invest in Digital and Data Infrastructure for Governance

Global coordination today is impossible without **data interoperability and digital trust**.

The hybrid model needs:

- **Real-time dashboards** for treaty compliance, resource allocation, and crisis alerts.
- **Secure cross-border identity verification**—especially for climate migrants, stateless persons, and digital citizens.
- **Open-source policy libraries**, enabling local leaders to adapt global best practices to national law.

To do this, we propose:

- A **Global Digital Public Infrastructure Fund**, seeded by G20 nations and tech companies.
- A **UN–Tech Compact**, requiring private platforms (Google, Meta, Amazon) to provide emergency data access during pandemics, conflicts, or disinformation attacks.
- A **Digital Ethics Protocol Council**, with binding recommendations on AI, surveillance, and algorithmic governance—co-chaired by state, corporate, and civil society leaders.

Technology must serve **participatory sovereignty**, not privatized control.

5. Democratize Global Engagement from the Bottom Up

No hybrid model will succeed without **public trust and legitimacy**.

Steps to democratize:

- Require all global agreements to be **subject to national parliamentary review or referenda**, depending on domestic systems.
- Introduce **citizen deliberation panels** for major global decisions (e.g., vaccine equity, migration, climate finance).
- Create **youth envoys and citizen councils** with standing input in treaty bodies and institutional reform processes.
- Fund global civic education initiatives to teach

the public about **how multilateral decisions affect daily life.**

A hybrid model is only as strong as its **social contract**—not just among states, but among people.

The Trillionaire Club and Global Duty

Let's begin with a question: **What happens when an individual becomes more financially powerful than most nations?**

As of the mid-2020s, the combined wealth of a dozen people exceeded the GDP of more than 100 countries. And within this decade, the world may see its first **trillionaire.**

This reality—of personal wealth outstripping public budgets—demands **a new kind of governance logic**, not based on envy or punishment, but on responsibility. Just as we require nations to participate in global treaties, perhaps we should require **the ultra-wealthy to participate in global stewardship.**

This is the premise of the **Trillionaire Club**: a hybrid mechanism that marries personal freedom with global duty, sovereignty with solidarity. It is **voluntary only until it must be mandatory**—a civic obligation tied not to citizenship, but to scale of impact.

1. Why Trillionaires Matter to the Global Order

A trillion dollars is not just wealth—it is **influence at planetary scale.**

With that money, a single person could:

- Fund clean water systems for every village on Earth.
- End extreme poverty for hundreds of millions.
- Transform education, eradicate malaria, or offset entire nations' emissions.

More importantly, **their investments shape the future:**

- Space infrastructure, AI development, biotechnology, and digital currencies.
- Their platforms govern speech, labor, and access to knowledge.
- Their supply chains dictate environmental norms, often across borders.

They already **govern by proxy**. The question is whether they should do so **alone**—or as part of a **collectively accountable framework**.

2. *The Trillionaire Council: A Framework for Shared Stewardship*

The Trillionaire Club proposal rests on four principles:

1. Membership Triggers Responsibility

Crossing the $1 trillion net worth threshold would automatically enroll the individual in a **global public service mandate**, administered by an international hybrid body (e.g., a council co-governed by the UN, regional unions, and public-private ethics panels).

2. Mandatory Participation with Autonomy

The individual must:

- Serve on a global advisory committee focused on humanitarian goals (e.g., food security, clean water, climate resilience).
- Fund public goods at a scale proportionate to their capacity (minimum threshold: 2.5% of net worth annually).
- Open designated philanthropic projects to **audits and democratic oversight**, ensuring transparency and avoiding PR-only charity.

3. Financial Penalties for Negligence

If the council fails to meet core goals (e.g., measurable hunger reduction, access to clean water), a **structured wealth tax** kicks in—progressive, automatic, and earmarked for a public trust fund managed by sovereign member states.

4. Voluntary Leadership Now, Legal Codification Later

The ideal path begins with voluntary adoption—by the first trillionaire, or a vanguard of tech billionaires. But in time, this would be enshrined in law by:

- G7 and G20 cooperation on enforcement and recognition,
- National legislation establishing a legal "trillionaire governance tier,"
- Integration with global compacts (e.g., UN Sustainable Development Goals, Paris Agreement).

3. Why This Is a Hybrid Model in Action

This idea is **neither a global wealth tax nor a libertarian free-for-all**. It's hybrid:

- **Sovereign nations** retain their tax codes and enforcement tools.
- **Global bodies** gain legitimacy and funding.
- **Private individuals** retain control of capital, but are subject to **ethical service obligations** at planetary scale.

It reflects a world where **the boundary between state and market, citizen and magnate, domestic and global** is increasingly fluid.

If a company like Amazon affects 150 countries, then its principal owner must **serve a community larger than any one nation.**

This is **sovereignty in scale—not just territory.**

4. Precedents and Feasibility

This may sound radical, but it echoes existing frameworks:

- **Draft registration** for military-age citizens.
- **Public trustee roles** for fiduciaries.
- **UN Goodwill Ambassadors**, representing global missions.
- The **B Corporation model,** where firms commit to public benefit alongside profit.

There's also legal precedent:

- U.S. tax law already treats ultra-high net worth individuals differently.
- International law has mechanisms for **universal jurisdiction** on issues like genocide or piracy—recognizing that some actions transcend borders.
- The **Global Magnitsky Act** allows countries to sanction individuals for human rights abuses, regardless of nationality.

If we can **punish individuals globally**, we can also **enlist them globally**—not with force, but with civic duty.

5. *Political Will and Public Support*

For such a council to succeed, three things must happen:

1. **Philanthropic buy-in**: Major billionaires must advocate for it—not just as charity, but as moral evolution.
2. **Public demand**: Citizens must see it as **restorative**, not punitive—a way to reconnect capital with community.
3. **Institutional design**: It must be accountable, representative, and free from capture—more New Deal than Davos.

Polling shows strong public support for tying ultra-wealth to public benefit:

- Over 70% of Americans support a global wealth duty to fund universal clean water access.

The United States of the World vs. The United Nations   253

- Even among high-income earners, a majority support **voluntary global service obligations** for extreme wealth holders.

The Trillionaire Club could become a **civic honor, not a penalty.**

6. What This Teaches Us About the Hybrid Future

This proposal isn't just about billionaires. It's about power and responsibility in a world where **scale matters more than borders.**

It shows:

- That sovereignty can be **tiered and flexible.**
- That participation in global governance can be **triggered by capability, not just nationality.**
- That shared stewardship of public goods is both **morally compelling and structurally possible.**

The hybrid path is not utopian. It is practical. It begins with ideas like this: ambitious, symbolic, implementable. It holds power accountable **not through punishment alone**, but through participation, visibility, and ethical service.

12

BUILDING A BETTER GLOBAL FEDERATION

THE ARCHITECTURE OF SHARED POWER

If the 20th century gave us the blueprints for international cooperation—treaties, alliances, conferences—the 21st century demands **a remodel**. The house of global governance is still standing, but the roof leaks, the stairs creak, and half the rooms are off-limits to the people who live there.

We don't need a global government. We need a **global federation**—a structure that empowers collaboration without imposing uniformity, that protects sovereignty while enforcing shared responsibility, and that builds **legal, political, and civic scaffolding** for a world that is already interconnected.

This part of the chapter sketches the foundational principles, design logic, and policy pathways for constructing such a federation—**not as utopia, but as infrastructure**.

1. What Is a Global Federation—and What It's Not

Let's define terms.

A **federation** is not a singular state. It is:

- A union of distinct political entities,
- Operating under **shared legal and decision-making frameworks,**
- With **delegated authority in specific areas,** and
- **Sovereign retention of local and national competencies.**

A global federation would NOT:

- Replace national governments,
- Control every domain of life,
- Abolish cultural, legal, or economic diversity.

It WOULD:

- Establish **binding yet limited supranational authority** in select areas (climate, pandemics, AI, migration),
- Create **democratic pathways** for decision-making and oversight,
- And function more like a **governance grid** than a pyramid—modular, layered, and interoperable.

2. *The Four Foundational Pillars*

A better global federation must rest on four institutional pillars:

1. A Democratic Global Forum

- Not just the UN General Assembly, which is symbolic, but a **new chamber with legislative**

authority—perhaps evolving from a **UN Parliamentary Assembly**.
- Representatives elected by **national parliaments or directly by global citizens**, apportioned by population but balanced to prevent hegemony.
- Powers limited to transnational concerns: **pandemics, global finance, climate, AI norms**, and large-scale humanitarian response.

2. A Judicial and Accountability Branch

- A **Global Constitutional Court**—not to override national constitutions, but to **arbitrate disputes** on treaty compliance, climate targets, digital sovereignty, and human rights.
- Empowered to issue **enforceable rulings**, subject to opt-in treaties and subsidiary enforcement via regional courts (e.g., European, African, Inter-American).

3. An Executive Coordination Council

- Comprised of elected heads of government (like the G20) and appointed technocratic commissioners (like the European Commission).
- Focused on crisis coordination, implementation of treaties, and convening of emergency action summits.
- Rotating leadership by region to ensure **no permanent dominance**.

4. A Civic Participation Infrastructure

- Global referenda for select decisions (e.g., climate taxes, digital standards).
- A network of **citizen assemblies, youth councils, and civil society panels.**
- **Transparency dashboards** and multilingual data hubs for public access to decisions, debates, and performance indicators.

This is not a bureaucratic behemoth. It's **an agile federation with participatory inputs**, legal clarity, and clear limits.

3. What Powers Would Be Federated?

The federation would not govern all things. It would focus on domains where:

- **Sovereign fragmentation leads to harm,**
- **Coordination has clear benefits,** and
- **Universal standards enable trust.**

Proposed areas:

- **Climate policy**: Enforcement of global emissions targets, carbon markets, and deforestation standards.
- **Pandemic response:** Shared data, coordinated production/distribution of vaccines and supplies, and movement protocols.
- **AI and cyber norms:** Shared ethical principles, risk audits, and threat reporting.
- **Migration and refuge:** Universal asylum

standards, resettlement quotas, and funding for frontline nations.
- **Transnational finance:** Minimum corporate tax standards, illicit finance tracking, and sovereign debt mediation.

Each of these areas would be subject to **national opt-ins** tied to treaty ratification and democratic approval.

4. How Would It Respect Sovereignty?

The central anxiety of global federation is the loss of control.

To mitigate this:

- **Opt-in mechanisms** must be structured around **referenda or parliamentary approval.**
- Nations retain the right to **exit frameworks**—though with graduated penalties if exit harms collective outcomes.
- Legal decisions **apply only within the domain of the treaty or authority delegated.**
- Cultural, educational, religious, and military policy remains entirely national—except in cases of **mass atrocities, genocide, or forced displacement**, already covered under universal jurisdiction.

Think of it as **sovereignty structured by covenant**—not ceded, but exercised together.

5. Can This Be Built Incrementally?

Absolutely. A global federation doesn't need to emerge overnight. It can grow:

- **Regionally:** Through expanded AU, ASEAN, Mercosur, EU-style federations with global liaison offices.
- **Functionally:** One treaty at a time (climate, tax, AI), each building its own participatory and enforcement mechanisms.
- **Civically:** Through global education initiatives, public referenda, and grassroots campaigns.

The goal is not centralization. It is **coherence across complexity**.

6. Why Now?

We are at an inflection point:

- Authoritarian governance is rising.
- Planetary thresholds are being crossed.
- AI could outpace regulation within years.
- The legitimacy of global institutions is faltering.

A global federation is not a luxury. It's an insurance policy for:

- **Preserving democracy through cooperation,**
- **Preventing catastrophic failure in shared systems,**
- And **balancing ambition with accountability**.

We need governance that is **scaled to the challenges we face,** but **rooted in the freedoms we cherish.**
Designing Regional Blocs as Federation Hubs

IF THE GLOBAL federation is to succeed, it must not be **imposed from above.** It must grow **organically, incrementally, and regionally.** That means looking not to New York or Geneva for every solution, but to **Abuja, Brussels, Jakarta, São Paulo, and Addis Ababa**—places where regional institutions already **negotiate sovereignty and solidarity** every day.

This part of the chapter explores how existing **regional blocs** can serve as **federation hubs**—handling the granular complexities of culture, language, and political alignment, while linking into a broader global architecture that is **modular, accountable, and cooperative.**

We focus on five regional models:

1. The European Union (EU)
2. The African Union (AU)
3. The Association of Southeast Asian Nations (ASEAN)
4. Latin American integrations (MERCOSUR, CELAC)
5. The Gulf Cooperation Council (GCC) and emerging regionalisms

1. The European Union: The Most Advanced Prototype

The **European Union** remains the world's most developed transnational institution. It has:

- A **common parliament** and executive commission,
- A **shared currency** among most members (the Euro),
- An independent **court of justice**,
- Coordinated environmental, agricultural, and migration policies.

It is **not a nation**, but it functions more like a **federation of states than an alliance**.

Strengths:

- Robust legal mechanisms with **binding authority**.
- Shared budget and development funds.
- Unified external trade policy and human rights charter.

Challenges:

- Democratic legitimacy questioned during crises (e.g., Greece debt bailout).
- Tensions over **immigration, cultural identity, and economic disparity**.
- The **Brexit precedent**, revealing public discomfort with perceived overreach.

Lesson: The EU model shows what's possible—but also warns against **technocracy without civic participation**. A global federation must **learn from both its strengths and its democratic growing pains**.

. . .

2. The African Union: Sovereignty, Unity, and Peace Architecture

The **African Union**, founded in 2002 as a successor to the Organization of African Unity, includes all 55 African states. It aims to:

- Promote **peace and security**,
- Coordinate economic development,
- Uphold **democratic governance and human rights**.

Key features:

- The **Peace and Security Council**, modeled loosely on the UN Security Council.
- **Continental free trade agreement (AfCFTA)**, launched in 2021.
- **Pan-African Parliament**, with consultative powers (limited legislative authority).

Strengths:

- Rooted in **anti-colonial identity** and Pan-African solidarity.
- Operates in multiple working languages (Arabic, English, French, Portuguese, Swahili).
- Responsive to regional security crises (e.g., AU missions in Somalia, Sudan).

Limitations:

- Dependent on external funding (EU, China, U.S.).

- Sovereignty concerns limit enforcement power.
- Electoral accountability and judicial mechanisms still developing.

Lesson: The AU demonstrates **a hybrid model of soft law and moral authority**—which could evolve into **a binding regional federation with stronger democratic infrastructure.**

3. ASEAN: Consensus Culture and Non-Interference

The **Association of Southeast Asian Nations** includes 10 member states with highly diverse political systems, religions, and economies.

Founded in 1967, ASEAN is based on:

- **Consensus decision-making,**
- **Non-interference in internal affairs,**
- Gradual, **dialogue-based integration.**

Key features:

- **ASEAN Charter** enshrines regional identity and common norms.
- Coordinated response to pandemics, disasters, and economic disruptions.
- Active security dialogues with the U.S., China, and Japan.

Strengths:

- Preserves sovereignty while encouraging regional trust.

- Provides a forum for conflict de-escalation (e.g., South China Sea).
- Emphasizes **"ASEAN Way": flexibility, mutual respect, and consensus-building.**

Challenges:

- Lacks binding enforcement powers.
- Struggles to address human rights violations (e.g., Myanmar).
- Economic integration slower than in EU or AU.

Lesson: ASEAN proves that **cooperation without coercion** can work—but stronger civic participation and legal enforcement mechanisms are needed for deeper federation alignment.

4. Latin American Integration: MERCOSUR and CELAC

Latin America has experimented with multiple integration efforts:

- **MERCOSUR** (Southern Cone trade bloc),
- **CELAC** (Community of Latin American and Caribbean States),
- **Andean Community, UNASUR**, and others—some now defunct or dormant.

Core goals:

- Economic integration,
- Regional identity without U.S. dominance,
- Social development and ecological cooperation.

Strengths:

- Deep cultural ties across language and colonial history.
- Shared interest in **autonomy from great power influence**.
- Increasing support for regional digital and green transformation.

Challenges:

- Political polarization among governments.
- Institutional instability—frequent rebranding and fragmentation.
- Dependence on commodity exports and external investment flows.

Lesson: Latin America's federative ambitions reveal **the importance of political alignment, civic trust, and institutional continuity**. With renewed investment and constitutional coherence, it could serve as a powerful node in a global federation.

5. GCC and Emerging Regionalisms: Potential Hubs Ahead

The **Gulf Cooperation Council (GCC)** and similar regional blocs (e.g., **CARICOM in the Caribbean, Pacific Islands Forum, Eurasian Economic Union**) offer models of:

- Shared security strategy,
- Infrastructure development,
- Cultural diplomacy and economic planning.

Most are **in early or partial stages of integration**, but they:

- Promote regional identity and negotiation leverage,
- Manage cross-border crises collaboratively,
- Establish economic frameworks that could evolve into **shared legal and civic institutions**.

Lesson: Not all regional blocs need to look like the EU. In a hybrid world, each can **function as a modular partner** in a federated network—customized to regional realities.

6. Federation by Region: A Coherent Global Vision

A successful global federation could be:

- **Coordinated through regional hubs**, each with its own civic, legal, and financial architecture.
- Connected by **treaty-based global institutions** that serve as unifying layers for crisis management and norm-setting.
- Designed to balance **centralized coordination with decentralized experimentation**.

In this model:

- **The EU ensures democratic precedent and legal rigor.**
- **The AU brings postcolonial ethics and peacekeeping leadership.**
- **ASEAN demonstrates flexibility and pluralism.**

- Latin America offers a social rights tradition and ecological vision.
- Other blocs contribute regional wisdom, language diversity, and adaptive design.

Together, they form the **backbone of a federated future.**

Enforcing Law Without Empire

ONE OF THE most persistent criticisms of global governance is that it lacks teeth. Treaties are signed, norms are declared, summits are held—and yet human rights are violated, emissions targets are missed, and financial crimes flourish. But when enforcement *is* attempted, it's often seen as selective, coercive, or neocolonial—especially when powerful nations **enforce rules they themselves do not follow.**

So what would *legitimate global enforcement* look like in a hybrid model?

This part of the chapter lays out the principles and tools for **holding states, corporations, and individuals accountable** to shared rules—*without sacrificing sovereignty, fairness, or democratic legitimacy.*

1. Why Enforcement Is the Achilles' Heel of Multilateralism

Let's be blunt: the UN can pass resolutions, but it can't compel compliance. The WTO can issue rulings, but powerful states ignore them. The ICC can indict war criminals, but enforcement depends on local cooperation.

This weakness stems from:

- **Overreliance on voluntary compliance,**
- **Absence of collective enforcement mechanisms,**
- **Unequal application of norms** (e.g., impunity for some, sanctions for others),
- And a fear—sometimes justified—of **global overreach and elite imposition.**

Result? Global law is often law in name only.

To fix this, we don't need an empire. We need **enforceable mutual accountability**, built on consent, capacity, and **reciprocity**.

2. *Principles for Just Enforcement in a Hybrid Model*

Any legitimate enforcement regime must be:

- **Proportional** – Punishments must fit the infraction.
- **Predictable** – Clear in scope and application, not arbitrary.
- **Participatory** – Designed with input from those affected.
- **Multilateral** – No single country can dominate or weaponize it.
- **Nested** – Global enforcement should align with national legal systems, not replace them.
- **Transparent** – Open reporting, review, and appeal mechanisms must be the norm.

The United States of the World vs. The United Nations 269

This means building **enforcement with legitimacy** at every level: legal, institutional, civic, and moral.

3. Enforcement by Consent: Treaty-Based Penalty Frameworks

The simplest hybrid mechanism is **pre-agreed consequences embedded in treaties.**

Examples:

- A climate agreement might include automatic penalties for missing emissions targets:
    - Temporary trade tariffs,
    - Withdrawal of green infrastructure funding,
    - Climate reparations adjusted based on historical emissions.
- A pandemic treaty could include:
    - Escalating sanctions for failing to report outbreaks,
    - Export restrictions on critical health supplies,
    - Coordinated travel bans applied multilaterally.
- A corporate tax accord might:
    - Impose fines on multinationals that shift profits,
    - Deny public procurement contracts to noncompliant firms,
    - Trigger "mirror legislation" across jurisdictions.

These are **not enforced by one power.** They are **codified by consensus**, reviewed by treaty bodies, and upheld by national courts **with global coordination.**

. . .

4. Multilateral Courts with Opt-In Jurisdiction

Rather than a single global court of supreme power, a hybrid model would rely on:

- **Specialized global tribunals:**
    - Climate court (for disputes over emissions and environmental harm),
    - AI ethics tribunal (for data misuse, algorithmic harm, surveillance abuses),
    - Corporate accountability court (for supply chain violations, tax abuse, labor exploitation).
- **Jurisdiction is opt-in, but binding once signed.**
- **Decisions enforceable via national courts** (like in the European model).
- Rulings subject to **appeals panels** and **public reporting**.

This model avoids overreach while **empowering principled enforcement**. It treats justice not as empire, but as **interlocking legitimacy**.

5. Civic-Driven Enforcement: Public Accountability Mechanisms

Top-down enforcement must be paired with **bottom-up pressure**.

Ideas:

- **Global whistleblower protection** laws for transnational crimes.
- **Citizen audits** of treaty compliance—e.g.,

emissions tracking, labor rights, pandemic response.
- Publicly funded **media collaboratives** that investigate treaty violations and hold institutions accountable.
- **Crowdsourced compliance platforms** where citizens track performance of corporations and states in real time.

Enforcement isn't just legal—it's **social and reputational**. Public visibility drives political will.

6. Enforcement Through Economic and Market Incentives

Markets can help enforce global norms—if properly structured.

Examples:

- **Carbon border adjustments** penalize high-emission goods entering green economies.
- ESG standards linked to **verified compliance**, not self-reporting.
- **Global ratings agencies** for treaty adherence, with investment premiums or penalties.
- **Sanction alternatives:** targeted tariffs, procurement bans, and corporate blacklists coordinated through **multilateral consensus**, not unilateral decree.

These tools make **non-compliance economically painful**, while avoiding military coercion.

. . .

7. *Preventing Abuse of Enforcement Mechanisms*

The risk in any enforcement regime is **political capture**—where powerful actors weaponize rules.

Safeguards:

- Require **rotating leadership** of enforcement bodies.
- Enshrine **whistleblower immunity**, judicial independence, and multi-region oversight.
- Allow **citizen or NGO complaints** to trigger reviews.
- Create **anti-retaliation shields**: countries or companies can't punish compliance.

Transparency is the antidote to tyranny. **Accountability works only when it's visible, plural, and reciprocal.**

8. *The Moral Legitimacy of Collective Accountability*

The hybrid model asks us to move beyond two bad options:

- Toothless cooperation, or
- Coercive domination.

Instead, it offers **accountability as mutual stewardship:**

- Sovereigns don't surrender autonomy—they **consent to co-govern.**
- Citizens don't lose control—they **gain tools to pressure, verify, and shape.**

In this way, enforcement becomes **a service, not a**

sentence—protecting shared goods while preserving rightful power.

Civic Identity in a Federated World

LAWS NEED LEGITIMACY. Institutions need imagination. And governance—at any level—requires more than rules. It requires **belonging**.

The success of a hybrid global federation will not depend solely on treaty signatures or enforcement mechanisms. It will rise or fall on whether people across nations, classes, and cultures can begin to see themselves as **participants in a shared civic project**. That doesn't mean erasing borders. It means **adding bridges**—building a layered sense of identity that spans local roots, national pride, and **planetary citizenship**.

This section explores how to cultivate that civic identity through **narrative, education, ritual, and inclusion**—the soft infrastructure that makes shared governance meaningful.

1. Why Identity Matters in Governance

Every durable political system has relied on **stories and symbols** to hold it together.

- The U.S. Constitution would be a relic without the story of "We the People."
- The European Union would have collapsed long ago without the narrative of peace after war.
- The African Union is sustained by the legacy of anti-colonial solidarity.

Civic identity turns obligation into participation, and abstract institutions into **homes of purpose**.

But global governance today lacks that emotional resonance. Most people don't know:

- Who represents them at the UN.
- What treaties their country has ratified.
- How their voice shapes international decisions.

Worse, globalism is often framed as **elite, abstract, or even threatening**. A civic identity for a federated world must be **the opposite**: tangible, rooted, and inviting.

2. *Nested Citizenship: Local, National, Global*

We don't need to replace national identity. We need to **layer it**.

Just as citizens can identify as both Texans and Americans, or Parisians and Europeans, so too can we build layered civic identities:

- **Local citizenship**: tied to community, tradition, and daily life.
- **National citizenship**: tied to shared language, law, and institutions.
- **Global citizenship**: tied to shared fate, rights, and responsibility.

Each level strengthens the others. Local pride doesn't preclude planetary duty—it can empower it.

A farmer who cares for her land should also care about **climate cooperation**. A teacher who shapes young minds should also value **global literacy**. A voter in

Michigan or Mumbai should understand that their choices ripple across **a connected civic ecosystem**.

3. Education for Global Citizenship

The foundation of civic identity is education. But global citizenship education must go beyond geography quizzes and UN acronyms.

Key elements:

- **Rights and responsibilities:** Teach not only the Universal Declaration of Human Rights, but also climate responsibilities, data ethics, and refugee solidarity.
- **Systems thinking:** Help students understand how supply chains, energy markets, and digital platforms connect them to others.
- **Empathy and ethics:** Encourage storytelling across cultures, simulations of global negotiations, and critical thinking about inequality and justice.
- **Civic action skills:** Train students in advocacy, coalition-building, and how to engage international institutions as citizens—not just spectators.

Pilot programs are already showing success:

- **Model UN simulations in secondary schools.**
- **Global service-learning exchanges.**
- **Digital classrooms connecting students across continents.**

A global civic identity is built **not through slogans, but through shared experience.**

4. Symbols, Rituals, and Collective Memory

Civic belonging needs **symbols and rituals** that bind people emotionally.

Imagine:

- A **Global Public Service Day**, where citizens around the world volunteer in their communities for a shared cause.
- A **World Citizenship Card**, verifying participation in transnational projects, youth summits, or treaty referenda.
- A **Global Anthem** or set of civic songs, written collaboratively across cultures, performed in schools or public events.
- A **Federation Charter Preamble**, signed or recited in ceremonies marking global citizenship milestones—like graduating from a civic education course or entering a service year abroad.

These may sound symbolic. That's the point. Symbols create stories. Stories create bonds. Bonds build legitimacy.

5. Participatory Institutions for a Shared Identity

To build civic identity, people need **a place to act it out.**

Institutions must be designed not just to govern, but to **include:**

- **Global Referenda:** Give citizens a voice in major treaties, like climate compacts or AI charters.
- **Citizens' Assemblies:** Select participants by lot from every region to deliberate on global questions.
- **Youth Parliaments:** Offer real advisory power to next-generation leaders.
- **Open Treaties:** Let citizens sign and track the treaties their governments ratify—similar to civic pledges.

The goal is to turn abstract policy into **personal action**. To give every person, regardless of nation, class, or creed, a sense that they are not just governed—but **governing**.

6. Media and Narrative: The Stories We Tell Ourselves

We cannot build a global civic identity if every international issue is framed as:

- A loss of control,
- A foreign imposition,
- Or an elite negotiation behind closed doors.

We need **journalism, storytelling, and popular culture** that portray:

- The drama of international collaboration,
- The courage of climate diplomats,
- The voices of displaced people seeking justice,
- The triumphs of shared science, aid, and culture.

This means:

- Funding independent global public media,
- Training journalists in constructive reporting on global affairs,
- Supporting creators who tell stories of **human connection across borders.**

Imagine a streaming series dramatizing the creation of a pandemic treaty. A podcast following the lives of five students navigating global climate service. A graphic novel about the first Trillionaire Club volunteer.

We build civic identity by **narrating belonging.**

7. Toward a Shared "We"

At the heart of it all is the simplest word: **we.**

A global federation cannot just be legal, procedural, or technocratic. It must be *civic*—felt, believed in, and practiced.

That begins with:

- A shared commitment to dignity,
- A willingness to listen across difference,
- A belief that humanity's story is not **a clash of civilizations,** but **a community of communities** learning to live together.

That is what a civic identity in a federated world means. Not replacing who we are—but expanding who belongs.

13

A UNIVERSAL BILL OF RIGHTS
FOUNDATIONS OF A GLOBAL RIGHTS FRAMEWORK

What gives a system of governance its soul?

Not just laws, institutions, or borders—but a **statement of shared values**, backed by enforceable commitments. In the United States, it was the Bill of Rights. In Europe, the Charter of Fundamental Rights. For South Africa, it was a post-apartheid constitution that reimagined what equality could mean.

A truly hybrid global federation—balancing sovereignty and cooperation—requires **its own declaration of rights**. Not to erase national constitutions, but to **underpin them** with universal standards: the rights of the individual, the responsibilities of the collective, and **the dignity that no border may deny**.

In this section, we trace the evolution, rationale, and foundational principles of a Universal Bill of Rights that could serve as **the moral compass of a federated world**.

1. The History Behind the Idea

The notion of universal rights is not new—but its implementation has always been **partial, aspirational, and contested.**

- **1948**: The **Universal Declaration of Human Rights (UDHR)** laid the groundwork—proclaiming the inherent dignity of all people, regardless of nation.
- **1966**: The **International Covenants** on Civil and Political Rights and Economic, Social and Cultural Rights (ICCPR and ICESCR) added legal heft.
- **1979 to 2007**: A series of treaties addressed race, gender, children's rights, torture, and disability.

But the current system suffers from:

- **Uneven ratification,**
- **Weak enforcement,**
- **Limited public awareness,**
- And **competing interpretations of sovereignty and culture.**

To build a better global order, we need to **upgrade the rights framework from declaration to integration**—from moral aspiration to legal foundation.

2. *Why Now?*

The urgency is real:

- **Climate change** threatens the right to life, health, and housing.

- **Digital surveillance** threatens privacy, speech, and autonomy.
- **Authoritarian creep** undermines press freedom, assembly, and dissent.
- **Mass displacement** raises questions about borders, belonging, and protection.

And as artificial intelligence, biotechnology, and planetary stressors converge, **the current rights architecture is outdated and fragmented.**

A Universal Bill of Rights would:

- Consolidate existing treaties into a coherent system,
- Define new rights fit for modern threats,
- Ensure enforceability through hybrid legal mechanisms,
- And reinforce civic identity in a federated world.

3. Key Design Principles

A viable Universal Bill of Rights must meet five criteria:

1. **Universality with Local Adaptability**

- Rights must apply everywhere, to everyone.
- Local cultures and legal traditions may **implement them differently,** but not deny their essence.

2. **Enforceability at Multiple Levels**

- Rights should be enforceable through:
  - **National courts,**
  - **Regional human rights tribunals,**
  - **Specialized global bodies** (e.g., climate, digital, refugee rights panels).

3. Legal Clarity and Justiciability

- Rights must be **clear, actionable, and subject to legal remedy**—not vague ideals.
- Obligations of states, corporations, and supranational institutions must be defined.

4. Balance of Rights and Responsibilities

- Rights come with civic duties:
  - To respect the rights of others,
  - To participate in shared governance,
  - To uphold sustainability, peace, and non-discrimination.

5. Living Framework

- The Bill should be **amendable through democratic global processes**, allowing new rights to emerge (e.g., data dignity, algorithmic transparency, ecological justice).

4. Core Rights for a Federated World

While details will follow in Part 2, a foundational Universal Bill of Rights would likely include:

- **Civil and political rights:**
    - Freedom of speech, religion, and association.
    - Right to due process and legal equality.
    - Protection from arbitrary detention, torture, and censorship.
- **Social and economic rights:**
    - Access to healthcare, education, and housing.
    - Fair wages, labor protections, and social safety nets.
    - Food and water security.
- **Environmental rights:**
    - Right to a healthy planet.
    - Protections against environmental destruction and forced migration.
- **Digital and technological rights:**
    - Data privacy, algorithmic accountability, and equitable access to the internet.
    - Right to protection from digital manipulation and surveillance.
- **Group and identity rights:**
    - Minority and Indigenous rights.
    - Gender equality, LGBTQ+ protections, and disability inclusion.
    - Cultural preservation and religious freedom.

These rights would be **non-exhaustive and future-ready**—anticipating shifts in technology, demography, and planetary limits.

5. Institutional Pathways to Codification

A Universal Bill of Rights could be advanced through:

- A **UN Convention on Global Rights and Responsibilities,** co-drafted by states, civil society, and regional blocs.
- Integration into existing charters:
    - EU Charter of Fundamental Rights,
    - AU's African Charter on Human and Peoples' Rights,
    - ASEAN's Human Rights Declaration.
- Ratification by national parliaments, with **opt-in enforcement protocols.**
- Creation of a **Global Human Rights Review Mechanism,** modeled on the Universal Periodic Review but with **binding follow-up procedures.**

The goal is not to impose, but to **align**—ensuring that every person lives under **a floor of rights, no matter where they live.**

6. A Moral Framework for the 21st Century

Ultimately, a Universal Bill of Rights is not just about legal safeguards. It is about **articulating what kind of civilization we want to be.**

- Will we treat AI decisions as final, or protect human dignity against automation?
- Will we defend the rights of future generations to a livable Earth?
- Will we honor the displaced, the vulnerable, the silenced—not just in charity, but in law?

A true federation is not just a contract. It is a **shared ethical commitment.**

This Bill would be its **beating heart**.

Rights in Practice—Global **Standards, National Implementation**

Declaring rights is easy. Implementing them is hard.

Every major rights declaration in history—be it the U.S. Bill of Rights, France's Declaration of the Rights of Man, or the post-WWII Universal Declaration of Human Rights—has faced the same challenge: **how to make rights real for people in radically different places and circumstances.**

In a hybrid global federation, the Universal Bill of Rights must be more than a poetic text. It must be a **living framework**, capable of operating across legal systems, political traditions, and cultural landscapes. That means balancing **universal norms with local adaptability**—and creating mechanisms that ensure **both compliance and contextual relevance.**

This part outlines the legal structures, enforcement tools, and civic pathways that would bring global rights into national life—without undermining identity or autonomy.

1. The "Floor Not Ceiling" Doctrine

The cornerstone of practical implementation is this simple principle:

Global rights set a minimum standard—never a maximum.

That means:

- Countries can go beyond the Universal Bill of Rights (UBR), but not below.
- Regional charters and national constitutions must **meet or exceed** these standards.
- No nation may use cultural, religious, or political justifications to **deny** the minimum—though they may interpret **how** those rights are applied.

For example:

- **Freedom of religion** is universal. How a country regulates worship spaces, holidays, or clerical status may vary—but it may not criminalize peaceful belief or apostasy.
- **Right to healthcare** is universal. Delivery systems can differ (public, private, mixed), but **denial of access due to class or race** violates the global standard.

This model respects diversity while maintaining **non-negotiable protections**.

2. *Legal Harmonization: Bridging Constitutions and Global Treaties*

A key challenge in implementation is legal alignment:

- Some countries enshrine international law **above domestic law**.
- Others (like the U.S.) treat international treaties as equivalent but not supreme.
- Still others ignore or selectively apply global norms.

To create a seamless system, the hybrid federation would promote **legal harmonization mechanisms:**

- **Compatibility Clauses:** Countries ratifying the UBR would amend their constitutions or statutes to declare the document **superseding in case of conflict.**
- **Judicial Concordance Councils:** Global and national judges would co-develop **case interpretation guidelines** to reconcile legal frameworks.
- **Implementation Protocols:** Tailored action plans for each country, negotiated at the time of ratification, ensuring feasibility and alignment with domestic law.

Think of this as **translating rights across legal languages**—without losing their essence.

3. Enforcement Through a Multilevel Judicial System

Enforcement must be **layered and pluralistic**, not centralized.

The UBR would be upheld by:

1. **National Courts,** empowered to apply global standards to domestic cases.
2. **Regional Tribunals,** such as:
    - European Court of Human Rights,
    - African Court on Human and Peoples' Rights,
    - ASEAN and Latin American rights panels.

3. **Global Special Chambers,** for transnational violations (e.g., climate injustice, digital rights abuse, systemic statelessness).

Cases would follow a **subsidiarity model:**

- First addressed domestically,
- Appealed regionally,
- Heard globally only when all other remedies fail or when the issue transcends borders.

Decisions would be **binding within ratifying states,** enforced through:

- National legal systems,
- Treaty-based penalties,
- Funding conditions from global institutions (e.g., trade, aid, development).

4. *Integrating Rights into Policy and Budgeting*

Declaring a right without funding it is **moral theater.** To make rights meaningful, states would be required to:

- **Include rights benchmarks in national budgets,**
- **Conduct annual impact audits,**
- Publish **UBR implementation scorecards,** accessible to citizens and civil society.

Examples:

- The right to education would be measured by enrollment rates, teacher-to-student ratios, and inclusivity.
- The right to clean air would be linked to emission targets, health outcomes, and local policy shifts.
- The right to housing would be tied to homelessness rates, rental affordability indexes, and slum clearance protections.

This turns abstract ideals into **policy mandates**.

5. Reconciling Cultural Norms and Universal Principles

One of the toughest challenges: What happens when global rights and local customs collide?

Some tensions are inevitable:

- Gender equality and patriarchal traditions,
- Freedom of expression and laws against religious insult,
- LGBTQ+ rights and conservative moral codes.

The UBR would address these through:

- **Transitional Implementation Plans:** Gradual compliance with defined milestones, supported by education and cultural dialogue.
- **Cultural Exemptions Review Boards:** Panels of jurists, ethicists, and cultural leaders to mediate disputes—aiming for **reinterpretation, not rejection** of rights.

- **Independent Watchdog Reports:** Publicly reviewing areas of tension, offering recommendations, and promoting inclusive civic dialogue.

The goal is not to erase culture, but to **evolve it through persuasion, participation, and moral reasoning.**

6. *Rights Education and Civic Literacy*

A right unknown is a right unenforced.

The UBR framework would require signatory states to implement:

- **Mandatory rights education** in school curricula (adapted to local context),
- **Public campaigns** about new rights and how to claim them,
- **Civic toolkits** in multiple languages and formats,
- **Rights ombuds offices** in every district—staffed with trained legal and civic personnel.

Education transforms people from subjects into citizens—from the governed into **participants in a rights-based democracy.**

7. *Rights and Emergencies: The Non-Derogable Core*

Even the best systems face crises. But emergencies cannot be used as excuses for **rights evaporation.**

The UBR would define **non-derogable rights:**

- No torture,

The United States of the World vs. The United Nations 291

- No extrajudicial killing,
- No discrimination,
- No arbitrary imprisonment,
- No statelessness.

Even during pandemics, wars, or disasters, these rights **must stand.**

Other rights may be temporarily limited **with strict oversight**—but only under:

- **Time-bound declarations,**
- **Judicial approval,**
- **Independent monitoring and review.**

This protects democracy **when it's most fragile.**

8. Monitoring and Review: Transparency as Enforcement

Every few years, signatory nations would undergo a **Global Rights Peer Review**—similar to the UN's Universal Periodic Review, but with binding follow-up.

Elements:

- Government self-report,
- Civil society shadow report,
- Public hearings with citizen participation,
- Outcome document with benchmarks, deadlines, and technical support offers.

Progress would be tracked on a **Universal Rights Dashboard**, accessible to all.

Transparency breeds accountability. And accountability sustains trust.

Rights and the Private Sector—Corporate Obligations in a Federated World

ONCE UPON A TIME, rights were framed as protections **from the state.** That's no longer enough.

Today, a person's access to information, mobility, employment, housing, banking, communication—even identity—is shaped as much by private platforms and global supply chains as by public law. A few dozen corporations now control the infrastructure of modern life: from search engines to social media, pharmaceuticals to cloud storage, microchips to shipping lanes.

To defend rights in the 21st century, the Universal Bill of Rights must confront a reality that legal theory often avoids: **sovereignty is shared—and so are duties.**

This section proposes legal, institutional, and financial mechanisms to ensure that corporations—not just governments—uphold the rights of the people they serve, employ, monitor, and affect.

1. The Expanding Power of the Private Sector

Let's start with the facts:

- **Tech platforms** determine what speech is visible, what data is collected, and what knowledge circulates.
- **Supply chains** dictate labor conditions, environmental degradation, and resource flows.
- **Finance institutions** decide which sectors thrive and which collapse.

- **Pharmaceutical giants** negotiate access to life-saving medicine.
- **AI developers** are building systems that influence everything from hiring to healthcare to policing.

This is not capitalism as usual. This is **corporate governance without democratic oversight**.

Unless the Universal Bill of Rights applies to these actors, it is incomplete—and increasingly, irrelevant.

2. Legal Theories for Corporate Responsibility

The modern legal system has ample precedent for **corporate obligations under public law**:

- **Corporate personhood** grants rights (e.g., to contract, to speech). But rights imply **responsibilities**.
- Companies already face legal liability for:
  - Environmental harm,
  - Workplace discrimination,
  - Product safety failures.

The shift needed is **not inventing responsibility, but internationalizing it**.

We propose the following legal innovations:

1. Rights-Based Corporate Chartering

- Require large corporations (over $10 billion revenue or operating in 5+ countries) to **adopt governance charters** that integrate the Universal Bill of Rights.

- Failure to comply may result in:
    - Fines,
    - Deregistration,
    - Denial of government contracts or international partnerships.

2. International Corporate Accountability Tribunal (ICAT)

- A new legal forum to hear cases where transnational corporations violate global rights.
- Jurisdiction triggered by:
    - Cross-border impacts,
    - Citizen petitions,
    - Whistleblower reports.
- Sanctions may include monetary penalties, mandated reparations, or operational suspension in violating regions.

3. Mandatory Human Rights Due Diligence Laws

- Already being adopted in the EU, these require:
    - Risk assessments,
    - Remediation plans,
    - Independent audits of labor, environmental, and digital practices.

Codifying these under the UBR framework makes them **universally enforceable**.

3. Corporate Duties Under Specific Rights Domains

The Universal Bill of Rights imposes **distinct obligations** on corporate actors in different sectors:

A. Digital & Tech Companies

- Respect user privacy (opt-in, transparent data policies).
- Prevent algorithmic bias and discrimination.
- Provide grievance mechanisms for deplatforming and moderation.
- Ensure equitable access to essential digital services (e.g., broadband as a right).

B. Industrial and Energy Sectors

- Comply with environmental protections under the Right to a Livable Planet.
- Respect Indigenous land rights and consult affected communities.
- Report transparently on emissions, spills, and remediation.

C. Finance and Investment Firms

- Conduct **social impact assessments** on major investment portfolios.
- Prevent tax evasion, money laundering, and extractive debt schemes.
- Include ESG (Environmental, Social, and Governance) criteria with **binding weight**, not just voluntary PR.

D. Pharmaceuticals and Health Corporations

- Prioritize affordability and access, especially in emergencies.
- Share vaccine or treatment IP under public health compacts.
- Allow for licensing during pandemics under the UBR's Right to Health clause.

These duties would be **codified through binding compacts**, signed by corporations, states, and watchdog organizations, and reviewed annually by **public interest commissions**.

4. *Mechanisms for Transparency and Accountability*

No rights framework can succeed without **visibility and enforcement**. We propose:

A. The Global Rights Impact Registry (GRIR)

- Publicly discloses annual rights impact reports from all large corporations.
- Includes third-party audits and whistleblower commentary.

B. The People's Platform for Corporate Justice

- A crowdsourced digital platform where workers, consumers, and communities can:
    - Report violations,
    - Upload documentation,
    - Track case responses.

C. Worker and Consumer Rights Councils

- Established within multinational companies,
- Elected by employees and users,
- Empowered to escalate rights concerns to regulators.

D. Penalty & Incentive System

- Fines for violations channeled into:
    - Reparations,
    - Development funds,
    - Independent compliance training.
- Tax breaks and procurement preference for companies with **high UBR compliance scores.**

This blends **stick and carrot**, law and market.

5. The Moral Argument: Private Wealth, Public Duty

Here's the principle in one sentence:

With transnational power comes transnational responsibility.

When companies:

- Mine our data,
- Shape our choices,
- Work across our borders,
- And affect our lives—

They must also be **answerable to our rights.**

This is not anti-capitalism. It's **post-feudal democracy.** No actor—public or private—should operate beyond accountability.

. . .

6. *From Philanthropy to Duty: The End of Voluntarism*

Too often, corporate responsibility has been framed as **charity**:

- Nice when it happens,
- Optional if inconvenient,
- A tool for brand management.

The Universal Bill of Rights says: *No more.*

- Responsibility is not optional.
- Compliance is not negotiable.
- Good PR cannot replace **justice**.

This is how we reclaim the public domain—not by ending markets, but by **making them ethical by design**.

The Rights of Future Generations—Intergenerational Justice in the Federation

You and I can vote. We can protest. We can sue. We can lobby for change.

But what about the unborn child who will inherit a coastline lost to rising seas, an atmosphere laced with carbon, a digital world built by opaque algorithms, and a food chain straining under extinction?

Governance without representation is tyranny—and nowhere is this more true than in our failure to represent the **interests of future generations.**

A hybrid global federation must be designed not only for the governed, but for the **not-yet-governed**. It must recognize **intergenerational justice** as a foundational principle—not an afterthought, not a footnote, but **a living commitment woven into every law, treaty, and investment.**

1. Why Future Rights Matter Now

The harms we fail to prevent today—climate chaos, technological overreach, biodiversity collapse, runaway debt—will be **the burdens our children bear.**

What makes these harms distinct?

- **Irreversibility**: Once coral reefs die or AI systems entrench bias, there is no easy rollback.
- **Lag effect**: Decisions made today create risks that materialize decades from now.
- **Power asymmetry**: The affected have no say, no vote, no veto.

This makes future rights **morally urgent and legally complex.** But complexity is not an excuse for delay. It's a call to **design governance structures that think in centuries, not just election cycles.**

2. Defining the Rights of Future Generations

A Universal Bill of Rights for a hybrid federation would explicitly include a **section dedicated to intergenerational justice.**

Core rights could include:

A. Right to Environmental Integrity

- The right to a stable climate, clean air, clean water, and thriving biodiversity.

- Enforceable through planetary boundaries benchmarks.

B. Right to Economic Sustainability

- Protection from policies that create unpayable sovereign debt, over-extraction of finite resources, or speculative bubbles that erode long-term stability.

C. Right to Technological Stewardship

- AI, biotech, and digital systems must be designed with long-term risks in mind.
- Mandated transparency, auditability, and ethical review.

D. Right to Cultural Continuity

- Future generations must inherit not only infrastructure, but language, history, knowledge, and sacred sites.
- This includes preservation of Indigenous lifeways and endangered cultural traditions.

E. Right to Participation-in-Absentia

- Legal recognition of the interests of future generations in all major policymaking, requiring special **guardianship representation**.

These rights would be embedded **into every other**

article, much like nondiscrimination clauses in modern constitutions.

3. Legal and Institutional Mechanisms for Enforcement

How do we enforce rights for those who don't yet exist?

By creating **guardianship institutions** and procedural mandates.

A. Future Generations Ombudspersons

- Independent offices at national, regional, and global levels.
- Mandate: Review policies, treaties, budgets, and technologies for long-term impact.
- Authority to issue **binding delay or mitigation orders.**

Examples already exist:

- **Hungary** and **Wales** have Future Generations Commissioners.
- The **UN Secretary-General** proposed a Special Envoy for Future Generations.
- These models can scale globally.

B. Intergenerational Impact Assessments (IIAs)

- Mandatory for:
    - Major infrastructure projects,
    - Climate-altering policies,
    - Technology deployment at scale.
- Includes simulations, risk matrices, and civic deliberation.

C. Citizens' Panels on Long-Term Policy

- A new form of democratic deliberation.
- Multigenerational juries review policy options, with expert guidance on future impact.

D. Constitutional Entrenchment

- Nations ratifying the UBR would amend their constitutions to include a "trust clause," requiring them to act as **stewards of resources held in trust for the unborn.**

This makes future justice **a legal norm, not a moral hope.**

4. *Financial and Environmental Accountability Across Generations*

Long-term thinking requires **new tools of accounting and responsibility.**

We propose:

A. Planetary Balance Sheets

- Every government must publish a periodic audit of its ecological debt and regeneration.
- Linked to access to development aid, IMF funding, and trade benefits.

B. Generational Budgeting

- Government and corporate budgets must estimate:

- 30–50 year risk horizons,
- Social and ecological debt projections,
- Resilience indices.

C. Intergenerational Equity Funds

- Mandatory investment in:
  - Clean energy,
  - Climate adaptation,
  - Public health infrastructure,
  - Cultural heritage preservation.

Funded through:

- Carbon fees,
- Windfall taxes,
- Resource royalties,
- And contributions from Trillionaire Club mandates (see Chapter 10, Part 4).

5. Cultural Transformation: The Seven-Generation Mindset

Governance reform is not enough. We need **cultural reorientation**.

Inspiration can be drawn from Indigenous traditions, such as the **Haudenosaunee Seventh Generation Principle**:

In every decision, consider its impact on the seventh generation from now.

This principle must be globalized:

- In education: Future impact as a core curricular value.
- In law: Sunset clauses and review requirements after 25+ years.
- In media: Narratives of continuity, guardianship, and time-honoring responsibility.

Civic rituals—like Future Days, intergenerational parliaments, or memory gardens—can embed these values **in public life.**

6. *The Ethics of Legacy and Inheritance*
At its core, this is a question of character:

- Will we be ancestors of pride—or regret?
- Will we pass down rights—or risks?
- Will the federated world be remembered as **a project of consumption or conservation**?

A Universal Bill of Rights must not end with us. It must **begin with them.**

A Bridge to Chapter 13: National Cultures, Local Rule—Autonomy Without Isolation

With the moral core of the hybrid federation now in place, we turn next to a critical balancing act: **How can global rights and frameworks be honored while protecting national identity, Indigenous sovereignty, and cultural pluralism?**

In Chapter 13, we explore how local governance, diverse

traditions, and constitutional autonomy can thrive **within a federated world**—proving that we can live together **without becoming the same.**

14

NATIONAL CULTURES, LOCAL RULE —AUTONOMY WITHOUT ISOLATION

SOVEREIGNTY REIMAGINED IN A FEDERATED WORLD

Let's be honest: the word "sovereignty" has taken a beating.

In some circles, it's framed as a relic—an obstacle to progress, a tool for repression, a refusal to cooperate. In others, it's clung to like a shield—a defense against foreign interference, elite globalism, and cultural erasure.

But sovereignty doesn't have to be binary. It's not either *absolute control* or *complete surrender*. In a federated global system, sovereignty must evolve—not vanish, but **transform into a layered, negotiated, and collaborative form of self-rule.**

This section reframes sovereignty for the 21st century. It explores how states, regions, Indigenous peoples, and communities can **maintain meaningful autonomy** while participating in shared governance—**without becoming isolated or adversarial.**

1. Classical Sovereignty vs. Interdependent Reality

Traditionally, sovereignty meant:

- Supreme authority within a defined territory,
- Non-interference from external actors,
- The state as the sole source of legitimate law.

This was the Westphalian model, born in 1648 and reinforced by decolonization, nationalism, and constitutional revolutions.

But the 21st century doesn't follow neat borders:

- Pandemics cross customs lines,
- Emissions ignore passports,
- Data moves invisibly,
- Investment and disinformation flow with little regulation.

Rigid sovereignty breaks under these pressures. But surrendering it altogether creates democratic panic and cultural resistance.

The hybrid solution: **sovereignty as dynamic autonomy**—exercised in some areas, shared in others, always anchored in **self-determined consent**.

2. *The Three Dimensions of Evolved Sovereignty*

To modernize sovereignty without erasing it, we propose a tripartite framework:

A. Political Sovereignty (Internal Autonomy)

- Control over electoral systems, local law, taxation, education, cultural policy, and policing.

- Protected against external imposition, unless in violation of global rights or treaty obligations.

B. Functional Sovereignty (Shared Authority by Domain)

- Voluntary delegation of certain powers (e.g., air travel safety, carbon accounting, global health protocols) to international bodies.
- Functions delegated **by treaty**, not taken by force.

C. Moral Sovereignty (Cultural and Civilizational Identity)

- Protection of language, religion, heritage, and Indigenous knowledge.
- Guaranteed within the federation as **an unalienable right**, not subject to harmonization.

This three-part model allows a state or people to say:

"We govern ourselves *here*, we govern *with others* there, and we remain *ourselves* always."

3. Federalism as a Bridge Between Identity and Order

Federalism isn't just a domestic tool—it's a **blueprint for global coexistence.**

Key features that apply globally:

- **Subsidiarity**: Decisions are made at the most local level capable of addressing them effectively.

- **Asymmetric integration:** Not all members share all powers—some opt into deeper cooperation than others.
- **Mutual recognition:** One polity doesn't have to agree with another to **co-goexist**.

Example:

- In the EU, Denmark opted out of the Eurozone. Poland accepts EU courts in trade but contests them in migration law. These tensions exist—**but the system holds.**

In a global federation, federalism enables:

- Autonomy without anarchy,
- Unity without uniformity,
- Integration without erasure.

4. Sovereignty in the Context of the Universal Bill of Rights

Can local law reject global rights?

Under the hybrid model: **no—but it can interpret them within cultural context.**

For example:

- A secular state and a religious monarchy may implement freedom of religion differently—but both must **guarantee it without coercion.**
- A collectivist culture may interpret property rights through community stewardship—not just individual ownership.

- An Indigenous government may integrate spiritual, ecological, and ancestral law into justice systems—so long as due process and dignity are upheld.

This is not relativism. It is **contextual constitutionalism**: upholding global principles **through local lenses**.

5. *Indigenous Sovereignty Within a Global Federation*

A truly hybrid federation must **center—not assimilate —Indigenous governance traditions**.

Steps to integrate Indigenous sovereignty meaningfully:

- **Recognize treaty nations and tribal governments** as legal actors in global forums.
- Ensure **reserved seats** for Indigenous leaders in global assemblies.
- Protect land, water, and ceremonial rights under the UBR's **Right to Cultural Continuity**.
- Support **legal pluralism**: Indigenous courts coexist alongside national systems, linked through constitutional compacts.

Federated governance allows for **nested sovereignties**—where an Indigenous nation governs its people while participating in planetary councils on climate, health, and knowledge preservation.

6. *Nationalism Without Isolationism*

Can patriotic citizens support global governance?

Yes—if we **reclaim nationalism from fear and fuse it with service.**

Healthy nationalism says:

"We love our home, and therefore we act as responsible neighbors."

In this spirit, nations would:

- Retain **civic holidays, flags, languages, and ceremonies,**
- Preserve **constitutional traditions and legal systems,**
- Assert **leadership in global conversations, not retreat from them.**

In short: **lead locally, contribute globally, remain proudly distinct.**

This is not the end of sovereignty. It is its renewal.

Case Studies in Cultural Autonomy within Cooperative Frameworks

IF A GLOBAL FEDERATION is to be legitimate, it must **honor not only shared values but unique voices.** Cultural autonomy—whether expressed through language, land, law, or lifeways—is not a barrier to cooperation. It is **the foundation for trust.**

This section explores real-world case studies that show how communities, nations, and regions have successfully **preserved cultural identity and legal autonomy while participating in broader political and institutional frameworks.** These are the building blocks of a hybrid federation that does not demand sameness—but celebrates a mosaic of self-governing parts contributing to a cohesive whole.

1. *Sámi Parliaments and Indigenous Cultural Sovereignty (Nordic Model)*

The **Sámi people**, an Indigenous nation spread across Norway, Sweden, Finland, and Russia, provide one of the clearest examples of **transnational cultural autonomy within regional governance.**

Key features:

- **Three Sámi parliaments** (Norway, Sweden, Finland), independently elected by Sámi citizens, with control over cultural, linguistic, and educational issues.
- Funded by national governments but **not subordinate to them** in cultural matters.
- Recognized as **permanent advisory bodies** in government consultations on natural resource use, land rights, and Indigenous knowledge.

Impact:

- Sámi languages are taught in schools and protected in media.
- Traditional practices, like reindeer herding and spiritual customs, are upheld by **customary law alongside national law.**
- Sámi Parliaments coordinate across borders to **represent their people globally,** including at the UN and EU Indigenous forums.

Lesson: When states **honor parallel governance systems**, they gain not just legitimacy, but **moral leadership on Indigenous inclusion.**

2. India's Asymmetrical Federalism

India is a vast federation of states, languages, and religious communities. It enshrines **differentiated autonomy** into its constitution.

Key examples:

- **Article 370** (until recently): Gave Jammu and Kashmir its own constitution and decision-making power in all areas except defense, foreign affairs, and communications.
- **Sixth Schedule:** Grants autonomous councils to tribal areas in Assam, Meghalaya, Tripura, and Mizoram.
- States control **language policy, education, police, and local taxation.**
- **Personal laws** differ by religion—Hindus, Muslims, Christians, and others have unique marriage, inheritance, and family codes.

Despite periodic political tensions, this model shows that **asymmetrical federalism can preserve pluralism at massive scale**—if supported by legal clarity and cooperative institutions.

Lesson: Cultural and religious autonomy **can coexist with democratic unity**, especially when backed by constitutional respect.

. . .

3. Nunavut and Inuit Self-Governance (Canada)

The creation of **Nunavut** in 1999 marked the most significant Indigenous land claim settlement in Canadian history.

Key elements:

- Inuit-majority territory carved from the Northwest Territories.
- Governance based on **Inuit Qaujimajatuqangit** (Inuit traditional knowledge) alongside Canadian law.
- Control over health, education, housing, and justice—with programs tailored to **Arctic realities and cultural norms.**
- Use of **Inuktitut and Inuinnaqtun as official languages** in schools and government.

While challenges remain (especially infrastructure and access), Nunavut represents **a hybrid legal and cultural order:**

- Indigenous leadership governs within a larger federation.
- Decisions reflect **Inuit worldviews**, not imposed western standards.
- Participation in Canada's federal system does not require cultural assimilation.

Lesson: Decolonization is not separation—it can be **reconstitutionalization through partnership.**

4. Catalonia and Cultural Self-Determination within Spain

Catalonia offers a complex case of **subnational autonomy and national tension**. While its 2017 independence referendum drew global headlines, the deeper story is one of **federative flexibility and its limits**.

Catalonia enjoys:

- Its own **parliament, police, education system, and official language** (Catalan).
- Control over local taxation and health services.
- Broad cultural self-determination under Spain's 1978 constitution.

But tensions arise over:

- Fiscal disparities (Catalonia contributes more than it receives).
- Cultural symbolism (flag, anthem, holidays).
- Limits of constitutional reform and independence rights.

Still, the existence of **deep cultural autonomy within a nation-state** shows that identities can **flourish without formal statehood**—when dialogue and decentralization are prioritized.

Lesson: Autonomy must be dynamic, not frozen—**capable of expanding when cultural demands intensify**.

5. *The European Charter for Regional or Minority Languages*

Adopted by the Council of Europe in 1992, this charter protects **linguistic diversity without requiring statehood**.

It obligates ratifying countries to:

- Offer minority languages in schools, media, public services, and courts.
- Promote use of regional languages in cultural and political life.
- Avoid assimilationist policies or neglect.

Impact:

- **Welsh, Basque, Breton, Sorbian, Romani**, and dozens more languages now enjoy legal protections.
- Regional identity is affirmed **within larger national frameworks.**
- Language becomes a **bridge to inclusion**, not a barrier to unity.

Lesson: Language is **not a threat to order—it's an anchor of dignity.**

6. *The Tlingit-Haida Compact in Alaska*

The **Central Council of the Tlingit and Haida Indian Tribes of Alaska** signed a historic self-governance compact with the State of Alaska.

Terms:

- Tribal control over child welfare, education, and law enforcement.
- Joint jurisdiction in overlapping legal areas.
- Mutual recognition of authority and adjudication.

This compact:

- Honors sovereignty while avoiding legal limbo.
- Creates a model of **co-regulation instead of jurisdictional competition.**
- Is rooted in **historical treaties and Indigenous law**—not delegated privilege.

Lesson: Sovereignty can be **layered, not siloed**—and **shared governance builds lasting trust**.

7. Key Takeaways Across Case Studies

Across these diverse contexts, five principles emerge:

1. **Cultural autonomy requires legal protection,** not just political tolerance.
2. **Self-governance can thrive within federations,** especially when tailored to local needs.
3. **Language and legal pluralism** are essential to dignity and trust.
4. **Asymmetry is strength,** not chaos—uniformity is not required for unity.
5. **Dialogue mechanisms are critical**—every cultural compact must include dispute resolution pathways grounded in respect and reciprocity.

Designing Local Autonomy Within a Global Rights Framework

LOCAL AUTONOMY IS the lifeblood of democratic life. It's where policy touches pavement. Where culture is lived, not theorized. And where identity is protected in practice, not merely acknowledged in principle.

Yet in a federated world—where global cooperation is essential to confront planetary challenges—**how do we ensure that local self-rule and global standards are not at odds?**

The key is structure. This section lays out how to design **a governance architecture that preserves local authority** while integrating universal rights and collective obligations. In other words: how to build **a bottom-up federation that is both principled and plural.**

1. Subsidiarity as Constitutional Principle

At the heart of this design is the principle of **subsidiarity:**

Decisions should be made at the most local level capable of resolving the issue effectively.

Applied globally, subsidiarity implies:

- Climate adaptation is best handled by cities and local tribes—while global carbon targets are set collectively.
- Cultural education should be localized—while access to education itself remains a universal right.
- Water policy might be regionally managed—while the **right to clean water** is protected globally.

This creates a **nested system of responsibility**, where power moves upward **only when necessary.**

We propose subsidiarity be enshrined:

- In **national constitutions,**
- In **the Universal Bill of Rights,** and
- As a **foundational clause in all global treaties.**

2. *Constitutional Design: Integrating Local Governance into National Law*

To ensure that local rule is not arbitrarily revoked or undermined, constitutions within the hybrid federation should include:

A. Protected Autonomy Clauses

- Guarantee authority over cultural, educational, linguistic, land, and religious matters.
- Enumerate the specific domains of local control and the process for modifying them.

B. Treaty Authority for Subnational Actors

- Allow local governments, Indigenous nations, or federated municipalities to enter **limited agreements** with international organizations—on climate, heritage, health, and more.
- These are reviewed for constitutional alignment, but not blocked without cause.

C. Legal Standing in Rights Disputes

- Empower local governments and community organizations to **bring cases directly to global or regional courts** in defense of cultural rights, environmental protections, or linguistic freedoms.

This recognizes **local bodies as full participants in the federated legal order**, not subsidiaries of national interest.

3. *Local Implementation Protocols for Global Treaties*

Every global treaty in the hybrid model would be accompanied by **Localized Implementation Protocols (LIPs)**.

These protocols:

- Translate global commitments into **locally relevant goals and mechanisms.**
- Are co-developed by **local governments, civil society, and cultural leaders.**
- Include budgets, timelines, monitoring systems, and flexibility clauses.

Examples:

- A global climate agreement requires reforestation. A tribal nation manages rewilding through **traditional ecological knowledge**, not corporate offsets.
- A human rights treaty mandates anti-discrimination. A rural district integrates these rights through **community-based mediation and public education** in local dialects.

LIPs protect both **sovereignty and solidarity**—honoring cultural reality while enforcing shared duty.

. . .

4. Legal Pluralism Within a Rights-Based Order

The hybrid model must accommodate **multiple legal traditions**—customary, religious, Indigenous—without abandoning universal rights.

We propose:

A. Recognition of Parallel Legal Systems

- Allow for dual or triple court systems in areas like family law, land disputes, and inheritance.
- Customary rulings are **binding** within their domain—unless they violate fundamental rights.

B. Mediation Mechanisms

- In cases of conflict between customary law and global rights, **mediation panels** composed of legal experts, cultural elders, and human rights advocates determine resolution.
- Goal: reconciliation, not domination.

C. Rights Consistency Reviews

- Every five years, local laws undergo a **consistency review** to ensure alignment with the Universal Bill of Rights.
- Noncompliance triggers dialogue, not immediate override.

This supports **cultural continuity while avoiding systemic abuse or exclusion.**

. . .

5. Local Institutions for Federation Engagement

To be more than symbolic, local governance must have **institutional voice** in the global system.

Proposed mechanisms:

A. Global Assembly of Local Governments (GALG)

- A permanent body within the global federation representing mayors, tribal councils, city managers, and regional leaders.
- Consulted on all treaties with local implementation.

B. Cultural Sovereignty Committees

- Within each country, a constitutional body made up of:
    - Local elected leaders,
    - Cultural scholars,
    - Rights experts.
- Reviews national policies for cultural impact and recommends alternatives.

C. Local–Global Treaties Pilot Program

- Authorize a small number of local governments or Indigenous nations to **negotiate directly with treaty bodies**—e.g., on climate adaptation, cultural repatriation, or sustainable development.

This builds **a feedback loop between local governance and global policymaking**, democratizing diplomacy.

. . .

6. Funding and Capacity Building

Rights without resources are rhetoric.
To empower local governance:

- Create a **Global Localism Fund**, seeded by:
    - Wealth taxes (see Trillionaire Club),
    - Climate finance,
    - Digital transaction levies.
- Support:
    - Civic education,
    - Legal infrastructure,
    - Translation and linguistic access,
    - Indigenous knowledge preservation.

Funding is allocated **by need, not geopolitical power**—and managed through **co-governance boards**.

This ensures local governments **aren't merely implementers of global policy, but shapers of it.**

7. Examples of Embedded Localism

- **Finland's constitutional law** protects the right of Sámi to maintain their language and culture, and requires all government services to be accessible in Sámi.
- **South Africa's constitution** recognizes 11 languages and allows for **traditional leadership structures** to govern in parallel with civil authority.
- **New Zealand's Treaty of Waitangi** serves as a living compact between Māori and the Crown—

used to negotiate water rights, school curricula, and environmental stewardship.

These examples are not anomalies—they are **proofs of concept for a pluralist federation.**

Pluralism as a Foundation for Global Solidarity

THERE'S a persistent myth in international affairs: that pluralism and unity are in tension. That to come together, we must dilute our cultures. That diversity breeds division. That shared governance means **erased identities and imposed values.**

This myth fuels:

- Populist backlash,
- Nationalist retrenchment,
- Fear of "global elites" overriding tradition.

But the hybrid model rejects this false choice. In its place, it offers a simple proposition:

Pluralism isn't the opposite of solidarity—it's the condition for it.

This section explores how to build **global cooperation grounded in difference**, not despite it. It calls for a federation that is **rooted in mutual recognition**, committed to protecting identity, and capable of **transforming cultural diversity into civic strength.**

1. The Power of Protected Difference

Too often, calls for unity have come with a demand for sameness:

The United States of the World vs. The United Nations 325

- Speak the same language,
- Obey the same legal code,
- Believe the same political ideals.

But experience—and history—suggest a different lesson: **cooperation endures not because we are identical, but because we are anchored in shared respect.**

Examples abound:

- **Switzerland** functions with four national languages.
- **India** thrives with multiple religions and legal systems.
- The **African Union** upholds both Islamic and secular member states.
- **Canada** enshrines multiculturalism and Quebecois autonomy in constitutional law.

What unites them? **Protected pluralism**—not imposed homogeneity.

2. *Global Solidarity Must Be Bottom-Up, Not Top-Down*

Solidarity can't be mandated. It must be **earned through trust, built through participation, and reinforced through shared outcomes.**

We propose three principles for bottom-up solidarity:

A. Inclusion Through Representation

- Local voices must shape global outcomes.
- This includes:
  - Indigenous leaders in climate negotiations,
  - Youth representatives in AI governance,

- Migrants in health system design.

When people see themselves in the system, they're more likely to defend and improve it.

B. Reciprocity Through Mutual Recognition

- Solidarity is not charity. It's **exchange**.
- Every culture, nation, and tradition offers wisdom:
    - Polynesian ocean stewardship,
    - Ubuntu philosophy from southern Africa,
    - Restorative justice from Indigenous courts.

A federated world must be **a forum of mutual contribution**—not a pyramid of influence.

C. Legitimacy Through Tangible Results

- Solidarity deepens when institutions **deliver real benefits**.
- Example: A treaty that ensures vaccine equity and protects local ritual health practices **builds more loyalty** than a speech about unity.

Pluribus Unum—out of many, one—is not just a motto. It's a method.

3. Cultural Security as a Civic Right

Just as people need food, safety, and shelter—they need **cultural security**:

- The right to speak and transmit their language,

- The right to worship, observe traditions, and teach their history,
- The right to name places, protect ancestral lands, and hold ceremonies without persecution.

In the hybrid federation:

- Cultural rights are not **secondary to civil rights**—they are **part of them.**
- Local cultures are not **obstacles to justice**—they are **vehicles for it.**

A person who feels seen, heard, and respected is more likely to:

- Trust institutions,
- Cooperate with shared goals,
- Reject extremism.

Pluralism creates **social glue,** not fragmentation.

4. The Dangers of Unchecked Universalism

Let's be clear: **universal rights do not mean universal uniformity.**

When global standards become rigid dogma, they risk:

- Silencing dissent,
- Flattening identity,
- Repeating colonial logics in new forms.

Examples:

- Forcing top-down democracy in places with traditional consensus systems.
- Imposing western gender norms without recognizing Indigenous gender fluidity.
- Equating secularism with progress, erasing spiritual governance models.

The hybrid model prevents this by embedding **pluralist review panels**, **local opt-in protocols**, and **cultural exemption processes**—balanced, of course, by **core rights safeguards**.

5. Building Rituals of Shared Belonging

Pluralism thrives when it's **practiced regularly**—not just promised in documents.

A federated world needs:

- **Shared holidays** that honor both local and global achievements (e.g., International Peace Day celebrated through local traditions).
- **Common symbols** that respect cultural variation—like multilingual oaths of citizenship or intercultural festivals tied to civic milestones.
- **Education systems** that teach both national history and global interdependence.

These rituals don't erase difference. They **ritualize our mutual investment in it.**

6. A Civic Identity Bigger Than Borders

The ultimate goal is not to abolish nationhood—it is to **layer it with planetary belonging.**

That means a child in Senegal, Serbia, or Saskatchewan can grow up knowing:

- They are **rooted in their place, their culture, and their story,**
- But also **connected to a global community of rights, responsibilities, and possibilities.**

Global civic identity isn't a threat to national pride. It's an **invitation to something larger**—a federation of communities protecting one another, learning from one another, and building a world no one culture could construct alone.

7. Pluralism and the Resilience of the Federation

A pluralistic federation is not fragile. It is **resilient.**

Because when one tradition falters, another can inspire. When one country retreats, another can lead. When one system fails, another can offer reform.

Diversity is **a form of collective insurance**—against cultural tyranny, policy blind spots, and spiritual decay.

It is not our weakness. It is our shield.

Autonomy Without Isolation, *Solidarity Without Assimilation*

We end this chapter where we began: with a question.

Can local cultures, spiritual traditions, and regional identities survive in a federated world?

The answer is not just yes—it is **they must.**

Because in their survival lies the key to:

- **Legitimacy** that reaches hearts as well as laws,
- **Stability** that grows from trust, not coercion,
- And **solidarity** that is rooted not in uniformity, but in mutual flourishing.

In the hybrid model, **difference is not a risk to manage—it is a gift to steward.**

15

A NEW ROLE FOR THE UNITED NATIONS

From Forum to Federation—Reimagining the UN in a Hybrid World

THE UN WAS FORGED in 1945, in the ashes of fascism and genocide, at a moment when the world longed for peace through cooperation. For nearly eight decades, it has been:

- A convener of states,
- A voice for diplomacy,
- A coordinator of global development, health, and humanitarian response.

And yet, today, it is also:

- **Accused of irrelevance** during crises (e.g., Syria, Ukraine, Myanmar),
- **Hamstrung by veto power** and institutional inertia,

- **Unable to enforce major treaties** or prevent global abuses,
- And increasingly seen as **too bureaucratic to lead, too weak to enforce, too elite to trust.**

In a federated world of shared sovereignty and participatory governance, the UN must **change its purpose, shape, and mechanisms**. It must move:

- From **symbol to structure**,
- From **recommendation to accountability**,
- From **exclusive state diplomacy to inclusive civic legitimacy.**

This section lays out the vision for a reformed UN—not abolished, but reborn as the **backbone of a hybrid global system.**

1. *The UN Today: Essential but Incomplete*
The UN remains indispensable in many domains:

- The **World Health Organization (WHO)** coordinates pandemic response.
- The **UN High Commissioner for Refugees (UNHCR)** delivers aid to millions.
- The **UN Environment Programme (UNEP)** tracks global ecological degradation.
- **Peacekeeping missions** prevent conflict in dozens of countries.

But these successes occur **despite** institutional design flaws, not because of them.

Structural weaknesses:

- **Security Council veto** paralyzes enforcement.
- **General Assembly resolutions** are non-binding.
- **Funding mechanisms** are dependent on voluntary contributions.
- **Civil society inclusion** is limited to consultative roles.
- **Accountability for failure** is almost nonexistent.

The UN today is a **forum of diplomats**, not **an engine of enforceable cooperation**. That must change.

2. Four Roles for the Reimagined UN

In a federated global system, the UN evolves into **four integrated roles:**

A. Constitutional Anchor

- Custodian of the **Universal Bill of Rights** and **Federation Charter**.
- Maintains the official registry of treaty ratifications, national implementation plans, and opt-in protocols.
- Hosts the **Global Court System** and mediates jurisdictional disputes.

B. Executive Coordination Hub

- Houses a **Global Council of Ministers** representing policy portfolios: health, climate, migration, AI, food, etc.

- Coordinates emergency responses, treaty compliance efforts, and institutional cooperation across blocs.
- Uses rapid deployment, cross-agency collaboration, and digital dashboards to manage crises.

C. Democratic Governance Platform

- Transforms the **UN General Assembly** into a **bicameral legislature:**
    - One chamber represents states (as today),
    - The second represents **global citizens**, elected directly or through national parliaments.
- Introduces **binding votes** on budget, rights enforcement, and emergency declarations.

D. Participatory Network-of-Networks

- Acts as **hub for cities, Indigenous nations, youth groups, NGOs, and professional guilds.**
- Facilitates global civic assemblies, cultural exchanges, and citizen juries.
- Develops open platforms for **crowdsourced policymaking** and public deliberation.

In this model, the UN becomes not the **manager of multilateralism**, but the **living structure of planetary self-governance.**

3. Key Reforms for Institutional Legitimacy

The United States of the World vs. The United Nations

To fulfill this new role, major structural reforms are necessary:

A. Security Council Democratization

- Expand membership to include **regional unions** (e.g., AU, EU, ASEAN).
- Replace permanent veto power with:
  - Qualified majority voting,
  - Emergency override mechanisms,
  - Independent conflict review panels.

B. Global Parliamentary Assembly

- Create a second chamber where **citizens are represented directly.**
- Seats apportioned by population but capped by region to prevent domination.
- Deliberates on global policy, monitors executive actions, and ratifies major treaties.

C. Enforcement Authority Through Treaty Design

- The UN's enforcement capacity grows **not by coercion,** but by **opt-in treaty frameworks.**
- Nations voluntarily agree to:
  - Jurisdiction of global courts,
  - Fiscal penalties for noncompliance,
  - Coordination of sanctions through **multilateral consensus.**

D. Budget Reform

- Move from voluntary contributions to:

- **Federated global taxes** (e.g., carbon fees, digital transaction levies),
- Treaty-mandated funding obligations,
- Weighted contribution systems tied to GDP, emissions, or rights impact.

This **financial independence** underwrites UN integrity.

4. Civic Visibility and Everyday Relevance

For the UN to matter, it must **show up in people's lives.** Proposals:

- **UN ID cards or digital apps** tracking individual rights, benefits, and civic participation.
- Local "UN Hubs" in cities and schools for public engagement, education, and advocacy.
- Direct **petitions to UN bodies** for environmental damage, human rights abuse, or treaty violations.
- **"UN in the Neighborhood"** campaigns connecting citizens with global goals and dispute resolution services.

We must build **civic imagination** around the UN—so it's no longer seen as distant and abstract, but as **a tool of shared protection and empowerment.**

5. Guardrails Against Elite Capture and Overreach

Critics warn: *Won't a more powerful UN become undemocratic? Unaccountable? A new empire of technocrats?*

That risk is real—and must be met with guardrails:

- **Rotating leadership and regional representation**, not permanent hegemony.
- **Open-source policymaking tools**, with citizen review panels.
- **Public ombuds offices** in every treaty body.
- Mandatory **annual review of UN decisions by national parliaments**.
- Full **transparency of budgets, votes, and deliberations**.

In other words: **Power must rise with accountability, or not at all.**

Operationalizing Global Authority with Democratic Consent

For the United Nations to truly serve as the foundation of a global federation, it must be more than an occasional forum for summitry or symbolic resolutions. It must become an **operational body** that translates shared global values into **tangible, enforceable actions**—and does so in a way that reflects the **legitimate will of the global population**, not just national governments or elite representatives.

This section lays out the **mechanisms, procedures, and pathways** for ensuring the UN's newfound power is **effectively exercised and democratically legitimized**.

1. Reimagining UN Decision-Making: The Global Legislature

In the reformed UN, the **General Assembly** must evolve into a **bicameral legislature** that reflects both state sovereignty and democratic participation.

A. The Chamber of States

- This chamber retains representation for national governments.
- It preserves the existing **one country, one vote** model but replaces the veto system with a **qualified majority voting mechanism**.
- Decisions require a **supermajority** (e.g., 60-70%) for major resolutions, such as the approval of new treaties or sanctions.
- Special decisions (like military interventions) require **dual approval**—both by states and by the **Global Parliament** (explained below).

B. The Global Parliament

- This new chamber represents the **global citizenry**, ensuring that the UN's decisions reflect **the voices of people, not just governments.**
- **Seats are apportioned by population**, but regions are **capped** to prevent overrepresentation by large states (e.g., no one region can dominate the chamber).
- **Direct elections** from citizens (through national elections or a global online system) ensure accountability and democratic legitimacy.
- The Parliament's duties include:
  - **Approving global budgets,**
  - Ratifying key international agreements (e.g., climate, trade),
  - Debating global crises and proposing actionable solutions.

C. Shared Decision-Making: Integrating the Chambers

- **Collaborative lawmaking:** Major treaties, including those related to climate change, human rights, and technological standards, must pass both chambers.
- **Checks and balances:** If the General Assembly and the Parliament cannot agree, **a reconciliation process** is triggered, with independent mediators or a global conciliation commission.

This system ensures that both **state sovereignty and global democracy are respected**, creating a **balanced decision-making framework** that represents both **state interests and individual rights.**

2. Crisis Management: Global Response Networks

The UN is tasked with addressing some of the world's most pressing crises—natural disasters, pandemics, armed conflicts, humanitarian emergencies, and climate catastrophes. But crises often expose the **UN's operational weaknesses**, especially its inability to respond swiftly and decisively.

To address this, we propose **a new Global Emergency Coordination Network** (GECN), which would include:

A. Rapid Response Units

- **Specialized global task forces,** pre-funded and pre-equipped to address specific types of crises, including:

- **Health emergencies (e.g., pandemics),**
- **Natural disasters (e.g., wildfires, floods),**
- **Food and water insecurity,** and
- **Peacekeeping and conflict mediation.**

These units would be **triggered automatically** by crises and would bypass the usual bureaucratic delays, responding within hours or days.

B. Crisis Response Assemblies

- Each major crisis would be overseen by a **Crisis Response Assembly**—a temporary body made up of:
    - Representatives from affected countries,
    - Experts from the relevant UN agencies (WHO, UNEP, FAO, UNHCR),
    - Civic representatives from global civil society, including those most impacted by the crisis.

The assembly would have the authority to:

- Mobilize emergency funds,
- Coordinate local, national, and international responses,
- Issue mandates to private-sector actors (e.g., pharmaceutical companies, tech firms).

C. Permanent Emergency Reserve Fund

- A **global insurance-style fund** would be established to finance rapid response to natural disasters, pandemics, and other emergencies.

- Funded by **global levies** (e.g., carbon taxes, digital transaction fees) and voluntary contributions from wealthy states and corporations.
- Managed by an independent **global humanitarian panel**, with transparent auditing and monitoring.

The GECN is designed to **shorten response times, streamline resources**, and **empower affected regions**, ensuring that the UN doesn't just talk about crises—it acts decisively.

3. Accountability and Legitimacy: Global Monitoring and Public Review

For the UN's expanded powers to be legitimate, **public accountability is essential**. In this reformed system, transparency and oversight will be built directly into its structure.

A. Independent Oversight Bodies

- **Global Audit Office:** This office would be responsible for auditing the UN's budget, projects, and programs. It would report directly to the **Global Parliament** and be accountable to civil society and the general public.
- **Global Accountability Commission:** Comprising global experts, civil society leaders, and representatives from regional organizations, this body would:
    - Review the implementation of international treaties,

- Ensure human rights, environmental protections, and social justice goals are met,
- Investigate allegations of corruption, human rights abuses, or policy failure.

These bodies would ensure that the UN's actions are **transparent, responsible, and answerable to the people** it serves.

B. Public Consultations and Citizen Input

- Every major UN decision—whether a new treaty, emergency response, or budgetary allocation—would go through a **global public consultation process**.
    - **Global digital platforms** will allow citizens to submit proposals, vote on key issues, and provide feedback.
    - Local councils, community representatives, and **Global Civic Assemblies** will hold hearings to engage in discussions on the UN's policies and goals.

This will enable **democratic oversight** and ensure that the UN's decisions are rooted in **global consent**, not just bureaucratic processes.

4. Sustainable Funding and Resource Allocation

For the UN to be effective in its expanded role, it must **build sustainable funding** mechanisms that aren't reliant solely on voluntary contributions from states.

A. Global Tax Contributions

The United States of the World vs. The United Nations 343

- The UN would begin to collect **small global taxes** on:
  - Digital transactions (e.g., a small levy on global tech firms),
  - Financial transactions (e.g., a financial transaction tax),
  - Carbon emissions.

These taxes would create a **stable and independent funding base** for UN programs, crisis management, and global governance.

B. Private Sector Accountability

- The UN would introduce **corporate taxes for global resources** (e.g., taxes on companies benefiting from global infrastructure or resources).
- A **Corporate Social Responsibility (CSR) Tax** could be introduced, where companies exceeding a certain threshold in profits contribute to global welfare and sustainability programs.

This will not only ensure that the UN is **financially independent**, but also **ethically accountable** to the global population it serves.

5. Global Transparency and Technology Infrastructure

The UN must leverage **cutting-edge technology** to ensure accountability, manage resources efficiently, and maintain **global transparency**.

A. Digital Transparency Platforms

- A **global dashboard** will track:
  - Treaty compliance,
  - Financial spending,
  - Emergency responses,
  - Human rights outcomes.

This platform will be publicly accessible, allowing citizens, policymakers, and journalists to **hold the UN accountable** at any moment.

B. AI for Crisis Prediction and Resource Allocation

- Artificial intelligence will be used to predict **emergencies**, optimize resource distribution, and manage **global supply chains** during crises (e.g., vaccine distribution during pandemics).

AI will also help track progress on **global goals** (e.g., SDGs), providing real-time analysis and recommendations for improvement.

Global Democracy at Scale—Expanding the Role of the People

IN EVERY HEALTHY DEMOCRACY, legitimacy flows from the people—not from tradition, not from technocracy, and not from abstract institutional structures.

But in global governance, **"the people" have long been missing**. The United Nations, despite its noble goals, is still a system of **governments representing populations**—not **populations representing themselves**. That model no longer suffices in a world where:

- Individuals face global challenges (climate change, pandemics, disinformation),
- Corporations and AI systems influence lives across borders,
- And citizens demand a greater say in shaping their collective future.

This part outlines how to **scale democracy globally**—not through unrealistic one-size-fits-all elections, but through **layered participation, digital platforms, civic innovation, and protected pluralism.**

1. The Democratic Deficit in Global Governance

Let's name the problem: **Global decisions are made without global voters.**

- Treaties are signed with no referenda.
- Trade deals are struck with no public oversight.
- Global health protocols are developed with minimal civic input.
- The Security Council can make war-and-peace decisions with **zero popular consultation.**

The result is **mistrust, disengagement, and populist backlash.** The way forward is not to eliminate global governance, but to **democratize it.**

We propose a layered approach to **Global Democracy 2.0**—where citizens engage at the local, national, and global levels, with real power, accountability, and voice.

2. The Global Parliament: Representation by the People

The proposed **Global Parliament**, introduced in Part 1, would be a **democratically elected chamber** representing people directly—not states.

Structure and Election

- Seats apportioned by **population**, capped per region to prevent dominance.
- Representatives elected through:
  - **National elections** using proportional allocation, or
  - **Global digital voting systems** certified by independent monitors.

Powers

- Approve budgets, treaties, and global regulations.
- Initiate investigations, reviews, and public hearings.
- Introduce **citizen-proposed legislation** (see below).
- Oversee all UN bodies, including the General Assembly and Global Councils.

Access

- Every global citizen aged 16+ may vote or run.
- Universal access guaranteed through digital identity tools, translated platforms, and public outreach.

3. Citizen-Initiated Global Legislation

In the hybrid model, **citizens are not passive subjects.** They can propose, review, and influence laws.

Global Initiative Platform (GIP)

- A secure digital system where any citizen can:
    - Propose legislation,
    - Gather endorsements (e.g., 1 million signatures from 10 countries),
    - Submit drafts to parliamentary committees.

Popular proposals are:

- Vetted for legality and feasibility,
- Reviewed in public hearings,
- Subject to **binding votes** if thresholds are met.

This system brings **global direct democracy into practice**, without replacing representative governance.

4. Deliberative Assemblies and Participatory Governance

Representation alone isn't enough. Many voices—especially from marginalized groups—require dedicated space.

Global Citizens' Assemblies

- Randomly selected citizens from across the world,
- Convene virtually or in person,
- Deliberate on major issues (e.g., digital rights, migration, climate),
- Issue **recommendations to the Parliament and UN agencies.**

Permanent People's Forum

- Ongoing consultative body composed of:
    - Civil society groups,
    - Faith and spiritual organizations,
    - Worker unions,
    - Disability and LGBTQ+ alliances,
    - Youth, elder, and Indigenous representatives.

This forum has:

- Right of **address to the global legislature**,
- Budgetary oversight privileges,
- Power to **flag rights violations or democratic crises.**

Participation is **not symbolic—it's procedural.**

5. *Digital Participation and Access to Global Governance*

Global democracy must meet people **where they are:** online, mobile, multilingual, and distributed.

Global Digital Civic Infrastructure

- A digital platform—accessible via phone or public access points—that allows citizens to:
    - Track votes and debates in real time,
    - Submit questions or feedback to representatives,
    - Vote in referenda,
    - Access civic education in their language.

This platform includes:

- AI translation across 100+ languages,
- Visual learning tools,
- Text-to-speech for accessibility,
- Voting verification mechanisms to prevent fraud.

Global democracy only works if **everyone can participate**, not just the connected elite.

6. *Global Referenda and Emergency Mandates*

Certain decisions—particularly those with civilizational consequences—require **direct public authorization**.

Global Referenda

- Called for decisions like:
  - Creation of new global taxes or enforcement mechanisms,
  - Major AI or biotechnology regulations,
  - Entry into binding climate pacts.

A referendum is triggered by:

- 2/3 vote of the Global Parliament, or
- Petition from 5 million verified global citizens from at least 20 countries.

Results are **binding**—enforced by the Federation Charter.

7. *Youth and Future Generation Representation*

Democracy must also include those **who will inherit its outcomes**.

Global Youth Parliament

- Elected or appointed body of citizens under 30,
- Advisory and legislative drafting roles,
- Dedicated to:
  - Education reform,
  - Sustainability,
  - Digital ethics,
  - Peacebuilding.

Intergenerational Guardianship Commission

- Oversees long-term policy impact,
- Reviews laws for fairness to future generations,
- May issue **advisory vetoes** on policies with catastrophic long-term harm.

In a federated world, democracy means **not only all voices now, but all voices yet to come.**

8. Guarding Against Democratic Manipulation

With new power must come **new protections**.

To prevent disinformation, manipulation, or disenfranchisement, the hybrid model ensures:

- **Independent electoral monitors**, not run by states or corporations.
- **Transparent algorithmic systems** for digital voting and public debate.
- **Global ethics commissions** to audit AI use in politics.

- **Civic education campaigns** tailored to region and language.

In short: **Democracy must be defended as it is expanded.**

Reforming the UN Charter—A Legal Blueprint for the Federated Future

THE CHARTER of the United Nations is often treated like sacred scripture—unmovable, untouchable, and written in the stone of post-war compromise. But the world has changed, and so must its institutions.

The **UN Charter is not immutable. It is amendable.** Article 109 provides the pathway. The question is not whether change is possible—but whether the political will can be mobilized, the process designed, and the transition managed with legitimacy and momentum.

This section lays out the **legal, procedural, and strategic roadmap** for how the United Nations could be transformed—**step by step, clause by clause, and country by country**—into the core of a truly participatory, enforceable, and just global federation.

1. The Charter Today: Foundations and Fault Lines

The existing UN Charter (1945) provides the structure for:

- The **General Assembly** (deliberative),
- The **Security Council** (enforcement),
- The **Economic and Social Council** (ECOSOC),
- The **International Court of Justice**,

- A **secretariat,** led by the Secretary-General.

Strengths:

- Universality: 193 member states.
- Legal personality: Treaties, immunities, and recognition.
- Legacy: Custodian of the Universal Declaration of Human Rights.

Weaknesses:

- **Security Council veto** grants five nations disproportionate power.
- **No democratic chamber** representing global citizens.
- **Limited enforcement authority** for resolutions and treaties.
- **No permanent funding mechanism,** dependent on voluntary contributions.

To become the scaffolding for a hybrid federation, the Charter must be reengineered to reflect **shared power, distributed legitimacy, and modern needs.**

2. *Legal Pathways to Charter Reform*
A. Article 109: The Built-In Amendment Process
Article 109 of the UN Charter states:

"A General Conference of the Members of the United Nations for the purpose of reviewing the present Charter may be held at a date and place to be fixed by a two-thirds vote of the General Assembly and by a vote of any nine members of the Security Council."

Amendments require:

- A **two-thirds majority in the General Assembly**,
- Ratification by **two-thirds of the Member States**, including **all five permanent members of the Security Council (P5)**.

Challenge:

- The **P5 veto** makes any sweeping reform difficult —especially if it reduces their power.

Response:

- **Treaty-based Charter override:** While formal Charter revision is ideal, many elements of a federated model can be **established through parallel treaties**, endorsed by a supermajority of nations.
- Over time, this de facto architecture **supersedes de jure power**—especially if backed by popular legitimacy and funding.

3. Priority Reforms and Draft Amendments

Here are the core Charter reforms needed to transform the UN into a federated anchor:

A. Bicameral World Legislature

Amendment to Chapter IV (General Assembly):

- Create a **second legislative chamber**—the **Global Parliament**—elected by global citizens or national parliaments.
- Define shared powers, including:
  - Budget approval,
  - Treaty ratification,
  - Legislative review.

B. Security Council Transformation
Amendment to Chapter V:

- Abolish or suspend **permanent vetoes**.
- Expand membership to include **regional blocs** (e.g., AU, EU, ASEAN).
- Introduce a **weighted voting system** (e.g., supermajority of members + population-based thresholds).

C. Binding Enforcement Authority
New Article under Chapter VI (Peaceful Settlement of Disputes):

- Treaties adopted by the UN General Assembly and Parliament, with sufficient ratifications, gain **binding legal status**.
- Create a **Global Compliance Tribunal** for dispute resolution and enforcement.

D. Rights Integration
Amendment to Chapter I (Purposes and Principles):

- Reference the **Universal Bill of Rights** as a core constitutional text.

- Mandate national alignment within 10 years of ratification.

E. Budget and Funding Reform
Amendment to Chapter XVII (Miscellaneous):

- Replace voluntary contributions with:
    - A **tiered dues model** (based on GDP, carbon footprint, or digital usage),
    - Federated taxes (e.g., financial transaction, carbon border tax).

These amendments form the **constitutional blueprint of the hybrid world order**—preserving sovereignty while strengthening cooperation.

4. Political Strategy for Adoption
Transforming the Charter requires not just legal arguments—but **movement strategy**.

A. Phase 1: Treaty Coalition Building

- Begin with a coalition of 50–70 willing states.
- Sign a **Charter Reform Treaty**, establishing the framework for:
    - The Global Parliament,
    - Enforcement architecture,
    - Rights obligations,
    - Citizen participation.
- Use this treaty as a **proof-of-concept**, running parallel to the existing UN.

B. Phase 2: Institutional Integration

- Gradually integrate the new federation into existing UN bodies:
    - Civic assemblies recognized by ECOSOC,
    - Parliament observers in General Assembly debates,
    - Joint funding and staffing with UNDP, WHO, etc.

C. Phase 3: Formal Charter Replacement

- Convene a **Global Constitutional Conference** under Article 109.
- Push for a revised Charter ratified by **at least two-thirds of member states**, even if P5 do not consent.
- Use civic pressure, treaty momentum, and **moral legitimacy** to isolate dissenting powers.

History shows that **when governance fails to evolve, it is bypassed**. This pathway offers peaceful transformation through **consent, pressure, and institutional patience**.

5. Legal Safeguards During Transition
To prevent destabilization during reform:

- **Non-derogation clauses** ensure current human rights, peacekeeping, and aid operations continue uninterrupted.
- **Interim institutions** (e.g., observer councils, transitional committees) manage overlap and confusion.

- **Sunset provisions** allow redundant or ineffective structures to be retired over 5–10 years.

The goal is **evolution, not revolution**—a peaceful remodeling of the house we already live in.

The UN Reborn—Scaffold of a New World

Reforming the UN Charter is not a dream. It is a **necessity for survival** and **a possibility within law**.

Done right, this transformation would:

- Embed democratic participation at the global level,
- Enforce rights and responsibilities fairly,
- End the impunity of powerful states and corporations,
- Empower people as planetary citizens,
- And finally fulfill the original promise of 1945— not just to prevent war, but to **build peace through justice, voice, and shared destiny**.

This is how the United Nations becomes not just the heart of multilateralism, but **the operational constitution of the federated future**.

16

THE IMPLEMENTATION CHALLENGE
THE GAP BETWEEN AGREEMENT AND ACTION

Every transformative idea, no matter how principled or rational, must pass through a crucible of politics, power, and practicality.

History is littered with beautiful blueprints—treaties signed, conventions declared, goals endorsed—only to wither from **lack of implementation**, political resistance, or public disengagement. The 21st-century hybrid global model risks the same fate unless we **close the gap between agreement and action.**

This section confronts that gap head-on. It analyzes the barriers to implementation—not to lament them, but to **understand, anticipate, and overcome them** through deliberate strategy.

1. Why Vision Isn't Enough

Let's start with a paradox: **Humanity is better than ever at agreeing on paper—and worse at following through in practice.**

Consider:

- The **Paris Agreement** was celebrated for its ambition—but emissions keep rising.
- The **Sustainable Development Goals (SDGs)** were adopted by nearly every country—yet poverty and inequality persist.
- Treaties against torture, pollution, and cybercrime are widely signed—yet daily violated without meaningful consequences.

What's behind this pattern?

A. Structural Barriers

- **No enforcement mechanism** for many treaties.
- **Lack of funding** or capacity in poorer nations.
- **Conflicting obligations** (e.g., trade vs. climate commitments).

B. Political Barriers

- **Nationalist backlash** to perceived loss of sovereignty.
- **Geopolitical rivalries** undermining collective action.
- **Short-term electoral pressures** overriding long-term global goals.

C. Psychological Barriers

- **Global problems feel abstract**, distant, and disconnected from everyday life.
- Citizens often feel **powerless to influence outcomes**.

- Media and political narratives emphasize division over shared destiny.

The result: a chronic **implementation deficit**. The solution? Strategic scaffolding for conversion from **global principle to local practice.**

2. *The Five Gaps of Implementation*

To understand what must be done, we identify **five distinct gaps** that plague global implementation efforts:

1. The Commitment Gap

- Countries sign agreements to signal goodwill—but don't follow through.
- Often due to **vague language, non-binding clauses,** or **lack of domestic political cost** for noncompliance.

Solution: Ensure future treaties include:

- **Concrete targets,**
- **Timelines with interim benchmarks,**
- **Public scorecards** to increase visibility,
- **Automatic penalties or funding suspensions** for failure to act.

2. The Coordination Gap

- Governments, agencies, and sectors often work in silos.
- Global decisions made by diplomats rarely reach:
  - **City planners,**

- Teachers,
- Small businesses,
- Tribal councils.

Solution: Create:

- **Interministerial implementation councils,**
- **Local–global liaison offices,**
- **Regional treaty coordinators** to translate goals into local law, policy, and budgets.

3. The Capacity Gap

- Many governments lack the **infrastructure, funds,** or **expertise** to implement ambitious goals.
- This is especially true in the Global South, but also affects rural and marginalized areas globally.

Solution:

- A **Global Capacity Investment Fund**, targeting:
  - Legal training,
  - Technical infrastructure,
  - Digital access,
  - Civic education.
- Priority access for countries committing to full compliance and data transparency.

4. The Continuity Gap

- Global initiatives often fade with changes in leadership or news cycles.

- Treaties survive administrations—but implementation plans do not.

Solution:

- Establish **multi-decade implementation compacts**, co-signed by:
    - Governments,
    - Civil society,
    - Youth representatives,
    - Independent monitoring bodies.
- Require **national implementation laws** that remain binding beyond electoral cycles.

5. The Credibility Gap

- Citizens often doubt whether global promises will affect their lives—or whether elites will follow the same rules.

Solution:

- Embed **citizen monitoring tools** in every treaty framework.
- Require **corporate compliance plans** for businesses operating across borders.
- Tie treaty ratification to:
    - **Public awareness campaigns,**
    - **School curricula,**
    - **Participatory budgeting mechanisms.**

Without visible benefits, **faith erodes.** With transparency and accountability, it builds.

3. The Risk of Elite Capture

Even well-meaning global initiatives can be hijacked—by:

- **Corporations seeking influence** over regulations,
- **Governments using treaties for surveillance or control,**
- **NGOs gatekeeping access to resources.**

To prevent this:

- Require **diverse representation** in implementation councils,
- Limit **lobbying power** through transparency rules,
- Rotate leadership roles to avoid institutional monopolies,
- Create **"Citizen Witness Panels"** to review abuses and issue public warnings.

In the hybrid system, implementation must be **polycentric and plural**—no single sector or institution can dominate.

4. Converting Global Goals into Domestic Law

One of the most practical barriers is this: *treaties don't self-execute.*

Without domestic legislation:

- Courts can't enforce commitments,
- Budgets can't allocate funds,
- Citizens can't invoke new rights.

Every treaty must be domesticated.
Tools:

- **Template legislation** included in every treaty annex,
- **Model municipal ordinances** for cities and Indigenous governments,
- **Federation Alignment Acts** passed by national parliaments to update laws with treaty requirements.

This ensures **alignment from the street level to the summit level.**

5. The Role of Civic Movements in Implementation

No global idea has ever succeeded without **grassroots pressure.**

Movements like:

- **Extinction Rebellion,**
- **Fridays for Future,**
- **Black Lives Matter,**
- **Indigenous Water Protectors,**

…have shaped agendas, exposed hypocrisies, and **forced accountability.**

To close the implementation gap, civic movements must:

- Be invited into treaty negotiations,
- Be funded to run public oversight campaigns,
- Be included in **joint monitoring bodies**,
- Receive legal standing to **sue for noncompliance.**

Implementation is not a technical process. It is a **political struggle**—and citizens must be empowered to fight for it.

Conclusion: *From Idea to Institution*

The dream of a hybrid global federation, with universal rights, pluralist governance, and shared authority, will **not collapse from lack of vision**. It will rise or fall on our ability to **implement it—everywhere, continuously, equitably, and visibly.**

This means:

- Building enforcement into every agreement,
- Translating global ideals into local policy,
- Funding capacity and inclusion,
- Embedding civic voice into every stage,
- And holding leaders—public and private—**accountable to the world they claim to serve.**

Catalysts for Change—Moments, Movements, and Momentum

THERE ARE times in history when the rules feel suspended, when windows open in the architecture of power, and when people can shape outcomes **not in decades—but in days.**

Political scientists call these moments "critical junctures." Sociologists call them "movement time." In spiritual traditions, they are kairos—**a sacred moment of reckoning.**

The implementation of a hybrid global federation will not move forward **because it makes sense.** It will advance because **the world demands it at a moment of fracture and potential.**

This section identifies the **key catalysts that can propel systemic reform**—and how to recognize, prepare for, and harness them.

1. Crisis as Catalyst

History shows that **crisis enables transformation**—if structures and movements are ready to respond.

Case Study: The Great Depression & the New Deal

- What began as economic collapse in 1929 birthed the **U.S. social safety net**, labor protections, and massive public infrastructure programs.
- FDR's administration had **policy teams on standby**, ready to act when political conditions allowed.

Case Study: World War II & the UN Charter

- The devastation of global war broke the world order—and out of its ashes came the **United Nations, Bretton Woods institutions, and human rights treaties.**
- These were not spontaneous. They were **drafted years in advance**, waiting for the crisis to make them possible.

Modern Analogs

- The COVID-19 pandemic revealed the failures of fragmented health governance and inspired **global vaccine equity conversations**.
- The climate crisis, already here, is a **chronic emergency** that could drive:
    - A new planetary constitution,
    - Mass mobilization for climate justice,
    - Climate reparations tied to new enforcement systems.

Crisis alone doesn't produce change—preparation does.

That's why every reform plan should include:

- **Crisis activation clauses** in treaties,
- **Emergency action teams** of legal drafters and civic leaders,
- Pre-positioned **civic communication platforms** for rapid public education.

2. Movement Alignment Across Borders

Single-issue protests can raise awareness. But **cross-border movements**, aligned around shared goals, can **change global institutions**.

A. The Climate Justice Movement

- Youth-led, decentralized, media-savvy.
- Demands go beyond emissions—they include:
    - Intergenerational equity,

- Indigenous rights,
- Economic redistribution.

With proper coordination, it could:

- Endorse the **Universal Bill of Rights**,
- Demand enforcement mechanisms,
- Drive ratification campaigns country by country.

B. Digital Democracy Advocates

- From open-source tech collectives to data privacy warriors, this movement:
  - Rejects authoritarian control,
  - Builds alternative tools for participation,
  - Champions transparency and civic power.

They are essential for:

- Building the **infrastructure of global voting**,
- Monitoring implementation data,
- Defending rights in the AI age.

C. Economic Justice Coalitions

- Debt-forgiveness activists, wealth redistribution advocates, fair trade groups.
- These movements offer **policy fuel** for:
  - Trillionaire Club legislation,
  - Global wealth taxes,
  - Reparations and social equity finance.

D. Global Indigenous Networks

- United by land protection, cultural sovereignty, and stewardship values.
- Offer moral leadership, legal pluralism models, and climate wisdom.
- Essential for rooting the federation in **spiritual and ancestral legitimacy.**

Synergy is the goal. A unified push across sectors, issues, and geographies **builds momentum greater than the sum of its parts.**

3. Technological Inflection Points

Certain innovations **rewire what's possible in governance.**

A. Decentralized Digital Identity

- Secure, portable IDs can enable:
    - Global voting,
    - Access to benefits,
    - Rights tracking and verification.
- A federated system could tie these identities to:
    - Treaty ratification participation,
    - Citizen assemblies,
    - Rights enforcement platforms.

B. Blockchain & Transparency Tech

- Smart contracts and immutable ledgers can:
    - Track compliance with climate targets,
    - Automatically release funds based on performance,
    - Reduce corruption.

C. AI for Policy Simulation

- AI can:
    - Predict impact of proposed laws,
    - Test equity implications,
    - Generate alternative scenarios.

Used wisely, these tools make implementation:

- **Faster, more adaptive, and more inclusive.**

But they must be democratized—not monopolized—by elite institutions or tech firms.

4. Cultural Shifts and Moral Reframing

Policy rarely leads culture. More often, **culture creates the conditions for policy.**

A. From Sovereignty as Isolation to Sovereignty as Stewardship

- A reframing campaign that teaches:
    - Nations are not fortresses—they are trustees of shared futures.
    - Autonomy and accountability are not enemies—they are **co-requisites**.

B. From Globalism as Elite Control to Globalism as Collective Protection

- Messaging and storytelling that:
    - Centers ordinary people's voices,
    - Celebrates diverse cultures working together,

- Redefines global citizenship as a **moral calling**, not a bureaucratic label.

C. Narrative Power

- Novels, films, music, and games that depict:
  - A world with a functional, participatory global system,
  - Youth leading policy summits,
  - Rights upheld across borders,
  - Trillionaires required to serve humanity.

We become what we imagine. The hybrid federation needs **a cultural canon**.

5. Legal and Political Milestones
Some catalysts are structural:

- **A landmark Supreme Court ruling** affirming global treaty supremacy.
- **A national referendum** ratifying the Universal Bill of Rights.
- **A first global tax** enacted by 30+ countries to fund planetary infrastructure.
- **A new Charter adopted by a regional bloc**, becoming a magnet for other nations.

Momentum is built **one domino at a time**.

Conclusion: *Be Ready Before the Window Opens*
Movements that wait for perfect conditions rarely

succeed. Movements that **prepare for the unexpected—and act with coherence when the window opens—make history.**

That's the goal of the hybrid model:

- Have **institutions in scaffolding,**
- **Treaties in draft,**
- **Platforms built,**
- **Narratives circulating,**
- And **people organized—**

So that when the moment comes, **we don't simply survive the next crisis. We transform the world through it.**

National Governments and Local Leaders—Implementers or Inhibitors?

When it comes to implementation, the story begins—not in the halls of the United Nations or the tech corridors of Silicon Valley—but in **parliaments, mayor's offices, tribal councils, and rural administrative districts.**

Because in the real world, **every global ambition becomes a local regulation.** Every treaty must pass through:

- **National legislatures,**
- **Judiciaries,**
- **Municipal planners,**
- **Customary authorities.**

And every visionary idea must contend with local

budgets, political incentives, and **the very human instinct to protect one's turf.**

This section explores **the dual role national and subnational leaders will play**: sometimes **champions of change**, sometimes **barriers to reform**—but always essential to the outcome.

1. National Governments: Gatekeepers of Legal Conversion

The first implementation hurdle for any global treaty or framework is **domestication**—the act of converting international obligations into **binding national law**.

But national governments vary in:

- **Legal structure:** Some have monist systems (treaties = domestic law), others dualist (treaties require legislative ratification).
- **Political will:** Some welcome global cooperation; others fear loss of control or backlash.
- **Institutional capacity:** Even supportive governments may lack the staffing, training, or budget to implement complex reforms.

Strategies to Align National Governments:
A. Treaty Incentive Packages

- Link treaty ratification to:
    - **Development finance,**
    - **Debt relief,**
    - **Technology transfers,**
    - Or preferential trade access.

B. Legislative Toolkits

- Provide **off-the-shelf legislation**, adaptable to each country's legal system, to speed up treaty conversion.

C. Intergovernmental Implementation Pacts

- Require governments to create "**Federation Alignment Plans**":
  - Budgeted,
  - Measured,
  - Publicly reviewed every two years.

D. Civic Pressure

- Equip domestic civil society to:
  - Monitor treaty promises,
  - Challenge noncompliance in court,
  - Use media to raise the political cost of inaction.

Governments must be **invited into leadership—but held to account through law and public demand.**

2. *Local Governments: The Hidden Levers of Global Power*

While national governments set frameworks, **local governments execute them:**

- Cities regulate carbon emissions.
- Municipalities oversee public health.
- School districts deliver human rights curricula.
- Tribal councils preserve linguistic and cultural continuity.

Yet too often, **global policy stops at the capital.**

A. Cities as Engines of Global Implementation

- Mayors and city councils are often **more nimble and pragmatic** than national leaders.
- Cities have led:
    - Climate pacts (e.g., C40 network),
    - Migration integration programs,
    - Smart infrastructure projects.

In the hybrid model:

- Cities should have **standing observer status at the UN,**
- Direct access to **federation development funds,**
- And authority to **pilot treaty implementation programs.**

B. Local Autonomy with Global Alignment

- Create a **"Local Treaty Mirror System"**:
    - Each local authority translates global treaties into local ordinances.
    - Peer-reviewed by a network of federated cities and legal experts.
    - Fed into the UN's **Global Implementation Dashboard.**

C. Decentralized Budgeting

- Allocate a portion of global treaty funding **directly to local governments,** bypassing inefficient national bureaucracies.

Cities and communities aren't just implementers. They are **co-authors of the future.**

3. *Indigenous and Customary Authorities*

In many parts of the world, especially in the Global South, governance is not only civil—it is **spiritual, customary, and relational.**

- 5,000+ Indigenous nations govern lands, resources, and peoples.
- Customary legal systems adjudicate conflict for millions outside the state.
- Ancestral land rights and cultural sovereignty are **not supplemental—they are constitutional** for those communities.

In the Federation:

- **Indigenous nations must be treaty subjects—** not just stakeholders.
- They should have:
    - **Legal recognition as subnational sovereignties,**
    - **Standing in global courts,**
    - **Access to treaty drafting and ratification processes.**

Examples of Engagement:

- The **Māori in New Zealand** negotiate directly with the Crown through the Treaty of Waitangi.

The United States of the World vs. The United Nations   377

- The **Sámi Parliaments** in Nordic countries represent cultural interests in education, language, and land.
- The **Zapatista autonomous zones** in Mexico maintain self-governance while engaging global solidarity networks.

Global implementation **fails if it disrespects sacred governance. It succeeds when it partners with it.**

4. Resistance from Within: Common Objections and How to Address Them

A. **"This undermines our sovereignty."**

Response: The hybrid model **protects national cultural and political autonomy**, while requiring shared accountability on rights and planetary survival.

B. **"We don't have the budget or capacity."**

Response: The federation includes **capacity investment tools** and **equity-based funding mechanisms**. No country is left behind.

C. **"We weren't at the table when this was drafted."**

Response: All governments and local authorities are invited into **ongoing participatory treaty processes**, with opt-in clauses and amendment pathways.

D. **"The public won't support this."**

Response: Civic education, referenda, and local implementation build **bottom-up legitimacy**—especially if people see **material benefits**.

5. Case Studies in Cooperative Implementation

A. **South Africa's Rights-Based Constitution**

- Post-apartheid South Africa didn't just ratify rights—it embedded them in law, education, and budgeting.
- Provinces and municipalities were required to **align with national human rights goals**.
- Result: a federated model of localized delivery of constitutional commitments.

B. Canada's Multi-Level Indigenous Recognition

- Treaty territories, tribal governance, and federal policies exist **in layered constitutional harmony** (imperfectly, but evolving).
- The Truth and Reconciliation Commission's 94 Calls to Action are examples of **intergovernmental implementation planning.**

C. Paris Climate Accord & Municipal Leadership

- After the U.S. federal withdrawal, **hundreds of American cities and states** pledged continued compliance.
- Demonstrates that **national withdrawal need not derail local implementation**—when cities are empowered.

6. Implementation Metrics for National and Local Bodies

Every government that signs onto the hybrid model commits to:

- **Annual Implementation Reports**, including:
  - Legislative progress,
  - Budget allocations,
  - Enforcement actions,
  - Civic engagement.
- Participation in the **Global Peer Review Process**, where:
  - Regions assess one another,
  - Issue **constructive compliance recommendations**,
  - Submit follow-up reviews to the Global Parliament.

This normalizes a **culture of performance and accountability**, not just signatures.

*Conclusion: **Make the Middle Matter***

Between global vision and individual impact lies the **middle tier of power**—national and local leadership.

To implement the hybrid federation:

- National governments must act as **legal engines**.
- Local leaders must serve as **translators and executors**.
- Customary and Indigenous authorities must be **guardians of rooted legitimacy**.

Global transformation is not only about building new institutions. It's about **activating the ones we already have—with new direction, new accountability, and new shared purpose.**

The Trillionaire Club and Global Economic Enforcement

THE WEALTH of a few individuals now rivals—and in some cases surpasses—that of entire nations. As of the mid-21st century, a small group of trillionaires controls vast networks of capital, land, technology, and data. Their choices affect:

- **Food supply chains,**
- **Climate emissions,**
- **Artificial intelligence infrastructure,**
- **Housing markets,** and
- **Public discourse** via digital platforms.

We live in a world where **extreme concentration of wealth has global consequences**—but lacks global accountability.

That ends here.

This section introduces the **Trillionaire Club:** a legally mandated **civic obligation and governance framework** for any individual whose net worth exceeds one trillion dollars (or equivalent threshold indexed to global GDP).

This isn't punitive. It's structural. It recognizes that **with great wealth must come binding responsibility,** particularly in a federated system where **no one—not even the richest—operates above the law of the people and the planet.**

1. Why the Trillionaire Club?
A. Scale of Influence
Trillionaires own:

The United States of the World vs. The United Nations 381

- Global logistics companies,
- Media conglomerates,
- Food and agriculture monopolies,
- AI platforms that regulate speech, employment, and mobility.

In the hybrid federation, such power cannot remain **voluntary, philanthropic, or opaque.**

B. Moral Precedent

Just as nations commit to **treaties** and citizens abide by **laws**, the ultra-wealthy must:

- **Declare assets globally,**
- **Submit to civic duty mechanisms,** and
- **Be held accountable for planetary stewardship.**

C. Political Necessity

Without public trust that **the richest contribute their share,** any global system risks:

- **Uprisings,**
- **Tax revolts,**
- **Collapse of legitimacy.**

The Trillionaire Club is a **symbol of fairness** and a **mechanism of enforcement.**

2. *Membership Is Mandatory, Not Voluntary*

There's no opt-out clause. Once a person's verified net worth crosses the **global wealth threshold**, the following conditions apply:

A. Legal Declaration

- Public, third-party-verified wealth disclosure,
- Comprehensive registry of:
  - Assets,
  - Trusts,
  - Shell holdings,
  - Digital currencies.

B. Binding Civic Contract

- Must sign and adhere to the **Federation Civic Wealth Mandate (FCWM),** which includes:
  - Required service,
  - Financial contributions,
  - Periodic reviews.

C. Enforcement Authority

- Refusal to comply results in:
  - **Global asset seizure** via treaty enforcement,
  - **Loss of cross-border business access,**
  - **Public designation as "Non-Cooperative Actor",** akin to a global economic sanction.

This is not punishment. It's participation.

3. Duties of the Trillionaire Club

A. Mandatory Service on the Global Human Security Council

- Members must serve 5–10 years on a **Global Human Security Council (GHSC)** responsible for:

- Coordinating global hunger eradication,
- Ensuring universal water access,
- Funding clean energy infrastructure in underserved regions.

Service includes:

- Attendance at quarterly summits,
- Contribution of technical and logistical expertise,
- Submission to **conflict-of-interest audits.**

B. Financial Contribution: The Global Contribution Mandate

- Minimum 5% of net worth annually toward:
  - **Federation Infrastructure Fund,**
  - **Universal Rights Enforcement Fund,**
  - **Climate Adaptation Fund,**
  - **Emergency Pandemic Reserves.**

This is not a tax. It is **a structural funding mechanism tied to global citizenship status.**

C. Transparency and Reporting

- Annual public reports reviewed by:
  - Federation Oversight Panel,
  - Global Parliament Economic Committee,
  - Civil society watchdogs.

Reports must include:

- Investment impact summaries,

- Philanthropic disbursements,
- Stakeholder consultation logs.

4. Rights of Members (Yes, They Have Rights Too)

The Trillionaire Club is **not punitive or confiscatory.** Members retain:

- Participation in governance,
- Opportunity to influence federation strategy,
- Rights of privacy, as long as **public interest and fiduciary duty are met.**

Additionally:

- Members may propose **innovation projects,**
- Co-invest in social R&D with the Federation,
- Access **legacy impact recognition programs** (think Nobel + civic awards).

This reframes civic service as **status redefined—not diminished.**

5. What This Solves (and What It Prevents)
It Solves:

- Chronic funding shortages for universal goals,
- Legitimacy crisis in the face of extreme wealth,
- The risk of wealth hoarding during systemic collapse,

The United States of the World vs. The United Nations 385

- Perception of unearned influence in global governance.

It Prevents:

- The emergence of **private planetary rulers**,
- **Economic feudalism** through unchecked asset control,
- **Capital flight** by tying asset use to global privileges,
- **Social unrest** driven by inequality and perceived injustice.

No global system will survive if it allows **two tiers of accountability**: one for everyone else, and none for the ultra-rich.

6. *Integration Into the Hybrid Model*

The Trillionaire Club is enshrined in the **Federation Charter** as:

- A standing body,
- A funding mechanism,
- A civic responsibility framework.

Each member state of the Federation must:

- Pass **domestic enabling legislation** for enforcement,
- Coordinate cross-border compliance and audits,
- Recognize Club members as **public fiduciaries**.

Federation courts oversee:

- Disputes,
- Allegations of evasion or corruption,
- Appeals for reform or exemption (e.g., in cases of catastrophic loss).

7. *The First Trillionaire: A Moral and Strategic Inflection Point*

Imagine this scenario:

A single individual becomes the world's first trillionaire. Headlines erupt. Protests spread. Politicians demand answers. And the question looms: **What now?**

This is the **activation moment** for the Trillionaire Club. If the Federation is in place, the answer is immediate:

- The individual is enrolled.
- Responsibilities are made clear.
- Contribution begins.

If the Federation is not yet fully established, the moment becomes a **rallying cry**—and the opportunity to say:

"You have achieved the pinnacle of private success. Now you are called to **public service on behalf of humanity**."

STRUCTURAL GENEROSITY *Is Civic Duty*

The Trillionaire Club reframes what it means to succeed.

It says:

- You can build empires.

- You can shape markets.
- You can innovate and inspire.

But once your wealth reaches the level where it can alter the fate of billions, it is **no longer yours alone**. It becomes **an asset of planetary concern, subject to law, ethics, and responsibility.**

This is not revolution. It is **the final stage of civic evolution**—where the highest privilege is matched by the highest duty.

17

FUNDING THE FEDERATION—GLOBAL FINANCE IN A RIGHTS-BASED WORLD

THE ARCHITECTURE OF PLANETARY ECONOMICS

Let's start with a blunt truth: the current global financial system is **not designed for fairness**. It was built to:

- Facilitate capital mobility,
- Protect investor rights,
- And optimize profit accumulation.

It has **no moral compass, no built-in obligation to the poor**, and **no accountability to future generations**.

That's fine—if the goal is efficiency without equity. But for a **rights-based global federation**, this architecture is both insufficient and dangerous. A new world requires a new economic foundation: one that **funds public goods, protects shared resources, and upholds the rights of all—without depending on charity or crisis**.

This section lays out the **core architecture of planetary economics** under the hybrid model, shifting us from **market-dominated globalization** to **morally governed global cooperation**.

1. *The Problem: An Economy That Privileges Capital, Not People*

Symptoms of Systemic Failure:

- **$1.8 trillion annually in fossil fuel subsidies,** while renewable transitions lag.
- **$500 billion lost yearly to tax havens,** while education and health systems falter.
- Rising inequality: The richest 1% own nearly half of global wealth.
- Sovereign debt crises spiral—while private creditors demand priority repayment.

These aren't accidents. They're the results of a system built without:

- **Universal floor protections** for basic rights,
- **Global enforcement of corporate responsibility,** or
- **Public control over transnational finance.**

The federation flips the script. It funds itself not through noblesse oblige, but through **mandatory contributions and embedded justice mechanisms.**

2. *The Four Pillars of Federation Finance*

To fund itself, the hybrid global federation rests on **four major economic pillars:**

A. Federation Contributions (Tiered Dues System)

- All member states contribute annually based on:
  - GDP,
  - Carbon emissions,
  - Historical responsibility (e.g., colonial legacy, resource extraction),
  - Population-adjusted need.

The formula is progressive:

- Wealthier nations pay more.
- Low-income countries pay symbolically—or contribute through in-kind governance roles.

Funds go to:

- Global health systems,
- Education and digital access,
- Human rights enforcement,
- Climate adaptation and migration infrastructure.

B. Global Resource and Transaction Taxes

Taxes are levied **at the point of planetary impact**, not national convenience.

Key mechanisms include:

- **Carbon Border Tax:** Importers pay based on the carbon intensity of their supply chains.
- **Digital Commons Tax:** Tech companies pay for bandwidth, data mining, and AI training use of public infrastructure.
- **Global Financial Transaction Tax (GFTT):** Small fee on high-frequency trades and speculative transactions.

- **Sea and Sky Levies:** Maritime and aviation sectors pay into environmental remediation funds.

Collected by national tax authorities, remitted to the **Federation Treasury**.

C. Trillionaire Club Contributions
(See Chapter 15, Part 4)

- High-net-worth individuals fund global public goods.
- Contributions are non-optional, transparently reported, and tied to citizenship privileges.

D. Regenerative Investment Funds

- The Federation operates **planetary investment banks:**
    - Clean Energy Bank,
    - Health Innovation Bank,
    - Cultural Restoration Fund.

Seeded by public contributions, these funds invest in:

- Sustainable infrastructure,
- Social enterprises,
- Ecological restoration projects.

Returns are **reinvested, not privatized**—creating **compound justice,** not compound interest.

3. Debt, Reparations, and Redirection

A. Canceling Illegitimate Debt

- The Federation commissions an independent audit of all sovereign debt.
- Odious, colonial, or extractive debts are:
  - Renegotiated,
  - Converted into equity in climate funds,
  - Or cancelled outright.

B. Climate and Colonial Reparations

- Wealthier nations and former empires contribute to a **Global Reparations Fund** for:
  - Infrastructure in formerly colonized countries,
  - Cultural repatriation,
  - Language revitalization programs.

C. Redirection of Military Budgets

- A planetary demilitarization initiative offers:
  - Matching incentives for military-to-civilian R&D reallocation,
  - Transition support for arms workers,
  - Global education scholarships funded by peace dividends.

Every billion saved from bombs becomes a billion invested in **books, bridges, and breathable air.**

4. Ensuring Transparency and Equity in Budgeting
A. Participatory Budgeting

- Annual Federation Budget includes:
  - Online public consultations,
  - Regional citizen assemblies,
  - Civic oversight panels.

Citizens vote on **spending priorities**, track implementation, and submit local needs for inclusion.

B. Rights-Based Budgeting

- Every budget line is evaluated for its **impact on the Universal Bill of Rights:**
  - Does it reduce inequity?
  - Protect the environment?
  - Empower marginalized groups?

Projects that **fail the rights test are denied funding.**

C. The Budget of Conscience

- An optional secondary budget is built through:
  - Private philanthropy,
  - Legacy giving,
  - Crowd-contributions to symbolic initiatives (e.g., refugee artists, global museums, climate reparations memorials).

It blends meaning with money—**a public expression of shared humanity.**

5. Currency and Digital Infrastructure

While the Federation does not issue a single currency, it facilitates:

- **Interoperability between digital wallets and national systems,**
- A **planetary stablecoin** for public procurement,
- Smart contracts tied to treaty benchmarks,
- AI-assisted corruption detection.

Every citizen can access:

- A **federation wallet** for:
    - Voting,
    - Rights tracking,
    - Universal basic services (UBS),
    - Climate dividends.

Digital sovereignty and privacy protections are hard-coded into the system.

Conclusion: *Toward an Economy of Enough*
The Federation does not seek unlimited growth. It seeks:

- Enough food for all,
- Enough shelter for all,
- Enough justice to ensure peace,
- Enough regeneration to preserve life.

This is not austerity. It is **abundance managed by conscience**, where economics is no longer separate from ethics—but **a daily expression of what we value together.**
Global Wealth Redistribution Mechanisms—Justice Beyond Charity

. . .

CHARITY IS NOT JUSTICE.

Aid is not equity.

Generosity is not obligation.

For too long, wealth redistribution at the global level has been structured as **voluntary, temporary, and conditional**. Even when well-meaning, it perpetuates a dynamic where:

- Rich nations act as benefactors,
- Poor nations remain dependent,
- And structural inequalities are obscured rather than dismantled.

The hybrid global federation flips this script. It doesn't ask, "Who wants to help?" It asks, **"What is owed, and how will it be delivered—equitably, sustainably, and without delay?"**

This section lays out the **institutional mechanisms for wealth redistribution**, designed to uphold the **Universal Bill of Rights** and implement the federation's **moral economy**.

1. Redistribution by Design: A New Paradigm

Wealth redistribution is not simply a matter of money—it is a matter of:

- **Correcting historical injustice,**
- **Investing in planetary resilience,**
- **Securing future dignity for all humans.**

In the hybrid model, redistribution is:

- **Systemic** (baked into budgets and taxes),

- **Transparent** (tracked publicly),
- **Democratic** (shaped by people's input),
- **Multilevel** (occurring between nations, regions, and individuals).

2. *The Three Arenas of Global Redistribution*
A. Fiscal Redistribution: Funding Equity Mechanisms:

- Progressive **Federation Dues** based on:
    - GDP per capita,
    - Emissions per capita,
    - Extractive legacy index.
- **Solidarity Transfers** from high-capacity states to low-capacity ones, tied to:
    - Climate resilience,
    - Education infrastructure,
    - Digital public goods.
- **Universal Planetary Services (UPS):**
    - Global health guarantees,
    - Water access and sanitation,
    - Universal minimum digital access (Wi-Fi, devices, translation AI).

This isn't "aid." It's **public infrastructure for a dignified life**—available to all citizens of the federation.

B. Structural Redistribution: Redesigning the Rules
Key Reforms:
1. Global Trade Equity Pact

- Revises WTO-style trade deals to:
  - Remove harmful agricultural and pharmaceutical subsidies in rich countries,
  - Prevent forced IP regimes that block access to medicine and tech,
  - Require fair labor pricing and ethical supply chains.

2. Tax Justice Compact

- Global agreement to:
  - Eliminate tax havens,
  - Implement **unitary corporate taxation** (profits taxed where value is created, not declared),
  - Enforce wealth registry transparency.

3. Digital Equity Accord

- Ensures that profits derived from global user data:
  - Are taxed locally,
  - Fund digital literacy and access,
  - Respect sovereignty over information.

These structural mechanisms **eliminate upstream injustice**, not just redistribute downstream harm.

C. Intergenerational Redistribution: Tomorrow's Justice Starts Today

Tools:

1. Futures Fund

- Seeded by carbon taxes and corporate levies.
- Pays for:
  - Climate adaptation infrastructure,
  - Education for displaced youth,
  - AI ethics and regulatory training.

2. Planetary Basic Inheritance (PBI)

- All citizens receive a **starting capital package at age 18**, regardless of birthplace.
- Funded by a mix of:
  - Trillionaire Club contributions,
  - Federation tax revenues,
  - Regenerative investment returns.

3. Intergenerational Climate Transfer

- Annual disbursement to low-lying, drought-prone, or otherwise climate-vulnerable nations, tied to:
  - Sea level risk maps,
  - Agricultural loss indices,
  - Migration exposure.

This redistribution isn't about guilt. It's about **planetary continuity**.

3. Democratizing Redistribution: Who Decides What Goes Where?

Redistribution must not become a new form of **technocratic paternalism**. Instead, it is governed by **civic and participatory institutions**:

A. The Federation Redistribution Council (FRC)

- Composed of:
    - Elected representatives from Global Parliament,
    - Economists and public interest lawyers,
    - Civil society leaders from historically disadvantaged communities.
- Tasks:
    - Allocate annual redistributive budgets,
    - Set contribution targets,
    - Monitor compliance and publicize results.

B. The Global Equity Dashboard

- Public, multilingual, real-time tool displaying:
    - Contributions by nation and corporation,
    - Distribution of services and funds,
    - Gaps in delivery or progress.
- Citizens can:
    - Submit claims of neglect,
    - Suggest new redistributive needs,
    - Track case status transparently.

C. Participatory Allocation Forums

- Held annually in each region,
- Citizen juries propose and debate:
    - Local needs,
    - Federation support priorities,
    - Ethical trade-offs.

Redistribution is not just what is given—but **who gets to define what is fair.**

4. Aligning Private Wealth with Public Purpose

No redistribution system can function if private capital **acts in opposition** to public goals.

The hybrid model requires all corporations operating across borders to:

- Submit a **Global Equity Plan (GEP)**:
    - Disclosing supply chain impacts,
    - Detailing tax contributions,
    - Outlining local reinvestment strategies.

Failure to comply results in:

- Loss of Federation market access,
- Brand risk via public compliance scores,
- Legal sanctions.

Private sector actors can opt to:

- Join the **Social Wealth Compact**,
- Invest in regenerative sectors,
- Co-fund universal basic services.

This is not a handout. It's **buy-in to shared prosperity.**

5. A New Narrative: From Redistribution as Threat to Redistribution as Civilization

To gain support, redistribution must be reframed—not as loss, but as **legacy**.

Imagine telling the story like this:

"Your taxes didn't just fund a government—they helped lift two billion people into health and safety. Your business didn't just turn a profit—it restored forests, repaired oceans, and rebuilt cities. Your vote didn't just choose a party—it shaped a planetary ethic."

This is not charity. It is **a civilization choosing to share power with itself.**

*Conclusion: **The Engine of Global Fairness***

Redistribution in the hybrid federation is not:

- A tax on success,
- A guilt trip for history,
- Or a policy of apology.

It is:

- A principled correction,
- A future investment,
- And the **economic architecture of dignity**.

In this world, wealth circulates not to concentrate—but to **liberate**, **repair**, and **sustain**.

PLANETARY INFRASTRUCTURE—WHAT **We Build Together**

. . .

A FEDERATION BUILT on rights and cooperation cannot survive on words alone. It must pour concrete, string fiber-optic cable, dig wells, and plant forests. It must **turn policy into pavement, treaties into taps, and declarations into data access points.**

This section explores the **universal infrastructure of the hybrid world**—not just physical, but digital, social, and ecological. It is the shared skeleton of global equity, resilience, and possibility.

1. The Philosophy of Shared Infrastructure

In the hybrid federation, infrastructure is not:

- A perk for elites,
- A trade-off for compliance,
- Or a development favor granted from one state to another.

It is a **birthright** of all planetary citizens.
Three principles guide its design:
A. Universality

- All humans must have access to:
    - Clean water,
    - Sanitation,
    - Electricity,
    - Healthcare,
    - Education,
    - Internet,
    - Safe shelter,
    - Public transit,
    - Cultural and civic space.

B. Sustainability

- Infrastructure is built to restore, not deplete.
- Materials, energy, and architecture support climate resilience, biodiversity, and circular economies.

C. Equity

- Priority is given to communities long neglected or harmed.
- Designs reflect local culture, climate, and capacity.

Infrastructure is where rights become **real, daily, and durable.**

2. *Federation Infrastructure Zones (FIZs)*

To coordinate infrastructure delivery, the federation designates **Federation Infrastructure Zones (FIZs)**—regions prioritized based on:

- Poverty levels,
- Climate vulnerability,
- Infrastructure gaps,
- Conflict recovery.

Each FIZ has a **5–15 year master plan,** co-created by:

- Local authorities,
- Civic organizations,
- Federation engineers and planners.

Features:

- Open, participatory budgeting,
- Contracts awarded with equity, ethics, and local employment quotas,
- Joint audits by public, private, and community stakeholders.

3. Eight Pillars of Shared Planetary Infrastructure
A. Water and Sanitation Networks

- Universal access to:
    - Clean drinking water,
    - Wastewater treatment,
    - Drought-adapted irrigation systems,
    - Flood prevention canals and wetlands.

Includes:

- Smart metering for equity,
- Gender-sensitive facilities,
- Indigenous water sovereignty protections.

B. Renewable Energy Grids

- Solar, wind, tidal, and geothermal power networks interconnected by:
    - Continental transmission superhighways,
    - Decentralized microgrids for remote areas,
    - Federated smart load-balancing platforms.

Fuels:

- Schools,
- Clinics,
- Factories,
- Homes.

C. Global Health Infrastructure

- Universal primary care clinics within 5 km of every person,
- Mobile health units,
- Planetary disease surveillance system with federated AI triage.

Features:

- Rights-based care (non-discrimination, confidentiality),
- Local languages and cultural integration,
- Open-access pharmaceutical R&D centers.

D. Planetary Education Grid

- Digital education access for every child by age 5:
    - Satellite-linked schools,
    - AI-assisted language translation,
    - Offline-first content systems.

Also includes:

- Universal early childhood education programs,

- Global curriculum on climate, rights, culture, and peace,
- Civic mentorship networks connecting youth across borders.

E. Sustainable Transport Corridors

- Low-carbon continental rail and electric bus systems,
- Bicycle and pedestrian infrastructure,
- Clean shipping ports and electric ferries.

Integration:

- Refugee-safe mobility lanes,
- Trade routes designed for local enterprise, not extractive megaprojects.

F. Digital Public Commons

- Planetary internet backbone offering:
    - Minimum guaranteed bandwidth,
    - Free civic tools (voting, education, banking),
    - Federated data storage protected by privacy law.

Ownership:

- Nonprofit global cooperatives,
- Open-source software standards,
- AI systems governed by public ethics boards.

G. Agroecological Food Systems

- Regional food sovereignty programs:
  - Seed banks,
  - Regenerative farming cooperatives,
  - Land tenure protections,
  - Anti-food waste infrastructure.

Resilience to:

- Floods, droughts, global trade shocks, corporate land grabs.

H. Climate Resilience Infrastructure

- Coastal protection and relocation frameworks,
- Reforestation and wetland restoration,
- Cooling centers in urban heat zones,
- Wildfire buffer zones.

Built not as charity—but **as a global obligation** to the future.

4. Design by Inclusion

The federation mandates that all infrastructure projects be:

- **Co-designed** with local communities, especially women, Indigenous peoples, and youth.
- Subject to **Free, Prior, and Informed Consent (FPIC).**
- Guided by **cultural heritage impact reviews.**

Projects receive a **Rights Implementation Score**, factoring in:

- Labor standards,
- Environmental justice,
- Access guarantees.

High scores unlock:

- Accelerated permits,
- Bonus funding rounds,
- Public recognition in federation reports.

5. Funding and Maintenance Models
Funded by:

- Federation core budgets,
- Trillionaire Club contributions,
- Local–global co-investment programs.

Maintained through:

- Local cooperatives trained by federation partners,
- Renewable finance loops (e.g., clean energy pays for school expansion),
- Smart infrastructure contracts with lifespan and resilience clauses.

No more broken pumps or abandoned clinics. The federation builds **to last.**

6. Federation Infrastructure as Peacebuilding

In conflict zones or divided regions, joint infrastructure becomes:

- A **neutral space** for cooperation,
- A **platform for reconciliation**,
- A **symbol of restored dignity**.

Examples:

- Joint water-sharing between border communities,
- Binational climate response teams,
- Cross-cultural schools with dual-language instruction.

Infrastructure doesn't just serve people—it **connects them.**

What We Build, Builds Us

Roads, wires, and walls shape the future just as much as constitutions and courts. In the hybrid federation:

- **Rights are delivered in concrete and code,**
- **Justice is wired into networks,**
- And **solidarity has a postal address.**

Planetary infrastructure is not just what we build together.

It's how we live together.

Transition Finance and Economic Risk Management

Every revolution in economic systems—whether feudal to capitalist, colonial to postcolonial, or fossil-fueled to clean—carries **transition costs**.

The hybrid global federation, committed to rights-based economics and planetary justice, is no different. The transition will:

- Restructure markets,
- Redefine global labor priorities,
- Demand new taxation and investment models,
- And reduce reliance on extractive industries, speculative finance, and privatized monopolies.

Done poorly, this risks:

- **Inflation and capital shocks**,
- **National resistance**,
- **Private sabotage**, and
- **Public disillusionment**.

Done wisely, it produces:

- **Equity-driven economic security**,
- **Post-carbon prosperity**,
- And a foundation for **intergenerational stability**.

This section offers the framework for **managing**

economic turbulence while implementing structural change.

1. *Anticipating the Shocks of Economic Rebalancing*

The hybrid federation doesn't pretend reform is painless. It anticipates the four major categories of risk:

A. Fiscal Shock

- Wealth redistribution and global investment may spur:
    - Inflation in under-resourced economies,
    - Volatility in currency and commodity markets,
    - Investor hesitation.

B. Employment Displacement

- Fossil fuel phaseouts,
- Military budget shifts,
- AI automation reforms will affect millions.

C. Capital Flight and Speculation

- The ultra-wealthy and multinationals may attempt:
    - Asset hiding,
    - Regulatory arbitrage,
    - Exit from high-responsibility jurisdictions.

D. Political Retrenchment

- Authoritarian regimes may:

- Reject federation treaties,
- Blame reforms for domestic economic pain,
- Incite nationalist backlash against "globalist takeover."

These are real risks—not reasons to stall, but signals for strategic design.

2. *The Federation's Transition Finance Framework*

To manage these shifts, the federation deploys **a phased Transition Finance Framework (TFF)**, grounded in five key pillars:

A. Transitional Stability Fund (TSF)

- A multi-trillion-dollar global reserve, pooled from:
    - Federation dues,
    - Trillionaire Club contributions,
    - Climate levies and wealth taxes.
- Purpose:
    - Stabilize currencies during reform cycles,
    - Provide liquidity for social safety nets during restructuring,
    - Offer conditional grants and zero-interest loans to states shifting from high-risk economies.

Managed by:

- The **Federation Economic Security Council**,
- With oversight from the **Global Parliament and regional assemblies.**

B. Sovereign Conversion Mechanism

- Countries opting into major reforms (e.g., closing extractive industries, embracing debt forgiveness, joining carbon exit treaties) gain:
    - **Temporary access to the TSF,**
    - A **currency swap facility** to buffer against speculation,
    - **Technical support teams** to implement budget realignment.

In exchange, they commit to:

- Transparent spending,
- Civic consultation,
- Rights-based economic planning.

3. Just Transition Guarantees for Workers and Communities

No reform survives if it throws people under the economic bus.

The federation ensures **Just Transition Guarantees:**

A. Universal Employment Transition Guarantee (UETG)

- Every worker displaced by:
    - Energy transition,
    - Demilitarization,
    - Digitalization,
    - Federation treaty compliance,
- Receives:
    - Guaranteed income for two years,

- Access to retraining programs,
- Local job placement or cooperative startup grants.

B. Sectoral Repurposing Funds

- Coal plants become solar hubs,
- Weapons factories become mobility labs,
- Military logistics converted into **emergency response teams.**

C. Economic Reparation Zones

- Areas historically dependent on **extractive colonial economies** receive long-term development grants to:
    - Diversify income streams,
    - Build sustainable local economies,
    - Retain youth through innovation incubators.

The goal is not just mitigation. It's **economic transformation with dignity.**

4. Safeguards Against Capital Subversion
To prevent sabotage by entrenched interests:
A. Global Anti-Evasion Compact

- Federation member states agree to:
    - Automatic cross-border asset disclosure,
    - Real-time financial data cooperation,
    - Joint prosecution of tax avoidance and wealth laundering.

Noncompliant actors:

- Are barred from bidding on public contracts,
- Denied access to federation markets,
- Flagged on the **Global Compliance Index.**

B. Corporate Re-Chartering Mandate

- All corporations operating above a designated revenue threshold must:
    - Be re-chartered under federation law,
    - Accept fiduciary duty to human rights and sustainability,
    - Participate in annual equity audits.

Violators risk:

- Charter revocation,
- Global license bans,
- Targeted financial sanctions.

This protects the economic transition from being **hijacked by profiteers.**

5. Inflation Control and Equity Indexing

To ensure equity-based redistribution doesn't trigger runaway inflation:

A. Inflation Equity Model (IEM)

- Combines:
    - Real-time inflation tracking by sector and geography,

- Tiered spending rollouts,
- Dynamic price controls on:
  - Food staples,
  - Housing,
  - Utilities.

B. Price Stability Pacts

- Public–private agreements to:
  - Cap executive profits during fiscal expansion,
  - Slow rent increases,
  - Prevent stockpiling of vital goods.

C. Progressive Repricing Tools

- Essential goods subsidized at the point of sale,
- Luxury items taxed through digital micropayments.

Stability and justice are **co-managed, not oppositional**.

6. Political Narrative and Civic Trust

A smooth transition is not just financial—it's psychological.

Governments and federated bodies must:

- Run **transparent communication campaigns**,
- Acknowledge pain while affirming purpose,
- Share timelines, trade-offs, and public decision points,
- Celebrate milestones, not just warn about costs.

Civil society plays a vital role in:

- **Framing sacrifice as service,**
- **Reframing economic citizenship** as global belonging.

BUILDING WHILE BRIDGING

Transitions are bridges. Dangerous if rushed, deadly if delayed, essential if we want to cross safely.

The hybrid federation's financial transition is not about swapping systems overnight. It is about:

- **Funding the possible,**
- **Protecting the vulnerable,**
- And **designing a dignified descent from extractive economics into regenerative global justice.**

If done well, it won't just avoid collapse—it will **anchor a better civilization.**

18

THE GLOBAL COMMONS—GOVERNANCE BEYOND OWNERSHIP

DEFINING THE COMMONS IN A FEDERATED WORLD

There are things too sacred to be bought. Too vital to be fenced. Too universal to be owned.

The commons—our shared air, atmosphere, oceans, forests, genomes, algorithms, knowledge, and planetary rhythms—have long existed in a paradox:

- **Everyone relies on them,**
- **No one owns them,**
- And **no system fully protects them.**

What's worse, they are routinely:

- Enclosed (privatized for profit),
- Extracted (mined, polluted, sold),
- Ignored (deemed too complex to regulate).

In the hybrid global federation, this ends. Commons are no longer **orphans of law** or **prey of power**. They become **legally protected, democratically governed, and**

ethically prioritized assets of humanity and the living Earth.

This section defines **what the commons are**, why they matter, and how their recognition marks a **civilizational turning point**.

1. What Are the Global Commons?

Traditionally, commons referred to resources like:

- Pastures,
- Waterways,
- Shared grazing lands.

Today, we extend the definition to **all essential, non-renewable or interdependent planetary systems** that:

- Sustain life,
- Transcend national borders,
- Cannot be privately owned without harming the whole.

The federation recognizes the following **primary commons domains:**

A. Ecological Commons

- Atmosphere and air currents,
- Oceans and marine biodiversity,
- Rainforests and carbon sinks,
- Freshwater aquifers and glacial systems,
- Soil microbiomes and pollinator networks.

B. Genetic and Biological Commons

- Seeds and plant genomes,
- Indigenous medicinal knowledge,
- Publicly sequenced DNA data,
- Microbial ecosystems and viromes.

C. Digital and Informational Commons

- Open-source code,
- Global public research,
- Open-access journals,
- AI language models trained on public content.

D. Cultural and Ancestral Commons

- Indigenous heritage and oral traditions,
- Sacred sites and shared history,
- Language diversity and traditional governance models.

E. Atmospheric and Extraterrestrial Commons

- Outer space (orbits, asteroid belts, solar radiation),
- Moon and planetary bodies,
- Global magnetic field monitoring systems.

The guiding premise is simple: **If we all depend on it, we must all protect it.**

2. *Why Market Logic Fails the Commons*

Markets operate on principles of:

- **Excludability** (you can deny access),
- **Rivalry** (if one uses it, another cannot),
- **Profit incentive.**

Commons are:

- **Non-excludable** (air circulates, oceans flow),
- **Non-rivalrous or co-dependent** (one breath doesn't deny another, but CO_2 affects all),
- **Without intrinsic market value until commodified.**

What happens when we try to fit the commons into market models?

A. Overuse and Collapse

- Fisheries depleted by open competition.
- Forests clear-cut because future value isn't monetizable.

B. Commodification of the Sacred

- Gene patents on Indigenous medicine.
- Privatization of water and seeds.

C. Digital Enclosure

- Big Tech companies training AI on public content—then locking it behind paywalls.
- Knowledge commons harvested, then sold back to the public.

Market efficiency becomes collective extinction. The

commons require **a different logic**—one based on stewardship, duty, and shared inheritance.

3. A Rights-Based Approach to Commons Governance

The federation treats the commons as:

- **Legal entities with protection,**
- **Stewarded by humanity,**
- **Intergenerationally governed.**

This approach embeds:

- **Universal ecological rights** (clean air, water, biosphere),
- **Custodial sovereignty for Indigenous and local communities,**
- **Shared benefit mandates** for research and digital tools,
- **Prohibition of extraction without consent and repair.**

Commons governance in the federation becomes:

- **Participatory** (citizens have a say),
- **Precautionary** (future risk matters),
- **Non-commercial** (value is ethical, not extractive).

4. The Federation Commons Covenant

All member states must ratify the **Federation Commons Covenant**, which includes:

A. Legal Recognition

- Commons are declared:
  - **Beyond ownership**,
  - Protected under **federation constitutional law**,
  - Insulated from privatization or exclusive exploitation.

B. Governance Structures

- Each commons domain has a:
  - **Global Stewardship Council** (scientists, Indigenous leaders, citizen-elected reps),
  - **Monitoring Observatory** (data and satellite tools),
  - **Commons Tribunal** (to adjudicate violations and enforce repair).

C. Reparative and Equitable Use

- If access to commons is granted (e.g., medicinal plant, orbital space), a **Commons Use Dividend** is paid to:
  - Affected communities,
  - The Commons Restoration Fund,
  - Future generations trust accounts.

This turns commons from legal ambiguity into **structured, enforceable protection.**

5. *A Moral Shift: From Ownership to Stewardship*

The Commons Covenant is not just legal—it is **spiritual**.

It reclaims an ancient understanding found in Indigenous law, religious teachings, and ecological ethics:

"We do not inherit the Earth from our ancestors. We borrow it from our children."

In practice, this means:

- No one owns the wind.
- No patent on a sacred ceremony.
- No monopoly on rain or sunlight.
- No exclusive mining rights on the Moon.

The shift is from "How do I profit?" to **"How do I preserve and share?"**

*Conclusion: **The Commons Are the Constitution of Life***

If the federation's financial system is its engine, the commons are its **lungs, rivers, nervous system, and memory**.

Protecting them is not a policy choice.

It is the **moral anchor of the hybrid world**.

To govern fairly, we must **protect what we all depend on, and none can own**.

The Commons in Practice—Case Studies in Shared Governance

When we talk about governing the global commons, we are not venturing into speculative fiction. **Communities, networks, and coalitions across the planet are already**

doing it—often without recognition, funding, or legal protection.

This section examines seven critical commons arenas where federated governance principles can be applied, scaled, and structured into enforceable rights and responsibilities.

1. Ocean Stewardship: The High Seas Treaty and Beyond
Context:

The high seas—those areas of the ocean beyond national jurisdiction—cover nearly **half the planet's surface**. They regulate climate, sustain biodiversity, and support billions of lives.

Problem:

Historically lawless, exploited by:

- Overfishing fleets,
- Deep-sea mining ventures,
- Plastic dumping.

Federated Approach:

- Building on the **2023 High Seas Treaty**, the federation:
    - Establishes **Marine Commons Zones (MCZs)**,
    - Grants **permanent seats to Pacific and Indigenous island nations** on the Marine Governance Council,
    - Prohibits unregulated resource extraction,
    - Funds marine restoration with taxes on maritime shipping.

Enforcement:
Satellite surveillance, drone verification, and automatic digital license suspension for violators.

Result:
Governance shifts from "freedom to exploit" to **custodial management and reparative action**.

2. *Atmospheric Governance: Carbon Budgeting and Air as a Human Right*

Context:
The atmosphere belongs to all. But some states—and corporations—have monopolized its absorptive capacity.

Problem:

- Carbon colonialism: rich nations overconsume while vulnerable ones face climate impacts.
- No enforceable legal claim to clean air.

Federated Approach:

- The **Air Commons Act** guarantees:
    - Right to breathable air,
    - Legal limits on national and corporate carbon budgets,
    - Global emissions caps enforced by the **Atmospheric Stewardship Court**.

Tools:

- Personal carbon footprint transparency dashboards,
- Automatic penalties for excess emissions,

The United States of the World vs. The United Nations 427

- Carbon dividends redistributed through climate justice funds.

This makes **air governance universal, accountable, and equitable.**

3. Indigenous Knowledge and Genetic Resources: From Exploitation to Consent

Context:

Indigenous communities have long held:

- Healing traditions,
- Agricultural techniques,
- Ecological stewardship knowledge.

Their wisdom often ends up in:

- Pharmaceutical patents,
- Biotech research,
- Corporate profit statements.

Federated Approach:

- **Biocultural Sovereignty Framework (BSF):**
  - Requires **Free, Prior, and Informed Consent (FPIC)** before any research or commercial use,
  - Establishes **benefit-sharing agreements** enforceable in global court,
  - Recognizes collective intellectual rights beyond Western IP law.

Example: The San people's partnership around the hoodia cactus—once exploitatively patented, now set as a precedent for **collaborative, reparative innovation.**

4. *AI and Digital Knowledge Commons: Transparency, Consent, and Sharing*

Context:

AI systems and language models are trained on:

- Public data,
- Private writing,
- Cultural artifacts.

Often without consent or benefit-sharing.

Problem:

- Big Tech enclosure of knowledge commons,
- Biased algorithms built on unaccountable datasets.

Federated Approach:

- **AI Commons Charter** requires:
    - Transparency of training datasets,
    - Consent for culturally sensitive data use,
    - Revenue-sharing from models trained on the commons.

Governance:

- A **Digital Commons Tribunal** hears cases of AI exploitation.

- **Global Data Cooperatives** allow users to vote on use and licensing of their contributions.

The result is an AI economy rooted not in extraction, but **shared authorship and consent**.

5. Forest Commons: Plural Governance for Plural Ecosystems
Context:
Forests—especially tropical rainforests—are:

- Carbon sinks,
- Biodiversity hotspots,
- Cultural homelands.

Problem:
Governance battles between:

- Governments,
- Corporations,
- Indigenous stewards.

Federated Approach:

- Establish **Transnational Forest Commons Trusts**, with:
    - Local communities as legal stewards,
    - Government co-regulators,
    - Federation monitors and funders.

Mechanisms:

- "No-Deforest" zones funded by global carbon taxes,
- Restoration employment programs for youth and ex-combatants,
- Forest guardianship recognition as a **salaried public service profession**.

Forests shift from being viewed as commodities to **cathedrals of planetary balance**.

6. Open Knowledge and Scientific Research
Context:

The majority of global research is:

- Publicly funded,
- Privately paywalled.

Knowledge inequality blocks:

- Health equity,
- Educational access,
- Scientific advancement in the Global South.

Federated Approach:

- **Federation Research License (FRL):**
    - All publicly funded research must be open access within 12 months.
    - Federated institutions must publish in accessible formats and languages.
    - AI models trained on public data must offer **public benefits in return**.

Enforcement:

- Research embargoes lifted by legal mandate,
- Academic funding tied to openness benchmarks.

Knowledge, like air, becomes **a right, not a product.**

7. *Extraterrestrial Commons: Governance Before the Gold Rush*

Context:

Space is no longer speculative. Nations and companies:

- Launch satellites,
- Plan asteroid mining,
- Eye Mars colonization.

Problem:

Space treaties from the 1960s are outdated.

- Private monopolies threaten resource wars.
- Orbital debris endangers life on Earth.

Federated Approach:

- **Planetary Orbit and Space Commons Act (POSCA):**
    - Prohibits property claims on celestial bodies.
    - Requires international review of all launches.
    - Sets orbital debris quotas and cleanup obligations.

Governed by:

- **Federation Space Stewardship Council,**
- With veto power by small states and environmental councils.

Before the Moon is mined or Mars is flagged, humanity must ask: **Do we govern space—or repeat Earth's mistakes in orbit?**

Conclusion: Governance by Example, Not Exception
These case studies show that commons governance is:

- Already happening,
- Technically feasible,
- Morally urgent,
- And institutionally ready to scale.

The task before us is not invention, but **integration**—weaving these fragments into **a cohesive, enforceable global framework.**
When we govern the commons, we don't just protect what we share.
We define how we share the world itself.
Commons Stewardship as Civic Identity

In most political systems, citizenship is defined by:

- Legal documents,
- Voting rights,
- Tax obligations,
- National affiliation.

In the hybrid global federation, **citizenship is defined not only by what one receives, but by what one protects.** At the heart of this expanded identity is **the role of steward**—a person whose life reflects responsibility for the well-being of all, through care for the shared systems that sustain life.

This section explores how **commons stewardship becomes not just policy—but culture.**

1. From Subject to Steward: A Civic Shift

In industrial and post-colonial models of citizenship, people were:

- **Subjects to rule,**
- Then **consumers of services,**
- Then **voters in a marketplace of policies.**

This left out a vital role: **guardian of the public good.**

In the federation, stewardship is **the fourth identity of the citizen,** where:

- One does not simply obey law or claim rights,
- But **actively protects that which is held in common trust**—air, water, soil, digital knowledge, and justice itself.

Citizenship evolves:

- From "What do I own?"
- To "What do we share?"
- To "What am I responsible for?"

2. Civic Education for Stewardship

Every child in the federation grows up with:

- A **Commons Curriculum**, teaching:
    - Ecological interdependence,
    - Indigenous worldviews on reciprocity,
    - Rights of nature,
    - Restorative justice.

Features:

- Hands-on stewardship (tree planting, data ethics, river monitoring),
- Debates on planetary ethics,
- Annual student-led audits of community commons.

By age 18, all citizens have completed:

- A **Commons Service Pledge**,
- A **Digital Literacy and Rights Exam**,
- A project in **local ecosystem repair or community knowledge sharing**.

Education creates not just graduates, but **guardians**.

3. Commons Service as a Civic Rite

Like national service or military duty in previous systems, the federation offers **Commons Service Programs**:
Federation Commons Corps (FCC)

- Voluntary or incentivized 1–2 year civic programs in:
  - Forest protection,
  - Clean water engineering,
  - Community mapping and land restoration,
  - Peacebuilding through cultural commons exchange.

Participants:

- Earn citizenship benefits,
- Receive public recognition,
- Contribute to global performance benchmarks.

FCC uniforms include **symbols of ecosystem affiliation** —not military rank, but biome allegiance (e.g., Desert Protector, Ocean Watcher, Cloud Forest Keeper).

This reshapes prestige around **protection, not conquest.**

4. Commons Citizenship as a Professional Path

In a rights-based world, stewardship becomes:

- A job category,
- A career trajectory,
- A funded public service.

Federation-recognized roles include:

- **Data Commons Architect,**
- **AI Ethicist,**
- **Forest Guardian,**

- **Commons Tribunal Lawyer,**
- **Ocean Pathways Navigator.**

Professionals receive:

- Salary parity with legacy industries,
- Cross-border licensing,
- Access to the **Commons Vocational Guild**, offering tools, education, and cooperative benefits.

The economy shifts: no longer rewarding exploitation, but **rewarding repair and regeneration**.

5. Rituals of Shared Belonging

Civic identity is built not only through law and work—but **through shared rituals** that bind people to place and planet.

Annual traditions in the federation include:

Commons Day

- A global celebration and civic service event:
  - Tree planting,
  - Public readings of the Universal Bill of Rights,
  - Community art on shared memory and future care.

Commons Oath

- Every 18-year-old and new citizen speaks:

"I pledge to protect what we all depend on, to restore what has been harmed, and to share what none can own."

Memory Gardens

- Parks or forest clearings where names of commons defenders are engraved beside species restored, rivers cleaned, or languages revived.

This creates **a living culture of civic inheritance**, not just national nostalgia.

6. *Commons Literacy in Public Media*

Every person in the federation has access to:

- Public media channels devoted to:
    - Planetary literacy,
    - Global commons storytelling,
    - Indigenous cosmologies.

Examples:

- Documentaries on seed-saving matriarchs in India,
- Interactive simulations of ocean acidification impacts,
- AI-narrated children's stories about rainforests told in 12 languages.

The commons are not only a topic for experts.
They are **a language of collective meaning**.

. . .

7. *Faith, Spirit, and Stewardship*

The federation honors the spiritual dimension of care.

Recognizing that many cultures understand the commons not just as resources—but as:

- **Relatives** (Mother Earth, Sky Father),
- **Ancestral spirits,**
- Or **gifts from the divine**—

Interfaith and interspiritual councils are invited to:

- Co-create ceremonies of reparation,
- Develop ecological theology education,
- Serve as Commons Chaplains in disaster relief zones.

This connects stewardship to **sacred duty**, not just civic code.

Conclusion: *The Commons Make Us Whole*

The global commons are not just the water we drink or the air we breathe.

They are:

- The memory of our ancestors,
- The responsibility of our present,
- And the inheritance we owe the future.

When stewardship becomes a civic identity:

- The Earth becomes safer,
- The people become stronger,

- And society becomes something more enduring than profit or policy—

It becomes **a culture of care.**

Enforcing the Commons—Laws, **Tribunals, and Reparations**

THE TRAGEDY of the commons was never about collective use—it was always about **the absence of collective law.**

In the old paradigm, harm to the environment or theft of shared knowledge went:

- **Unpunished** (no one "owned" it),
- **Unrepaired** (no enforcement or restoration mechanism),
- **Unrecorded** (impacts were diffuse and displaced).

But in the hybrid federation, **commons violations are no longer invisible, abstract, or consequence-free.** They are codified, monitored, prosecuted, and repaired—by a **formal system of global environmental and digital justice.**

This section lays out **the enforceable legal framework that upholds the rights of the commons and the responsibilities of all who interact with them.**

1. The Commons as Legal Persons
In federation law, designated commons—such as major

rivers, forests, aquifers, or digital knowledge domains—are granted **legal personhood**.

This means:

- They can be represented in court,
- They can receive reparations,
- Their interests can be defended, independent of state or corporate agendas.

Examples:

- The **Whanganui River in Aotearoa (New Zealand)** already has legal personhood.
- Under federation law, **the Amazon Rainforest, the Arctic Ocean, and the Global Data Archive** receive similar status.

Legal personhood ensures that **the commons speak for themselves—through stewards, advocates, and civic councils.**

2. *Federation Commons Courts (FCCs)*

The federation establishes a tiered legal system specifically for commons protection:

A. Local Commons Tribunals

- Hear cases of small-scale environmental harm, cultural theft, or localized digital misuse.
- Often include **citizen juries**, restorative justice panels, and traditional dispute resolution methods.

B. Regional Commons Courts

- Handle transboundary issues like:
    - Cross-border pollution,
    - Forest destruction affecting multiple nations,
    - River usage disputes.

C. Global Commons Court (GCC)

- Final arbiter for cases involving:
    - High-seas exploitation,
    - Atmospheric emissions,
    - Space resource governance,
    - Major AI/digital infrastructure harms.

The GCC has the power to:

- Issue binding judgments,
- Levy reparations,
- Revoke digital licenses,
- Temporarily halt extractive projects.

3. Standing and Access to Justice

Who can file a case?

The federation guarantees **broad standing** for:

- Affected communities,
- Commons stewards,
- Civic groups,
- Federation officials,

- Youth and future generations via ombudspersons.

Features of Commons Litigation:

- **No-cost filing options** for marginalized groups,
- Rapid action timelines for emergency harms,
- Translators and tech support for digital commons cases,
- AI-assisted evidence gathering and environmental damage modeling.

Justice is not just symbolic—it is **accessible, timely, and rooted in real-world consequences.**

4. Sanctions and Penalties for Commons Violations
A. Corporate Violations

- Illegal bioprospecting, emissions breaches, or AI data exploitation can result in:
    - Fines proportional to harm (with multipliers for intent),
    - Global market access bans,
    - Mandatory commons reparations investments,
    - Open-source release of closed IP derived from stolen commons data.

B. State Violations

- Examples: river redirection harming downstream

nations, illegal deforestation, unauthorized space launches.
- Penalties include:
  - Loss of federation privileges,
  - Carbon or emissions caps with financial bonds,
  - Mandated payments into the **Commons Reparations Fund**,
  - Suspension from voting in commons governance bodies until rectified.

C. Individual and Institutional Violations

- For wealthy individuals, academic labs, or cultural institutions engaging in commons theft:
  - Revocation of licensing or credentials,
  - Public listing on **Commons Violation Registry**,
  - Federation-funded reconciliation processes.

5. *Reparations and Restoration*
A. Monetary Reparations

- Calculated using:
  - The **Federation Environmental Damage Index (FEDI)**,
  - Cultural harm impact assessments,
  - Lost use valuations over time.

Reparations are paid to:

- Impacted communities,
- Commons Restoration Trusts,
- Global Future Generations Fund.

B. Ecological and Cultural Restoration

- In some cases, **repair must precede profit**:
    - Illegal logging companies must fund reforestation before reapplying for contracts.
    - Cultural institutions holding stolen heritage must **return and fund the rebuilding of knowledge systems**.

C. Truth and Commons Commissions

- For large-scale or historical violations, the federation convenes **truth commissions**:
    - Hear testimonies,
    - Establish official records,
    - Propose long-term remediation pathways.

Example:
A federation commission on Arctic oil exploitation could lead to **a 100-year polar healing plan**, funded by oil majors and implemented by Indigenous governments.

6. Commons Compliance Index (CCI)

The federation maintains a **Commons Compliance Index**, ranking:

- Corporations,
- Countries,

- Cities,
- Institutions,

…on their adherence to commons protection laws. Publicly accessible and updated quarterly, it includes:

- Color-coded trust ratings,
- Detailed violations and improvement efforts,
- Commons stewardship achievements.

CCI becomes a **reputation tool** for procurement, investment, and civic trust.

7. *Technology and Enforcement Infrastructure*
Enforcement is powered by:

- **Satellite-based environmental monitoring** (e.g., forest cover, methane leaks),
- **Digital commons tracking systems** (e.g., AI training dataset audits),
- **Blockchain for restorative funding transparency,**
- **Federated whistleblower protection platforms.**

The result is not just more rules—but **a living system of visibility, trust, and real consequences.**

Justice for What Cannot Speak
In past centuries, the law protected:

- Property,

- Power,
- And privilege.

In the hybrid federation, the law protects:

- **Life without voice,**
- Systems without borders,
- And people without previous standing.

Commons enforcement is not a burden—it is **the backbone of civilization at scale.**

19

BORDERLESS RIGHTS—MOBILITY, MIGRATION, AND HUMAN BELONGING

FEDERATION MOBILITY LAW—FROM BORDERS TO PATHWAYS

A right is only real if it comes with a pathway to access it.

The hybrid federation's approach to mobility is built on that premise. It does not abolish all forms of migration management—but it **dismantles the global apartheid of mobility by replacing arbitrary barriers with structured, rights-based pathways.**

This section outlines the **legal framework of Federation Mobility Law**, which:

- Ends border violence,
- Protects displaced people,
- Clarifies residency and labor rights,
- And redefines citizenship as a dynamic, participatory relationship—not an inherited entitlement.

1. The Federation Mobility Code (FMC)

The legal foundation of borderless rights is the **Federation Mobility Code**—a globally binding legal system that replaces:

- Detention,
- Deportation,
- Statelessness,
- And arbitrary migration bans.

Key features include:
A. Universal Residency Recognition

- Every person, regardless of passport, has the right to:
    - Reside in a Federation member territory,
    - Apply for local integration,
    - Access essential services after a brief registration process.

Residency is no longer tied to nationality, but to **presence and participation**.
B. Mobility Passports

- All global citizens receive a **Federation Mobility Passport** (FMP) that tracks:
    - Residency history,
    - Work authorization,
    - Health and education access (not policing data).

It is **non-biometric, privacy-protected**, and issued regardless of nationality or legal status.
C. Migration Pathways, Not Exclusion Lists

- The federation establishes:
  - Climate Migration Pathways,
  - Labor Mobility Channels,
  - Humanitarian Corridors,
  - Education Exchange Pathways.

No human is illegal.
No reason for movement is invalid.

2. Redefining Citizenship: Participation Over Inheritance

In the federation, **citizenship is not a fixed asset inherited by birth or wealth.** It is a **participatory legal and moral status** based on engagement, stewardship, and residency.

A. Federation Citizenship Model

Citizenship is acquired through:

- Time-based residency,
- Completion of civic education modules (available in all languages and formats),
- Participation in community service or democratic processes.

This prevents:

- Statelessness,
- Inherited privilege,
- Gatekeeping by elite passport regimes.

B. Multiple Citizenship Is Normalized

- Federation citizenship coexists with national, tribal, or ancestral affiliations.
- No requirement to renounce original identity or legal recognition.

Citizenship becomes a **layered experience**, not a zero-sum belonging.

3. Federation Visa System: Simplified, Transparent, Universal

Visas are not eliminated—but they are **streamlined into six universal categories**, all of which are rights-protected:

1. **Humanitarian Protection Visa**
   - For those fleeing persecution, violence, or disaster.
   - Approved in under 14 days with remote application access.
2. **Climate Adaptation Visa**
   - For people displaced by sea-level rise, drought, or climate collapse.
   - Includes relocation subsidies, language training, and family integration.
3. **Family Reunification Visa**
   - Immediate access for spouses, children, parents, and long-separated kin.
   - No income or employment thresholds.
4. **Open Labor Visa**
   - For work in any field or sector across federation economies.
   - Portable benefits and labor protections guaranteed.
5. **Educational Mobility Visa**

The United States of the World vs. The United Nations 451

- For formal or informal learners at any age.
- Includes free access to digital or physical education.

6. **Civic Engagement Visa**
    - For migration tied to arts, activism, spiritual engagement, or cultural preservation.
    - Validated by community-based organizations.

All visas are:

- Renewable,
- Convertible to residency and citizenship,
- Processed by **digital civic agents**, not border militaries.

4. Ending Detention and Deportation
Under Federation Mobility Law:

- **No person can be detained solely for migration status.**
- Deportation is replaced with:
    - Mediation,
    - Voluntary return with full support,
    - Or local regularization.

Migrants must be treated:

- As **rights-bearing humans,** not security threats.
- With access to legal counsel, language services, and trauma-informed care.

5. *Digital Rights in Transit*

All migrants retain:

- **Data sovereignty** over their personal information,
- Control over what governments, employers, or agencies can access.

The Federation Mobility Passport uses:

- **Decentralized storage**,
- **End-to-end encryption**,
- **Consent protocols**.

Migrants also receive:

- Free mobile connectivity,
- Legal hotline access,
- Real-time alerts in their language regarding rights and resources.

6. *Local Integration and Belonging*

Migrants are supported by:

- **Federation Welcome Networks**—community hubs offering:
    - Translation,
    - Housing cooperatives,
    - Employment coaching,

The United States of the World vs. The United Nations 453

- Language immersion.
- **Commons Service Exchange Programs**—where new arrivals:
    - Contribute time to community projects,
    - Build social ties,
    - Gain federation credits convertible into benefits or voting points.

Belonging is not just policy—it's **co-created through participation**.

7. *Remittances, Diasporas, and Transnational Families*
Remittances are not taxed or penalized.
Diaspora contributions are recognized through:

- Voting rights in multiple jurisdictions,
- Diaspora civic councils,
- Transnational family protections (e.g., joint guardianship recognition).

Migration no longer fragments families—it **creates living bridges between places**.

CONCLUSION: *A System That Moves with People*
Federation Mobility Law reimagines the entire structure of global movement.
It says:

- You do not need permission to be human.
- You do not lose rights when you cross a line on a map.

- You do not have to wait to belong.

It replaces exclusion with invitation.

It transforms migration from problem to **pathway of possibility**.

Climate Migration **and the Right to Stay**

Climate migration is not a future problem.

It is the present reality for millions.

- Entire villages in the Arctic are relocating due to thawing permafrost.
- Pacific islands are watching their shorelines disappear.
- Sub-Saharan farmers are walking north, not for better jobs, but **for breathable air and drinkable water.**
- Cities like Jakarta and Lagos face chronic flooding and rising temperatures—pushing out residents one storm, one heatwave, one landslide at a time.

And yet, **there is still no legally binding international framework** to protect those displaced by climate.

The hybrid federation changes that—by **recognizing climate displacement as a rights issue**, not just a humanitarian emergency.

This part outlines how the federation:

- Classifies climate migration,

The United States of the World vs. The United Nations 455

- Builds legal pathways,
- Offers resettlement and restoration options,
- And defends the right to stay, adapt, and thrive in place.

1. *Who Are Climate Migrants?*
Climate migrants are people who:

- Move temporarily or permanently because of environmental degradation,
- Lose access to food, land, or water due to climate impacts,
- Relocate preemptively before disaster strikes,
- Are trapped in place, even as conditions worsen (known as "climate-immobile").

They are not:

- Recognized under the 1951 Refugee Convention,
- Guaranteed asylum or international protection,
- Tracked systematically by any global body.

They are often **invisible to the law, but hypervisible to crisis.**

2. *Categories of Climate-Linked Displacement*
The Federation Mobility Code (FMC) creates new categories of protected climate movement:
A. Sudden-Onset Displacement

- Hurricanes, wildfires, floods, or earthquakes.
- Individuals may evacuate temporarily or relocate permanently.

B. Slow-Onset Displacement

- Sea-level rise, desertification, salinization, glacial melt, or drought.
- Communities may migrate gradually, over generations.

C. Planned Relocation

- Federated programs to relocate entire villages, regions, or low-lying cities with:
    - Full consultation,
    - Rights to land and compensation,
    - Cultural preservation protections.

D. Trapped Populations

- People who want or need to leave, but cannot due to poverty, disability, war, or systemic exclusion.
- Federation policies prioritize safe corridors, airlifts, or funding for relocation assistance.

3. The Climate Displacement Protocol (CDP)
The CDP is a legally binding federation treaty that:

- Grants **protected status** to all climate-displaced persons,
- Bans the criminalization or deportation of climate migrants,
- Establishes a **Federation Climate Displacement Authority (FCDA)** with power to:
  - Monitor displacement hotspots,
  - Coordinate emergency responses,
  - Distribute resettlement funds,
  - Oversee long-term integration.

Climate migration is treated not as a security threat, but **a civic emergency with global responsibility.**

4. The Right to Stay: Climate Adaptation as Sovereignty

While some will move, others **wish to remain—and must be supported to do so.**

The hybrid federation recognizes the **right to stay as foundational**—not only to preserve homes, but cultures, identities, languages, and ecosystems.

Federation Adaptation Guarantees:

- Infrastructure investment in climate-vulnerable regions,
- Renewable energy microgrids and freshwater desalinization systems,
- Disaster-resistant housing upgrades,
- Support for climate-resilient agriculture,
- Compensation and subsidies for lost ecosystems or livelihoods.

Adaptation is treated not as a privilege—but **as a public right owed to frontline communities.**

5. *The Climate Migration Solidarity Fund (CMSF)*

Funded by:

- Trillionaire Club contributions,
- Carbon border taxes,
- Federation climate dues (scaled by historical emissions),

...the CMSF supports:

- Community-led relocation planning,
- Youth education and reskilling in both origin and host regions,
- Infrastructure in new settlement zones (schools, clinics, housing),
- Mental health and trauma support.

Access is granted not only to nations, but:

- Tribal governments,
- Displaced cooperatives,
- Migrant-led organizations.

The Fund operates by **bottom-up proposal**, not top-down allocation.

6. *Cultural Continuity and Land Memory*

Migration is not just physical—it is **cultural and spiritual**.

Federation policies protect:

- Land memory archives: oral histories, sacred sites, ancestral planting practices.
- Cultural continuity zones: where relocated communities retain:
    - Naming rights,
    - Language use,
    - Educational autonomy.

Example: If a coastal Indigenous community from Vanuatu is relocated inland, the new community center is still:

- Named by the original people,
- Run by their elders,
- And supported to practice their governance traditions.

7. Case Study: Federated Climate Citizenship in Action
Scenario:

- A low-lying Pacific island declares permanent relocation to a higher-elevation federation partner (e.g., New Zealand or a Pacific climate corridor nation).

The Federation Response:

1. **Climate Citizenship Treaty** enacted.
2. **Collective citizenship granted**—not individual asylum.
3. **Community-designated relocation zones** offered with land tenure rights.
4. **Cultural heritage contracts** signed to protect songs, designs, burial practices.
5. **Federation Mobility Passports issued** to all residents, regardless of former documentation.

The result:

- **No one becomes stateless,**
- The culture continues,
- And the people help design their new life **with dignity and democratic voice.**

Climate Mobility Is a Global Duty

The era of climate displacement is here.

The choice is not whether people will move—but **whether we will meet them with rights, respect, and resources—or barbed wire, bureaucracy, and blame.**

The hybrid federation ensures:

- You may stay, and be supported.
- You may move, and be welcomed.
- You may belong, anywhere.

Because in a just world, **the climate does not determine your worth.**

20

FROM VISION TO REALITY
AMERICA'S OPPORTUNITY—AND OBLIGATION

Why the U.S. Is Uniquely Positioned to Lead This Transition

AT EVERY CRITICAL juncture in global history, the United States has played a role—sometimes as architect, sometimes as saboteur, always as a pivot.

- After World War II, it helped design the United Nations and the Bretton Woods system.
- In the Cold War, it framed democracy and capitalism as the guardians of freedom.
- In the digital age, it produced the tools and companies that now shape global discourse.
- And in the 21st century, it has become a paradox—**a superpower in crisis, a divided democracy that still holds enormous global sway.**

This moment demands that America confront its legacy—not to apologize for it, but to **redeem and realign it** with the shared destiny of humanity.

Why the U.S.? Because it is uniquely positioned to lead the hybrid federation into being.

1. *Structural Influence: The Power to Move Systems*

No other single nation has the combination of:

A. Economic Reach

- The U.S. dollar is still the world's dominant reserve currency.
- U.S. corporations shape global labor markets, technology, and investment flows.

By endorsing hybrid economic reforms, such as:

- Global wealth redistribution,
- Tax justice frameworks,
- Climate reparations funds, ...the U.S. can **accelerate system-wide change by flipping a single economic switch.**

B. Military Infrastructure

- With 750+ military bases in 80 countries, America's footprint is planetary.
- It spends more on defense than the next ten nations combined.

By repurposing its global infrastructure toward:

- Peacekeeping logistics,
- Climate response,
- Commons protection, ...it can **redefine security as service, not domination.**

C. Cultural and Narrative Reach

- American media, music, and universities shape global imagination.
- U.S.-based movements (civil rights, feminism, tech innovation) ripple worldwide.

If America begins telling a new story—of **shared**

responsibility, of planetary democracy, of borderless belonging—the world listens.

2. Foundational Paradox: A Nation Born of Revolution and Empire

The United States is not an innocent player. It carries:
- The burden of slavery and genocide,
- The shadow of interventionism,
- The scars of inequality and surveillance capitalism.

Yet it also carries:
- The DNA of revolutionary ideals,
- A written Constitution capable of amendment and reform,
- Generations of activists who have expanded democracy in the face of backlash.

This paradox is not a weakness. It is a mirror for the world.

The hybrid federation requires nations willing to say:

"We have erred, and we evolve. We are not perfect, but we are committed."

No nation better symbolizes **that ongoing struggle between ideal and reality** than the United States.

3. Constitutional Flexibility and Legal Precedent

The U.S. Constitution, though written in the 18th century, is:
- **Amendable,**
- **Interpretable by courts,**
- **Open to treaty commitments.**

It already recognizes:

- International law as binding via the Supremacy Clause (Article VI),
- Treaties as enforceable by courts,
- Executive agencies as instruments of transnational coordination.

This gives the U.S. an **internal legal framework compatible with global federation principles**—from ratifying new rights to implementing hybrid governance models domestically.

Where other nations may need revolutions, **America needs amendments, legislation, and interpretation.**

4. Democratic Traditions and the Crisis of Democracy

America's institutions are aging—but resilient:

- Local governance,
- Civic organizing,
- Independent media,
- State-federal balancing systems.

While these are under threat, they also provide **models for scaled governance:**

- National–state hybrid structures mirror federation–nation relationships.
- Civil rights law offers precedent for enforcing universal protections.
- Participatory budgeting, local ballot measures, and state-level experimentation make **American federalism a usable analogy for global hybrid governance.**

America does not need to invent new systems—it needs to **extend its best ones beyond borders.**

5. Youth, Multiculturalism, and Global Identity

The rising generation in the U.S. is:
- Majority non-white,
- Globally connected,
- Disillusioned by nationalism,
- Inspired by justice movements and digital pluralism.

They:
- Learn Korean pop and Nigerian film alongside English classics,
- Work remotely across continents,
- Mobilize for climate, racial justice, and democracy.

This generation **already lives a hybrid, federated identity**. U.S. leadership in a new global structure would **reflect its youth, not its institutions.**

6. Foreign Policy Realignment Opportunities

U.S. policy already includes the tools to support the hybrid vision:
- **State Department global democracy funds,**
- **USAID support for human rights**, health, and education,
- **Defense Department climate-readiness initiatives,**
- **National Science Foundation AI ethics research.**

All that's needed is **reframing and realigning** these tools toward federation goals:
- Ending food and water insecurity,
- Supporting digital commons and planetary infrastructure,
- Funding universal health, education, and ecological protection.

In short: **turning soft power into shared power.**

. . .

7. Global Perception: Credibility Through Action

The U.S. has often preached what it does not practice. To lead the federation, it must **do both:**

- **Implement domestic reforms** (see Part 2),
- **Model rights-based foreign engagement.**

Actions that would establish credibility:

- Join and strengthen the International Criminal Court,
- Lead in ratifying a Global Bill of Rights,
- Enforce carbon border adjustments that fund climate justice,
- Repurpose overseas bases for ecological stewardship and humanitarian aid.

Moral leadership must be visible, verifiable, and viral.

Conclusion: A Legacy Worth Leading Into the Future

America stands at a crossroads:

- One path leads deeper into isolation, nationalism, and decline.
- The other leads into **a new kind of leadership—not of dominance, but of dignity.**

The hybrid global federation will happen—with or without the United States.

But if the U.S. leads:

- It can **help design a system worthy of the Constitution's highest ideals,**
- It can **repair its reputation through reform, not rhetoric,**
- And it can become **not an empire in retreat—but a republic in rebirth.**

How Domestic Reform Strengthens Global Credibility

. . .

IN THE 20TH CENTURY, American leadership rested on two pillars:
- **Economic scale**, and
- **Moral narrative.**

It claimed:
- "We are the arsenal of democracy."
- "We are the land of opportunity."
- "We are the free world's protector."

But the 21st century has exposed contradictions:
- Skyrocketing inequality,
- Disinformation-fueled elections,
- Gun violence, mass incarceration, and voter suppression,
- A democratic system vulnerable to minority rule and corporate capture.

For the United States to lead the hybrid federation, it must **align its internal political practices with the external moral vision it promotes.** That means **rebuilding credibility from the inside out**—not with slogans, but with structural reform.

1. Campaign Finance Reform: Ending Legalized Corruption

No reform is more essential to restoring U.S. moral authority than **removing the grip of money on politics.**

Problem:
- Citizens United v. FEC (2010) opened the floodgates for unlimited corporate and dark money.
- Billionaires and special interests now dominate elections at every level.
- Policy outcomes often reflect donor interests, not voter will.

Federation Implications:

- A nation that cannot regulate its own democratic process **cannot design a legitimate global one.**

Required Reforms:

- Overturn Citizens United via constitutional amendment or new judicial precedent.
- Enact public financing of campaigns.
- Mandate real-time transparency of all contributions and expenditures.
- Ban lobbyist bundling and foreign-influenced corporate spending.

These reforms restore **the principle that governance flows from the people—not from wealth.**

2. Electoral Integrity: Protecting the Voice of Every Citizen

The U.S. electoral system faces:

- Gerrymandered districts,
- Outdated voter rolls,
- Disenfranchisement of formerly incarcerated individuals,
- Partisan voter suppression laws.

To be a model of democracy, the U.S. must ensure that **every person can vote, and every vote counts equally.**

Reform Actions:

- Enact automatic, universal voter registration.
- Establish independent redistricting commissions in every state.
- Guarantee voting access through early voting, mail-in ballots, and election holidays.
- Restore voting rights to incarcerated and formerly incarcerated citizens.

Federation credibility demands that **the U.S. model voting as a right, not a battleground.**

. . .

3. Civic Education and Participation: Reviving the Public Mind

Democracy is not just a procedure—it is a culture.

The U.S. has suffered decades of:

- Declining civic education,
- Polarization,
- Public mistrust,
- And the erosion of shared facts.

A federation that depends on **informed planetary citizens** requires America to reawaken its **civic soul**.

Reform Actions:

- Mandate comprehensive, nonpartisan civic education in all K–12 curricula.
- Create public forums for deliberative democracy.
- Fund youth civic engagement programs and national service options.
- Support local media and fact-checking cooperatives.

Rebuilding civic trust at home is **preparation for fostering civic trust abroad.**

4. Racial Justice and Reparative Democracy

The moral leadership of the U.S. cannot rest on democracy alone—it must be founded in **justice**.

The U.S. bears unhealed wounds:

- Enslavement and structural racism,
- Indigenous displacement and genocide,
- Mass incarceration and economic exclusion.

These are not just domestic issues—they are **global symbols** of hypocrisy when unaddressed.

Federation Alignment Requires:

- Truth commissions on racial violence and systemic injustice,
- National reparations program for Black and Indigenous communities,
- Land return and tribal governance recognition,
- Dismantling of carceral systems built on racialized control.

A country that teaches the world about rights must **show how it repairs the denial of those rights.**

5. Reclaiming the Commons at Home

The U.S. must also **model the federation's economic and environmental vision** by reclaiming its domestic commons.

Examples:

- Transitioning water, energy, and broadband systems to public cooperative ownership.
- Enshrining clean air, water, and housing as constitutional rights.
- Protecting ancestral lands and biodiversity from extractive industries.
- Creating local food, transportation, and healthcare networks as **community rights**, not commodities.

This becomes the prototype for **planetary commons governance—grounded, tangible, and democratic.**

6. Immigrant Justice and Border Reform

America cannot lead a federation of borderless rights while:

- Jailing asylum seekers,
- Separating families,

The United States of the World vs. The United Nations 471

- Militarizing its southern border,
- And denying refugees access to basic care.

Required Reforms:

- End detention of migrants and refugees.
- Provide pathways to legal residency and citizenship for undocumented residents.
- Restore and expand asylum protections.
- Create binational border commissions for human mobility and ecological protection.

Immigrant justice is not a wedge issue. It is a **litmus test of federation values.**

7. Aligning Domestic Institutions with Federation Principles

To truly lead, the U.S. must align its institutions with the federation charter:

- Congress must ratify global treaties on climate, migration, and human rights.
- The Supreme Court must recognize international obligations as part of constitutional interpretation.
- Federal agencies must integrate **federation scorecards and rights audits** into operations.
- Local governments must be empowered to implement federation-aligned programs with full funding and legal backing.

Governance becomes **an act of coherence**—domestic and global policies mutually reinforcing.

Conclusion: Repairing to Lead, Leading by Repair

The United States cannot export what it refuses to practice.

But neither must it be perfect to lead. It must be honest. It must be accountable. And it must be willing to **transform itself into the kind of democracy it believes the world deserves.**

Domestic reform is not a detour from global leadership.

It is the **only legitimate path toward it.**

America's opportunity is real.

Its obligation is clear.

Its future is still unwritten.

The Moral Responsibility of Global Leadership

When the future asks what role the United States played in humanity's defining century, the answer will not be measured in GDP or military budgets. It will be measured in **moral courage.**

- Did it lead when others hesitated?
- Did it repair when it could have denied?
- Did it make room for others at the table—or reinforce its throne?

Global leadership is not a birthright. It is a responsibility—one earned not by declaring values, but by **demonstrating them, at home and abroad.**

1. The Decline of Coercive Legitimacy

Historically, empires maintained global influence through:

- Colonization,
- Economic coercion,
- Military power,
- And control of trade routes and resources.

Today, that model is **unsustainable and morally bankrupt.**
- Military supremacy cannot solve climate breakdown.
- Corporate monopolies cannot rebuild ecological balance.
- Propaganda cannot generate trust.

The hybrid federation model **rejects coercive legitimacy.** It calls instead for:
- Voluntary alignment,
- Rights-based governance,
- Participatory leadership.

For America to lead, it must renounce its status as hegemon and **redefine itself as a convenor of common cause.**

2. What Leadership Looks Like in a Hybrid World

In the hybrid federation, leadership is not dominance. It is service.

A leading nation:
- Shares technology without monopolizing it.
- Pays its fair share to planetary institutions.
- Accepts binding legal frameworks for accountability.
- Protects the commons rather than privatizing them.
- Models democratic participation in every sphere.

America's leadership potential lies in:
- Its ability to mobilize resources,
- Influence narratives,
- And coordinate systems rapidly and at scale.

But that power must be exercised **with humility, transparency, and solidarity.**

. . .

3. Responsibility Scaled to Power

The federation does not flatten responsibility—it **scales it.** The greater a nation's historical impact, emissions, military reach, and financial leverage, the greater its duty to:

• **Fund the transition** to regenerative systems,

• **Uphold universal rights** even when politically inconvenient,

• **Submit to enforcement mechanisms** that apply equally to all,

• And **make space for emergent voices**, especially from the Global South, Indigenous communities, youth movements, and marginalized populations.

Leadership means **carrying more—not commanding more.**

4. Moral Repair as Foreign Policy

The United States has a unique global footprint of:

• Military intervention,
• Cultural influence,
• Economic dominance.

It must also develop a **doctrine of moral repair**, which includes:

A. Acknowledgment

• Official recognition of historical harms (slavery, coups, land theft, etc.).

• Support for truth commissions and people's tribunals.

B. Restitution

• Reparations funds for nations and communities harmed by U.S. policy.

• Return of stolen cultural artifacts.

• Cancelation of unjust debts and unfair trade pacts.

C. Reinvestment

- Redirecting military aid toward climate adaptation.
- Funding public health, education, and infrastructure in post-conflict regions.
- Empowering civil society networks, not corrupt gatekeepers.

Moral repair becomes **foreign policy in practice—not just language in speeches.**

5. *The Opportunity to Model a New Social Contract*

The United States has the constitutional, institutional, and cultural tools to model what the hybrid federation aspires to become.

This includes:
- A **Bill of Rights** reinterpreted for the 21st century to include housing, climate, and digital access.
- **Local-federal relations** that resemble how nations might relate to the federation.
- A tradition of **civil resistance, legal reform, and pluralist debate** unmatched in scale and reach.

The U.S. doesn't need to invent the future from scratch. It needs to **align its past innovations with its future responsibilities.**

6. *From Fear-Based Exceptionalism to Purpose-Based Leadership*

American exceptionalism has long been a double-edged sword:
- A source of aspiration,
- And an excuse for avoiding accountability.

To lead the hybrid transition, the U.S. must **replace exceptionalism with example.**

Not "We're different, so we opt out,"
but **"We're responsible, so we step up."**
The shift is from:
- *Dominance to partnership,*
- *Immunity to alignment,*
- *Control to contribution.*

This is not weakness. It is **a new form of greatness.**

7. *The Call of History*

Future generations will not ask how the U.S. preserved its primacy.

They will ask:
- Did it prevent collapse?
- Did it protect the vulnerable?
- Did it build the scaffolding of planetary peace?

We are living through **a constitutional moment for the world.**

Just as 1776 marked the beginning of American democracy,
and 1945 marked the birth of international cooperation,
this century demands a new milestone:

The rise of a **just, participatory, enforceable global system—led not by power, but by principle.**

The United States can be a midwife to that future.

Or it can be a footnote in its origin story.

CONCLUSION: *From Empire to Earth Steward*

America has a choice:
- To cling to empire in decline,
- Or to lead **as Earth's steward—anchored in rights, powered by conscience, and guided by solidarity.**

The path forward begins not with domination, but with a new declaration:

"We hold these truths to be planetary:

that all people are created equal,

that dignity is indivisible,

and that the rights of the many shall be defended by the power of the willing."

America's opportunity is not to rule the future.

It is to help **build a world where no one has to.**

21

THE PATH FORWARD
A SUMMARY OF THE HYBRID MODEL

Let us begin with a reminder of the crisis.

The 21st century presents a paradox that no nation-state, corporation, or ideology can resolve alone:

- **Interdependence without cooperation.**
- **Shared crises without shared governance.**
- **Global systems ruled by local interests, and local lives endangered by global neglect.**

The hybrid model of global governance is **the bridge between sovereignty and solidarity**. It is a **blueprint for coordination without colonization, for enforcement without empire, for belonging without erasure.**

This section distills the model into its most essential components: its **governing logic, institutional framework, legal foundation, civic identity, and transformational aims.**

. . .

1. What Is the Hybrid Federation Model?

The hybrid global governance model is a transnational framework that:

- Respects national sovereignty while elevating global obligations;
- Replaces unaccountable global elites with **representative planetary institutions**;
- Balances enforceable law with pluralistic local governance;
- Guarantees universal rights without erasing cultural and political difference.

It is not a **world government**, but it is **more than international cooperation.**

It is a **federation of federations**—a legally binding, ethically grounded system of multilevel coordination between:

- Nations,
- Cities and regions,
- Civil society networks,
- Commons stewards,
- And planetary institutions.

2. Foundational Values and Guiding Principles

The hybrid model is based on **five core values:**

1. Dignity

- Every person deserves access to life-sustaining goods, rights, and voice.
- No one is illegal. No one is disposable.

2. Responsibility

- Power must be accountable to people and planet.
- The more power one holds, the more responsibility one bears.

3. Reciprocity

- Nations, institutions, and individuals are bound by mutual obligation—not zero-sum competition.

4. Pluralism

- Difference is protected. Cultural, spiritual, and linguistic diversity is a global asset—not a threat.

5. Planetary Stewardship

- The Earth is a shared home, not a commodity.
- Governance must ensure the continuity of life, not just human convenience.

These values inform the **legal, economic, and civic structures** of the federation.

3. The Institutional Architecture
The hybrid federation includes:
A. A Global Parliament

- Democratically elected,
- Representing people—not just states,

- With legislative authority to:
    - Enact planetary rights,
    - Fund public goods,
    - Oversee transnational institutions.

B. A Federation Council of States

- Composed of national and regional governments,
- Votes on shared security, resource allocation, treaty interpretation.

C. Planetary Judiciary

- Interprets the Universal Bill of Rights,
- Resolves transboundary disputes,
- Prosecutes violations of commons and dignity.

D. Federation Agencies and Commissions

- Responsible for:
    - Climate justice,
    - Digital governance,
    - Commons protection,
    - Global health and migration systems,
    - Trillionaire contribution compliance.

E. Civic Oversight Mechanisms

- Participatory budgeting,
- Citizens' assemblies,
- Independent media and transparency tools,

- Civil society panels with veto power on high-risk projects.

It is a system of **checks and balances—across borders, classes, and sectors.**

4. The Legal Framework: Binding, Enforceable, Legitimate
The hybrid model enforces law at three levels:
1. International Treaties Reimagined

- Treaties on rights, climate, AI, and migration gain enforcement power via:
  - Federation judiciary,
  - Public compliance tracking,
  - Penalties and reparations for noncompliance.

2. The Universal Bill of Rights

- Every citizen, regardless of nation, is guaranteed:
  - Access to clean water, food, and shelter,
  - The right to movement, culture, health, and education,
  - Digital and ecological protections.

3. Commons Protection Protocols

- The atmosphere, oceans, seeds, AI training data, and other commons are:
  - Legally recognized,
  - Governed by planetary institutions,
  - Protected through reparations frameworks and stewardship mandates.

Laws are not suggestions. They are **tools of justice, structured for durability.**

5. *Economic Foundations: A Moral Economy*

The hybrid model transforms economics from a private game to a public contract.

Key Components:

- **Federation Tax Base:** Progressive dues, carbon taxes, transaction fees, and Trillionaire Club contributions.
- **Universal Services:** Healthcare, education, housing, digital access provided as a global minimum.
- **Commons Investment Funds:** Profits reinvested in ecological repair, cultural resilience, and innovation.
- **Debt and Reparations Reform:** Illegitimate debt canceled; colonial and climate reparations legally mandated.

Economics becomes a **vehicle for dignity—not domination.**

6. *Citizenship and Civic Identity: Belonging by Participation*

Under the hybrid model:

- Citizenship is earned through **residency and contribution**, not ancestry or wealth.
- Everyone receives a **Federation Mobility Passport**, guaranteeing rights across borders.

- Belonging is affirmed through **service, participation, and mutual care.**

You don't belong because you were born in the right place.

You belong because **you are willing to protect and serve the whole.**

7. *Transition Strategy: Evolution, Not Imposition*

The hybrid model allows for:

- **Voluntary adoption** via treaty accession.
- **Nested alignment** with existing institutions (e.g., EU, AU, UN agencies).
- **Domestic experimentation,** where nations adopt federation-aligned laws internally.
- **Multi-stakeholder integration,** bringing cities, Indigenous nations, and civic networks into shared governance.

This is not a coup against sovereignty. It is a **constitutional evolution for the planet.**

Conclusion: *The Vision, Made Real*

The hybrid model is not a utopia. It is:

- A scaffold,
- A charter,
- A system born of necessity and shaped by centuries of struggle.

It builds what the old system cannot:

- Trust,
- Accountability,
- Equitable coordination at planetary scale.

It asks every country, institution, and person to make a choice:
Will you govern together—or perish separately?
This is the summary.
In the next section, we lay out the specific **actions that bring this vision to life.**
Short-, Medium-, and Long-Term Policy Recommendations

CHANGE HAPPENS ON TIMELINES. But timelines must be **anchored in possibility, urgency, and political feasibility.**

The hybrid federation can only emerge through **strategic staging**, where short-term actions build political momentum, medium-term policies create legal infrastructure, and long-term commitments lock in planetary transformation.

This three-tiered roadmap begins with today—and stretches toward a more just tomorrow.

1. Short-Term: Foundations for Transition (0–3 Years)

These actions can begin immediately, using existing political, legal, and institutional tools. They lay the groundwork for planetary cooperation and legitimacy.

A. National and Local Governments

- **Ratify the Universal Bill of Rights** (draft included in Appendix B).
- Enact **domestic campaign finance and voting rights reforms.**
- Join existing global compacts on:
  - Climate (rejoining Paris and beyond),
  - Digital cooperation (data sovereignty and open-source governance),
  - Commons stewardship (e.g., oceans, forests, AI).
- **Declare cities and municipalities "Federation-Aligned Zones,"** piloting local universal services and commons governance.
- Reallocate military funding toward:
  - Disaster preparedness,
  - Ecological restoration,
  - Civic employment corps.

B. International Institutions

- Reform UN voting to give **weighted input to regional blocs, cities, and civic networks.**
- Establish a **Global Commons Monitoring Body** (precursor to full federation enforcement mechanisms).
- Open **transparency dashboards for treaty compliance,** hosted by a third-party, open-data coalition.
- Empower regional unions (AU, EU, ASEAN, CELAC) to prototype federation frameworks.

C. Civil Society & Movements

- Launch **citizen assemblies on planetary rights**, modeled after climate and constitutional forums.
- Begin **public education campaigns** on federation values and structures.
- Coordinate a **Global Federation Convention** to simulate treaties, charters, and deliberations with public input.

D. Trillionaire Engagement

- Establish voluntary **Trillionaire Club councils** with publishing, philanthropy, and ethics oversight.
- Begin channeling 0.5% of global billionaire wealth toward:
  - Universal clean water,
  - Federated education platforms,
  - Digital commons infrastructure.

2. Medium-Term: Structural Development (3–10 Years)

Once the foundation is laid, the hybrid model's core structures must be codified, funded, and enforced.

A. Governance Structures

- Create and elect the **Global Federation Parliament**:
  - Proportional, direct representation,
  - Ensures participation of stateless persons, youth, and Indigenous populations.
- Form the **Federation Council of States** with ratified member governments.

- Establish the **Federation Commons Court and Universal Rights Tribunal**.

B. Legal Systems

- Integrate federation law with national constitutions via:
    - Treaty domestication clauses,
    - Dual-law sovereignty protocols.
- Operationalize the **Commons Charter** as binding global law.
- Embed **digital and climate rights** into national Bills of Rights and corporate law.

C. Economic Frameworks

- Launch the **Federation Universal Services Fund**, delivering:
    - Global healthcare baseline,
    - Digital access,
    - Federated public transportation.
- Implement **federation-wide tax protocols**:
    - Global transaction taxes (e.g., Tobin tax),
    - Carbon pricing,
    - Trillionaire Club dues.
- Establish **planetary reparations programs** for:
    - Climate displacement,
    - Colonial extraction,
    - Cultural appropriation.

D. Mobility & Migration

- Operationalize the **Federation Mobility Code**:

- Recognize climate migrants,
- Issue Mobility Passports,
- Support regional resettlement corridors.
- End detention-based border enforcement globally.

3. Long-Term: Cultural and Planetary Integration (10–30 Years)

The goal is not merely policy reform. It is **civilizational alignment around dignity, sustainability, and participation.**

A. Cultural Infrastructure

- Redesign education systems to center:
  - Ecological literacy,
  - Global history,
  - Interfaith ethics,
  - Civic stewardship.
- Institutionalize **Federation Holidays** and civic rituals (e.g., Commons Day, Mobility Oath).
- Fund global **arts exchanges** across movement-impacted regions and cultural traditions.

B. Spiritual and Ethical Integration

- Create **Interfaith Federation Councils** to protect sacred sites and moral pluralism.
- Fund spiritual peace missions during planetary crises.
- Recognize Earth-based traditions as **sovereign knowledge systems,** not folklore.

C. Deep Economic Realignment

- Transition private wealth systems into:
  - Social inheritance funds,
  - Earth restoration trusts,
  - Cooperative financial governance models.
- End global dependence on:
  - Fossil fuels,
  - Extractive agriculture,
  - Surveillance capitalism.

D. Constitutional Milestones

- Amend national constitutions to:
  - Recognize planetary obligations,
  - Include universal rights as enforceable law,
  - Limit corporate influence over democracy.

E. Measurement and Feedback

- Implement the **Hybrid Participation Scorecard** (Appendix C) to assess:
  - Alignment with federation values,
  - Rights compliance,
  - Civic engagement metrics.
- Publish **Federation Reports to Humanity** every 5 years, detailing global progress, failures, and transformations.

A Timeline Built for Courage
The hybrid model is not a leap into chaos.

It is **a staircase into shared responsibility**, built step by step by those who believe in the long arc of justice—and are willing to bend it.

Some changes begin today.

Some require a decade of struggle.

Some will take generations.

But the future is not a mystery.

It is a project.

And this is the blueprint.

A Call to Governments, NGOs, Activists, and Ordinary Citizens

A PLAN without people is just a document.

This book has laid out a hybrid model for global governance—legal, moral, and structural. But ideas do not walk, speak, or build themselves.

People do.

This final part offers concrete pathways for participation—tailored to the unique leverage points of the world's most influential actors. Not everyone can pass legislation or sign a treaty. But **everyone can shift the system from where they stand.**

1. Governments: Ratify, Reform, Realign

Governments—national, regional, and municipal—carry the authority to codify rights, enforce laws, and allocate budgets.

Action Steps:

- Begin **ratifying the Universal Rights Proposal** (Appendix B).

- Join or establish a **Regional Federation Bloc** with neighbors.
- Create domestic legislation aligned with:
  - Commons protection,
  - Mobility rights,
  - Trillionaire contribution frameworks.
- Offer **pilot partnerships with cities** to test local federation governance models.
- Reform campaign finance, courts, and civic structures to model federation transparency and inclusion.

Message to Governments:

Your legitimacy will no longer be judged by GDP or border control.

It will be judged by **how well you uphold dignity—within and beyond your borders.**

2. *Multilateral Institutions: Evolve or Be Replaced*

Institutions like the UN, IMF, WTO, and regional unions must **adapt to hybrid structures** or risk irrelevance.

Action Steps:

- Reform governance to include:
  - Cities,
  - Civic networks,
  - Commons stewards.
- Make **compliance data open-source and citizen-auditable.**
- Redirect financing from military growth to:
  - Universal basic services,
  - Ecological repair,

- Public digital infrastructure.
- End fossil fuel subsidies and reallocate funds to the **Federation Services Fund.**

Message to Institutions:
You were designed to avoid world wars.
Now you must evolve to **prevent world collapse.**

3. NGOs and Foundations: Align Impact with Governance

Non-governmental organizations, philanthropies, and think tanks must **treat democracy and rights as structural goals,** not just service delivery.

Action Steps:

- Publicly endorse the Hybrid Global Governance Framework (Appendix A).
- Commit funding to:
  - Civic education,
  - Local participatory budgeting,
  - Treaty advocacy campaigns.
- Share data and research into **federation-aligned global commons management.**
- Use your convening power to bring together:
  - Youth movements,
  - Municipal coalitions,
  - Diaspora communities.

Message to NGOs:
You've fought symptoms long enough. Now join the fight for **systemic structure and planetary sovereignty.**

. . .

4. Social Movements and Grassroots Activists: Claim the Federation

Movements for climate justice, racial equity, Indigenous sovereignty, LGBTQ+ rights, disability justice, and labor must see themselves as **foundational architects of this transition.**

Action Steps:

- Co-create local federation chapters and global solidarity networks.
- Translate the Universal Bill of Rights into local languages and customs.
- Host **People's Conventions** to build constitutional proposals from below.
- Create public art, ceremonies, and storytelling spaces around:
  - Commons stewardship,
  - Migration dignity,
  - Climate courage.

Message to Movements:

This isn't just a policy fight. It's **a soul fight** for the kind of world your ancestors hoped for—and your children deserve.

5. Trillionaires and Private Wealth: Step into Stewardship

If you control billion-dollar portfolios, data centers, or AI platforms, **you are already governing global systems.** The only question is whether you'll do so **ethically and transparently.**

Action Steps:

- Publicly accept the **Trillionaire Club Charter** (Appendix D).
- Voluntarily allocate **5–10% of personal wealth** toward:
    - Global water security,
    - Climate mitigation,
    - Commons-based technology.
- Support digital cooperatives and public data infrastructure over monopolies.
- Submit your companies to:
    - Equity audits,
    - Commons compliance tribunals,
    - Federation-aligned governance models.

Message to Trillionaires:

You cannot escape responsibility. But you can **choose how history will remember you.**

6. Artists, Educators, and Faith Leaders: Shape the Imagination

Before systems change, cultures must.

You carry the **moral and symbolic power** to:

- Name injustice,
- Reveal possibility,
- And teach new generations **what it means to belong.**

Action Steps:

- Create content that elevates:
    - Planetary ethics,
    - Federation values,

- Borderless belonging.
- Design rituals of welcome and grief for displaced communities.
- Teach children:
  - The languages of justice,
  - The stories of shared responsibility,
  - The tools of democratic action.

Message to Cultural Leaders:
Build the songs and symbols that make this real.
Without your vision, policy has no soul.

7. Ordinary Citizens: Start Where You Stand

You don't need permission to begin. You need purpose.
Action Steps:

- Read the Universal Bill of Rights aloud. Translate it. Share it.
- Host a Federation Reading Group or teach-ins in your town or online.
- Audit your workplace or city using the **Hybrid Participation Scorecard** (Appendix C).
- Contact your elected officials and demand:
  - Commons protections,
  - Migration justice,
  - Federation treaty alignment.
- Plant trees, host welcome ceremonies for new arrivals, join cooperatives.

Message to You:
You are not powerless.

You are **part of the power that is rising to replace the old world with a livable one.**

From Witnesses to *Builders*

History will not remember how we explained collapse.

It will remember how we **chose to build after understanding it.**

This is the path forward.

Not a fantasy. Not a theory.

A project. A plan. A plea.

For those willing to act—now.

Let this be our declaration:

"We are not waiting for permission to create a world of rights, justice, peace, and shared responsibility.

We are claiming our place in the great work of humanity's repair, reimagination, and moral awakening."

The hybrid federation is no longer a question.

It is your invitation.

22

CONCLUSION

THE FUTURE IS FEDERATED—IF WE CHOOSE IT

We stand at the edge of an age that will be defined not by our ideologies, but by our decisions.

The 20th century offered us two incomplete maps:

One, a world of nations, flags, borders, and exceptionalism.

The other, a world of treaties, forums, and global cooperation often too weak to bind.

One promised power. The other, peace.

But neither has delivered the justice, dignity, and sustainability that our survival demands.

This book is not an argument against sovereignty or globalism.

It is an invitation to **transcend their limits**—to construct a third path: a hybrid federation of shared governance, enforceable rights, cultural pluralism, and planetary accountability.

We have shown that this model is **structurally viable**, **morally compelling**, and **democratically participatory**. We have mapped how it can be implemented by nations, regions, cities, and citizens. We have written a charter of universal rights not as poetry, but as policy. We have named the real-world engines of inequity and proposed the means to reintegrate wealth, law, and governance with the Earth and its people.

But books alone do not change the world. **People do.**

The hybrid model will only be built if those who read this rise—not with utopianism, but with *courage*, *memory*, *imagination*, and *organization*.

We are the transitional generation.

The builders. The bridge.

If we act now—with clarity, conviction, and solidarity—

we may yet live to see a world where no one is stateless,

where nature is not a commodity,

where power answers to people,

and where the borders that once divided us

become the blueprints of a world finally governed by the **whole of its humanity**.

This is your call.

This is your time.

The future is federated—**if we choose it.**

APPENDIX A: THE HYBRID GLOBAL GOVERNANCE FRAMEWORK

Appendix A: The Hybrid Global Governance Framework
Section 1: Core Institutional Architecture

1. Global Parliament (Legislative Branch)
Purpose:
Represents the people of Earth—directly elected through proportional, multi-region voting.
Powers:

- Draft and pass binding global legislation on rights, climate, commons, technology, and peace.
- Approve budgets, taxation, and oversight commissions.
- Conduct hearings, inquiries, and emergency resolutions.

Structure:

- Seats allocated by regional population blocs.
- Guaranteed quotas for:
    - Stateless people,
    - Indigenous nations,
    - Youth representatives.

Checks:

- Subject to judicial review by Federation Courts.
- Budgetary proposals require dual ratification with the Council of States.

2. Council of States (Executive Coordination Body)
Purpose:
Bridges national governments with planetary policy implementation.
Powers:

- Ratify treaties and executive directives from Parliament.
- Coordinate intergovernmental responses to planetary crises.

- Approve appointments to key Federation agencies.

Structure:

- Each recognized state (or national union) receives one vote.
- Decisions reached via **qualified majority**, not veto-based unanimity.

Key Innovation:

- States may delegate representation to regional blocs (e.g., EU, AU, Mercosur) to vote collectively.

3. Federation Judiciary
Purpose:
Ensures rule of law across all levels of the federation.
Courts Include:

- **Universal Rights Tribunal** – Enforces the Global Bill of Rights.
- **Commons Court** – Handles environmental and digital commons violations.
- **Mobility and Migration Bench** – Protects the rights of climate migrants and stateless people.

Powers:

- Adjudicate disputes between nations, corporations, and individuals.
- Order reparations and binding compliance measures.
- Nullify laws or policies that violate federation charters.

4. Federation Agencies and Commissions
These include the **operational arms** of the federation. They function much like ministries in national governments.
Key Agencies:

- **Federation Tax Authority** – Collects dues, carbon taxes, wealth transfers.
- **Climate Resilience Corps** – Coordinates response to extreme weather, displacement, and food crises.

Appendix A: The Hybrid Global Governance Framework

- **Federated Mobility Bureau** – Manages migration, visa harmonization, and passport systems.
- **Digital Commons Commission** – Regulates AI, platform governance, and data rights.
- **Trillionaire Compliance Council** – Audits contributions, enforces penalties, manages redistribution plans.

Each agency is:

- Staffed through a mix of civil service appointments and rotating citizen juries.
- Audited by independent transparency bodies every two years.

5. Participatory and Civic Governance

To democratize planetary governance, several structures ensure citizen participation beyond voting.

A. Citizens' Assemblies

- Randomly selected, demographically representative panels.
- Empowered to review legislation and propose amendments.
- Required to be convened annually in every federated region.

B. Participatory Budgeting Platform

- Citizens vote directly on how to allocate portions of the global budget for health, education, or climate repair.

C. Civic Tribunals

- Hear cases brought by civic networks (NGOs, youth coalitions, worker cooperatives).
- Issue formal findings and have veto authority on extractive projects deemed harmful by supermajority vote.

6. Commons Stewardship Architecture

The hybrid model recognizes non-state governance over key domains.

A. Commons Steward Councils

- Include Indigenous nations, scientific communities, and climate-vulnerable populations.

- Issue impact reports and legal warnings when commons are at risk.

B. Commons Compliance Network

- Uses satellite and AI monitoring to detect:
  - Deforestation,
  - Ocean pollution,
  - Unauthorized space exploitation,
  - AI model misuse.

Data is made public, enforceable by judicial ruling, and used to trigger emergency planetary actions.

7. Federation Ombuds Network
Purpose:
Receives complaints, whistleblower reports, and rights violation alerts.
Features:

- Anonymous, multilingual reporting tools.
- Regional coordinators with local enforcement power.
- Annual human rights and environmental scorecards per member state.

The Hybrid Global Governance Framework
Section 2: Decision-Making and Participation Flowchart

Overview: The Seven-Stage Process
The hybrid federation's lawmaking and enforcement process follows a **seven-stage flow:**

1. **Proposal Initiation**
2. **Deliberation and Public Review**
3. **Parliamentary and Council Passage**
4. **Judicial Pre-Certification**
5. **Implementation by Federation Agencies**
6. **Compliance Monitoring and Audit**
7. **Civic Evaluation and Recourse**

Each stage is designed to:

Appendix A: The Hybrid Global Governance Framework

- Enable **participation by multiple actors,**
- Prevent abuse of power,
- Ensure enforceability, and
- Promote **transparency from start to finish.**

Let's examine each step.

1. Proposal Initiation
Who can initiate legislation or treaty proposals?

- Members of Parliament
- Recognized states or regional blocs
- Federation Agencies
- Citizens' Assemblies (via consensus)
- Commons Steward Councils
- Civic movements with 1 million verified cross-border endorsements

Types of proposals:

- Universal rights amendments
- Commons protections
- Budgetary allocation frameworks
- Digital governance statutes
- Federation treaty expansion or revision

Initial review conducted by:

- Federation Legal Drafting Council, to ensure structural and constitutional compatibility.

2. Deliberation and Public Review
Goal:
Create a transparent, participatory environment for shaping and challenging the proposal.
Deliberation Channels:

- **Public hearings** livestreamed globally and archived in the Federation Library.

- **Citizen feedback portal** with multilingual AI-assisted summaries and voting.
- **Participatory translation networks** (especially for non-colonial and Indigenous languages).
- **Youth deliberation panels** and **Global University Forums** to gather intergenerational feedback.

This phase lasts **30 to 120 days**, depending on scope and urgency.

If a proposal garners more than 40% disapproval in a citizen survey during this phase, it must:

- Be amended,
- Or undergo **a second Citizens' Assembly review** before proceeding.

3. Parliamentary and Council Passage

The proposal moves simultaneously through two legislative channels:

A. Global Parliament

- Requires **simple majority** to pass ordinary legislation.
- Requires **2/3 majority** for rights amendments or budget reallocation above 10%.

B. Council of States

- Each nation or regional bloc casts one vote.
- **Qualified majority required** (⅔ of voting members *representing at least 60% of global population*).

Disagreement Resolution Mechanism:

- If Parliament and Council diverge:
    - A **Joint Reconciliation Forum** is convened,
    - Composed of 15 members from each body,
    - Mediated by a randomly selected Citizens' Assembly.

If deadlock persists, the matter may be referred to the **Federation Constitutional Court**.

4. Judicial Pre-Certification

Before implementation, every major proposal undergoes:

Appendix A: The Hybrid Global Governance Framework 507

- **Judicial review** by the Federation Judiciary,
- To certify:
  - Constitutional alignment,
  - Non-violation of existing rights,
  - Conflict checks with regional laws.

Commons-specific legislation is reviewed by:

- A hybrid bench of legal scholars,
- Indigenous legal experts,
- Environmental scientists,
- And citizen observers with standing.

Outcomes:

- Greenlighted,
- Returned for amendment,
- Or blocked (pending appeal or overhaul).

This **pre-certification stage** ensures that "bad laws" don't become binding rules.

5. Implementation by Federation Agencies

Once approved and certified, the legislation is handed to the relevant **Federation Agency** or Commission.

Each agency must:

- Publish an **Implementation Roadmap**,
- Conduct **stakeholder consultations in each region**,
- Translate policies into **national and local guidance packages**,
- Allocate funds from the Federation Treasury.

Oversight:

- Implementation teams must report quarterly to:
  - The Federation Budget Office,
  - The Oversight Council for Public Trust (a civic audit body),
  - A public dashboard for citizen tracking.

Implementation is **not private bureaucracy—it is public and participatory.**

6. Compliance Monitoring and Audit
The Federation operates a **multi-layered compliance system**, drawing on:

- Satellite and digital monitoring (for climate, deforestation, emissions, etc.)
- Decentralized ledgers (tracking digital rights violations or budgetary use)
- Commons Citizen Review Boards (community-based watchdog groups)
- **Annual Scorecards** generated by:
    - The Federation Ombuds Network,
    - The Hybrid Participation Scorecard system (see Appendix C)

Agencies and states **must respond publicly** to noncompliance scores. Severe violations may trigger:

- Budget suspension,
- Legal action at the Federation Courts,
- Veto rights suspended at Council of States.

7. Civic Evaluation and Recourse
Once laws are implemented and enforced, **people still have power** to revise, repeal, or reform them.
Mechanisms include:

- **Annual Policy Referenda**, where any law can be flagged for public review,
- **Commons Tribunals**, where stakeholders can present challenges or propose amendments,
- **Federated Recall Petitions**, allowing for agency leadership reviews,
- **Score-based Sunset Clauses**—laws must meet defined metrics to remain active beyond 5–10 years.

This closing loop means **governance is never final—it is always living, accountable, and renewable.**

The Hybrid Global Governance Framework
Section 3: The Federated Cooperation Matrix

Overview: A System of Nested Sovereignties

The hybrid model is *not* a world government that overrides national autonomy. Instead, it is a **shared governance framework** that enables:

- National independence,
- Regional cooperation,
- Local experimentation,
- And global accountability—

...simultaneously.

This matrix shows how **different actors contribute to and are held accountable by** the federation, each with **defined roles, influence, and obligations.**

We explore seven categories of actors:

1. Nation-States
2. Regional Blocs
3. Cities and Municipalities
4. Indigenous and Ancestral Nations
5. Non-Governmental Organizations (NGOs)
6. Transnational Corporations
7. Commons and Civil Society Coalitions

1. Nation-States
Role:

- **Primary treaty signatories** to the Federation Charter and Universal Bill of Rights.
- Responsible for domestic legal alignment and budgetary contributions.

Powers:

- Full vote in the **Council of States.**
- Nominating authority for regional judiciary representatives and agency appointments.

Obligations:

- Align national law with federation treaties within 5 years of ratification.
- Participate in federation monitoring and scoring mechanisms (e.g., carbon caps, digital compliance).
- Uphold commons protections within borders.

Federation Supports:

- Transition funding for sovereignty-compatible reforms.
- Federation legal liaison office in national parliaments.
- Access to global adaptation and reparations funds.

2. Regional Blocs (e.g., EU, AU, Mercosur, ASEAN)
Role:

- Act as **intermediary governance entities** coordinating collective positions among member states.

Powers:

- Collective voting in certain Council decisions (e.g., regional migration corridors, economic compacts).
- Ability to propose treaties, agency functions, and rights additions.

Obligations:

- Ensure regional harmonization with federation principles.
- Establish internal mechanisms for federation alignment review.

Federation Supports:

- Regional civic assemblies,
- Federation Parliament seats allocated to regional delegates,
- Shared climate, digital, and mobility infrastructure platforms.

3. Cities and Municipalities
Role:

Appendix A: The Hybrid Global Governance Framework

- Serve as **pilots and innovation hubs** for local implementation of federation rights and systems.

Powers:

- Can declare "Federation-Aligned Cities," gaining funding and priority for participation.
- Submit independent reports to Federation Ombuds Network.

Obligations:

- Must uphold baseline rights (housing, migration, climate resilience) to maintain alignment status.
- Participate in participatory budgeting and public data reporting.

Federation Supports:

- Federation Welcome Hub infrastructure (for mobility, education, arts),
- Budget subsidies for commons stewardship,
- Legal protections for sanctuary cities.

4. Indigenous and Ancestral Nations
Role:

- Recognized as **sovereign partners and guardians of ecological and cultural commons.**

Powers:

- Permanent representation on Commons Steward Councils,
- Veto power on proposals affecting sacred lands or biocultural zones,
- Ability to propose rights additions to the Universal Bill of Rights.

Obligations:

- Maintain communal governance in line with rights-based and non-extractive principles.

Federation Supports:

- Land restitution and legal recognition,
- Funding for language, knowledge, and governance revival,
- Protected status for migratory and ecological sovereignty.

5. Non-Governmental Organizations (NGOs)
Role:

- Operate as **civil society delivery partners and watchdogs.**

Powers:

- File cases with the Federation Judiciary and Commons Tribunals,
- Sit on implementation and oversight committees.

Obligations:

- Submit annual transparency and governance audits,
- Avoid partisan alignment with national electoral interests.

Federation Supports:

- Access to Federation Grants for Rights Delivery (FGRD),
- Participation in the Global Commons Data Network,
- Legal standing in citizens' legislative proposals.

6. Transnational Corporations
Role:

- Recognized as **regulated economic actors,** not governance partners.

Powers (Limited):

- May consult in agency rule-making when invited,

Appendix A: The Hybrid Global Governance Framework 513

- Required to comply with Federation labor, tax, and digital governance laws.

Obligations:

- Submit to Federation Scorecard evaluations (Appendix C),
- Open algorithmic transparency (for digital companies),
- Commons contributions proportional to revenue and ecological impact.

Federation Restrictions:

- No legislative voting rights,
- No private enforcement powers,
- Sanctions or revocation of market access for rights violations.

7. Commons and Civil Society Coalitions
Role:

- Serve as **living stewards of rights and resources** beyond the state.

Includes:

- Worker cooperatives,
- Climate justice alliances,
- Youth and diasporic networks,
- Migrant-led advocacy platforms.

Powers:

- Can propose amendments, resolutions, and initiatives to Parliament and Tribunals.
- Access to Civic Representation Slots in legislative and judicial bodies.

Obligations:

- Practice inclusive governance,
- Document participatory processes,

- Submit contributions to the Federation Knowledge Archive.

Federation Supports:

- Seed funding,
- Protection against retaliation or state suppression,
- Data sovereignty and open-source infrastructure for organizing.

From Power Hierarchies to Cooperative Interdependence

The Federated Cooperation Matrix **flattens governance without flattening identity**. It enables:

- States to remain autonomous,
- Cities to innovate locally,
- Indigenous nations to govern ancestrally,
- Civil society to hold power accountable,
- And commons to be stewarded, not sold.

Power is no longer a vertical pyramid—it is a **horizontal lattice of responsibilities and reciprocal governance,** with the Earth itself at the center.

APPENDIX B: UNIVERSAL RIGHTS PROPOSAL

Appendix B: Universal Rights Proposal
Pillar 1: Core Human Rights

Article 1: Right to Life with Dignity
Every person has the right to:

- Safe and sufficient food,
- Clean water and sanitation,
- Adequate shelter,
- Healthcare without discrimination,
- Personal safety and bodily autonomy.

Governments and institutions must:

- Ensure universal access to these life-supporting conditions,
- Prevent deprivation through policy, neglect, or economic exclusion.

Article 2: Right to Mobility and Belonging
Every person has the right to:

- Leave any place, migrate freely, and seek safety without fear of detention or persecution.
- Reside, participate, and belong in any federation-aligned region.

States must:

- Recognize climate migrants, stateless persons, and forcibly displaced people as full rights-holders,
- Guarantee integration pathways based on residency, not origin.

Article 3: Right to Cultural and Spiritual Identity
Every person and community has the right to:

- Maintain and express language, culture, faith, and ancestral practices,
- Access and protect sacred sites and traditional knowledge.

Governments must:

- Protect minority and Indigenous cultures from erasure or forced assimilation,
- Support cultural preservation in all education, media, and public funding.

Article 4: Right to Education and Knowledge Access

Every person has the right to:

- Free, inclusive, and decolonized education from early childhood through adulthood,
- Access to public knowledge, science, and truth-based historical memory.

Federation institutions must:

- Remove barriers to education based on geography, status, or disability,
- Prevent privatization of essential knowledge systems.

Article 5: Right to Health and Wellbeing

All persons are entitled to:

- Preventative and emergency healthcare,
- Reproductive autonomy and gender-affirming care,
- Mental health services,
- Protection from environmental harm.

States must fund universal healthcare systems and prohibit denial based on:

- Nationality,
- Legal status,
- Ability to pay.

Appendix B: Universal Rights Proposal

Article 6: Right to Economic Security and Fair Labor
Every person has the right to:

- A living income,
- Safe working conditions,
- Freedom of association,
- Access to collective bargaining.

The federation recognizes **care work, informal work, and commons-based labor** as valuable and compensable.
Forced labor, exploitative platform work, and algorithmic wage theft are violations of this right.

Article 7: Right to Privacy and Bodily Autonomy
All persons have the right to:

- Refuse surveillance,
- Control their personal data,
- Be free from biometric and behavioral profiling.

States and corporations may not:

- Exploit data without consent,
- Use predictive analytics for policing, border control, or commercial manipulation.

Article 8: Right to Self-Determination
Communities—including Indigenous nations, stateless peoples, and occupied populations—have the right to:

- Govern themselves,
- Steward their territories,
- Participate in global decisions that affect their survival.

Federation institutions must respect non-Western governance systems as legitimate political forms.

Article 9: Right to Safety from Oppression
No one shall be subject to:

- Violence based on race, gender, class, religion, sexuality, disability, or origin,
- Arbitrary detention, torture, or extra-legal punishment.

This article applies to:

- State actions,
- Corporate practices,
- Digital harms.

Remedies must be accessible in the **Federation Judiciary** regardless of national legal status.

Article 10: Right to Redress and Restoration
Every person or community harmed by:

- State policy,
- Corporate conduct,
- Climate impact,
- Commons violation…

…has the right to:

- Truth and accountability,
- Reparations (monetary or structural),
- Restoration of land, rights, and dignity.

Restorative justice must be **prioritized over punitive enforcement.**

Pillar 2: Planetary Rights and Commons Protections

Article 11: Rights of Nature and the Living Earth
Nature is not a resource. It is a subject of law.
The Earth, its ecosystems, and all living species possess:

- The right to exist, flourish, regenerate, and evolve without exploitation.

Specific guarantees include:

- Rights of rivers to flow freely,

Appendix B: Universal Rights Proposal

- Rights of forests to self-regenerate,
- Rights of soil to retain fertility,
- Rights of species to habitat continuity.

Legal Standing:

- Nature may be represented in court by Commons Stewards, scientists, or Indigenous representatives.
- Legal remedies include:
  - Restoration orders,
  - Prohibition of extractive activity,
  - Rewilding mandates.

Article 12: The Right to a Stable Climate

Every person and every generation has the right to:

- A livable, predictable, and just climate.

States and corporations must:

- Halt greenhouse gas emissions exceeding scientifically defined planetary limits,
- Transition to zero-carbon economies by binding dates,
- Pay climate reparations proportionate to historical emissions and current capacity.

This right includes:

- Climate refugees' rights to migrate and receive care,
- Community rights to adaptation infrastructure and early warning systems,
- Cultural rights of climate-vulnerable peoples to maintain identity.

Article 13: The Right to Safe Water and Clean Air

Water and air are sacred and shared—never owned, sold, or denied. Every person has the right to:

- Access safe, affordable drinking water and sanitation,
- Breathe clean, unpolluted air,

- Be protected from atmospheric contamination caused by war, industry, or extraction.

Federation enforcement requires:

- Ban on water privatization for basic services,
- Phaseout of fossil fuel–linked pollution within 15 years,
- Global water justice fund, paid into by highest industrial polluters.

Article 14: The Right to Commons Stewardship
Every person and every community has the right to:

- Participate in the protection and regeneration of local and planetary commons.

This includes:

- Seeds and genetic heritage,
- Oceans, coasts, and fisheries,
- Mountains, glaciers, and watersheds,
- Open-source digital and cultural knowledge.

Commons must be governed by:

- Participatory legal frameworks,
- Science and ancestral ecological knowledge,
- Transparent, non-commercial custodianship.

Stewardship is **not ownership—it is civic guardianship** with shared obligations and benefits.

Article 15: The Right to Food Sovereignty
Every community has the right to:

- Control their food systems, seeds, and agricultural practices,
- Eat culturally appropriate, locally grown food,
- Reject genetically modified or corporately patented seed monopolies.

Federation protections include:

Appendix B: Universal Rights Proposal

- Support for small farmers and Indigenous cultivators,
- Bans on agri-corporate land grabs,
- Rights of territories to regulate foreign food imports and defend local economies.

Article 16: The Right to a Healthy Biosphere

The planet's biodiversity—including plants, animals, fungi, and microbial life—has intrinsic value and must be protected for current and future generations.

This right guarantees:

- No species shall be intentionally extinguished by human action.
- Ecosystem fragmentation must be reversed through corridor restoration.
- Synthetic biology and geoengineering are subject to commons oversight and moratoria unless democratically authorized and scientifically justified.

Article 17: The Right to Equitable Resource Use

Natural resources extracted for human use must be:

- Equitably distributed,
- Transparently governed,
- And taxed to fund repair and redistribution.

This includes:

- Rare earth minerals,
- Timber,
- Fossil fuel phaseout revenue,
- Water access in drought zones.

Excessive or monopolistic resource use is considered a **violation of planetary equity** and subject to sanctions.

Article 18: The Rights of Future Generations

Unborn generations have:

- The right to inherit a livable, beautiful, and biologically intact world.

Current generations are stewards, not owners.
Governments and institutions must:

- Submit major infrastructure, energy, or environmental decisions to **future impact assessments,**
- Fund **intergenerational equity trusts** that ensure youth participation and long-term planetary care,
- Enshrine this article in national and regional constitutions as enforceable law.

Pillar 3: Digital and Participatory Rights

Article 19: Right to Digital Access and Sovereignty
Every person has the right to:

- Affordable, high-speed internet access,
- Federated digital identity not linked to corporate or state surveillance,
- Safe and censorship-free expression in digital spaces.

Federation mandates:

- Universal broadband as a public utility,
- Public infrastructure for data storage, identity, and encryption,
- Protection of decentralized platforms from corporate capture.

Article 20: Right to Data Ownership and Consent
All personal data is:

- The property of the individual,
- Non-transferable without clear, revocable consent.

This includes:

- Biometric, financial, medical, behavioral, and location data.

Federation protections include:

- A "right to be forgotten,"

Appendix B: Universal Rights Proposal

- Consent dashboards and data passports,
- Bans on coercive or hidden data extraction (e.g., from children, migrants, or in emergencies).

Article 21: Right to Algorithmic Justice
Every person has the right to:

- Know how decisions affecting them are made by machines,
- Contest and appeal algorithmic decisions,
- Demand fairness, transparency, and explainability in AI systems.

This applies to:

- Employment,
- Policing,
- Credit scoring,
- Migration screening,
- Education,
- Access to public benefits.

AI systems used in governance must be:

- Open-source,
- Publicly audited,
- Certified for bias and harm mitigation.

Article 22: Right to Digital Assembly and Civic Expression
All people may:

- Organize,
- Protest,
- Vote,
- Fundraise,
- Form associations—

...in digital spaces, with equal protection to physical rights of assembly.
Federation responsibilities:

- Prevent shutdowns and censorship of peaceful protest,

- Regulate platform moderation under universal rights standards,
- Ensure linguistic and cultural accessibility in digital governance portals.

Article 23: Right to Platform Accountability and Choice
All people have the right to:

- Use alternative platforms without penalty,
- Receive information free of algorithmic manipulation,
- Participate in content governance.

Federation mandates:

- Platform cooperatives must receive public funding equal to dominant private platforms,
- Monopolistic tech practices (data lock-in, surveillance ads, shadow banning) are outlawed,
- Users must have access to **auditable feeds and reverse chronological timelines** on social media.

Article 24: Right to Digital Rest and Disconnection
All people have the right to:

- Periods of digital disconnection without economic, civic, or social penalty.

This right protects:

- Children and youth from compulsive digital harm,
- Workers from 24/7 availability expectations,
- All people from exploitation of attention and dopamine systems.

Federation encourages:

- Design ethics for humane tech,
- Cultural rhythms of sabbath, silence, and rest.

Article 25: Right to Participatory Governance
All persons have the right to:

Appendix B: Universal Rights Proposal

- Participate meaningfully in the design, passage, and review of laws that govern their lives.

This includes:

- Citizens' Assemblies at local, regional, and global levels,
- Participatory budgeting at all federation spending levels,
- Civic design input on urban development, health policy, education, and commons management.

Participation is not a privilege—it is the foundation of planetary legitimacy.

Article 26: Right to Truth and Information Integrity
Every person has the right to:

- Access truthful, verified, and pluralistic information about the world.

Federation obligations:

- Fund public media cooperatives with citizen oversight,
- Ban disinformation campaigns (state or corporate),
- Require transparency in news sourcing, AI-generated content, and influence operations.

This is essential for:

- Public health,
- Democracy,
- Crisis response,
- Cultural survival.

Article 27: Right to Language, Access, and Translation
All people have the right to:

- Understand and shape public policy in their language, ability, and cultural context.

Federation policies must:

- Translate core documents into all living languages,
- Ensure full accessibility for persons with disabilities,
- Fund Indigenous language revitalization through public platforms and arts.

Without this, **participation is performative—not real.**

The Digital Commons as a Human Right
This final pillar affirms that the **digital world is not exempt from justice.**
It must be governed:

- By dignity, not dominance;
- By access, not algorithms;
- By shared infrastructure, not data monopolies.

Digital life is no longer optional.
Therefore, **digital justice is no longer negotiable.**

Final Synthesis: One Charter, Three Pillars, One Planet
Across all three pillars—Human, Planetary, and Digital—the Universal Rights Proposal sets the legal foundation for:

- The end of extractive governance,
- The rise of regenerative systems,
- And the construction of a world where law is built on life, not domination.

These rights are:

- **Enforceable** through judiciary structures,
- **Funded** through federation taxes and contributions,
- **Renewable** through civic assemblies and participatory revision,
- And **guaranteed** to all persons, everywhere—*not by geography, but by existence.*

APPENDIX C: HYBRID PARTICIPATION SCORECARD

Appendix C: Hybrid Participation Scorecard
A Civic Tool for Alignment, Accountability, and Activation

Overview: Why a Scorecard?
The scorecard serves several critical purposes:

1. **Benchmarking** — Tracks progress toward alignment with federation principles.
2. **Transparency** — Provides a publicly auditable record of state and institutional behavior.
3. **Motivation** — Encourages cooperation through recognition and feedback loops.
4. **Incentivization** — Connects alignment scores with eligibility for federation funding, voting privileges, and cooperative frameworks.

It is intended to be administered:

- Annually by each federation member and applicant,
- With oversight from independent civic auditors,
- Open to public review and civic counter-submission.

0
No compliance, active violation, or regression
1
Minimal progress or symbolic engagement
2
Partial implementation, limited in scope
3
Substantive policies in place, early enforcement
4
Broad implementation with strong accountability
5
Full alignment with federation standards and civic integration
Each section includes indicators, examples, and action prompts.

Appendix C: Hybrid Participation Scorecard

Category 1: Rights Alignment (Max Score: 25)
1.1 – Core Human Rights

- Does the jurisdiction guarantee universal access to water, shelter, food, health care, and education?
- Are these rights enforceable by law, with accessible remedies?

1.2 – Planetary Protections

- Are commons protected legally?
- Is climate justice codified and funded through progressive taxation?

1.3 – Mobility and Belonging

- Are climate migrants recognized?
- Is detention-based immigration policy prohibited?

1.4 – Data Sovereignty

- Does every person control their data?
- Are surveillance and biometric profiling restricted?

1.5 – Access to Culture and Language

- Are all laws and platforms accessible to linguistic and ability-diverse populations?

Action Prompt: Draft local legislation incorporating the Universal Rights Proposal.
Score Threshold for Eligibility to Vote in Council of States: ≥ 15

Category 2: Participatory Structures (Max Score: 25)
2.1 – Citizens' Assemblies

- Are deliberative bodies convened annually with randomly selected, representative participants?

2.2 – Participatory Budgeting

- Is at least 5% of the public budget citizen-directed?

- Are project outcomes published and monitored?

2.3 – Civic Education

- Is civic education universal, nonpartisan, and integrated across generations?

2.4 – Local Autonomy

- Are cities, tribal regions, and Indigenous governments empowered to self-govern within federation norms?

2.5 – Public Access to Lawmaking

- Can citizens propose legislation?
- Are laws available in readable formats with comment periods?

Action Prompt: Publish your participatory mechanisms in the Federation Participation Archive.
Score Threshold for Commons Tribunal Access: ≥ 18

Category 3: Commons Stewardship (Max Score: 25)
3.1 – Legal Recognition of Commons

- Are forests, water, air, and ecosystems recognized as rights-bearing entities?

3.2 – Community Governance

- Are commons co-managed by public, civic, and Indigenous actors?

3.3 – Extraction Limits

- Are there limits on resource exploitation tied to planetary boundaries?

3.4 – Ecological Reparations

- Does the jurisdiction fund restoration and pay historical climate debts?

3.5 – Biodiversity and Seed Sovereignty

- Are native species protected?
- Are seeds owned and stewarded by the public, not monopolies?

Action Prompt: Establish a Commons Council in your city or region.
Minimum Score for Environmental Trade Eligibility: ≥ 20

Category 4: Institutional Transparency and Justice (Max Score: 25)
4.1 – Public Audits

- Are all institutions subject to regular, public, and civic-partnered audits?

4.2 – Open Data Systems

- Is information (budgets, votes, environmental impacts) accessible in real time?

4.3 – Independent Judiciary

- Is there a judiciary capable of ruling against powerful actors without retaliation?

4.4 – Anti-Corruption Systems

- Are political donations and lobbying transparently regulated?

4.5 – Reparative Justice Mechanisms

- Is there a functioning Truth, Reparations, or Healing Commission?

Action Prompt: Convene a People's Tribunal to audit transparency performance.
Eligibility for Federation Grants: Score ≥ 15 in this category

Appendix C: Hybrid Participation Scorecard

Category 5: Global Engagement and Solidarity (Max Score: 25)
5.1 – Treaty Ratification

- Has the jurisdiction ratified the Federation Charter and the Universal Rights Proposal?

5.2 – Financial Contribution

- Is the jurisdiction meeting its dues, reparations, or Trillionaire Club obligations?

5.3 – Transnational Solidarity

- Is it providing aid to climate- or conflict-impacted communities?

5.4 – Federation Delegation Inclusion

- Do marginalized and stateless populations have representation in international delegations?

5.5 – Peace and Demilitarization

- Is military spending reduced in favor of peace, health, and education?

Action Prompt: Publish your solidarity portfolio and submit to Civic Oversight review.
Minimum Score for Federation Parliament Voting Seat: ≥ 17

Total Maximum Score: 125
Score Tiers:
Scoring Method
Each area is evaluated on a **0–5 scale**:

Federation Standing

100–125
Aligned
Full privileges, voting, grants, and access
75–99

Participating
Partial access to platforms, under review
50–74
Observer
Non-voting, eligible for assistance and civic mentoring
Below 50
Non-Compliant
Subject to public audit, sanction, or conditional engagement

APPENDIX D: TRILLIONAIRE CLUB DRAFT PROPOSAL AND FRAMEWORK

Appendix D: Trillionaire Club Draft Proposal and Framework

1. Purpose and Rationale
The Trillionaire Club is founded on three principles:

- **Responsibility scales with power.**
- Those with disproportionate control over capital, technology, and infrastructure must bear **commensurate responsibility for planetary outcomes.**
- **No wealth beyond contribution.**
- Private accumulation beyond $1 trillion is a *civic and ecological liability* if left unchecked. The Club ensures **wealth is transformed into justice, not hoarded as privilege.**
- **Legitimacy requires accountability.**
- No one—not corporations, not dynasties, not billionaires—may exist **outside the system of planetary obligations.**

This framework makes clear: **trillionaire wealth must be treated as a form of public trust**, not private indulgence.

2. Eligibility, Triggers, and Legal Definitions
2.1 – Eligibility Criteria
Any individual, family trust, or corporate executive structure is subject to Trillionaire Club requirements if they meet one or more of the following:

- **Personal Net Worth** exceeds USD $999 billion,
- **Control of Data Infrastructure** that governs more than 1 billion digital users,
- **Asset Management Authority** over portfolios exceeding USD $5 trillion,
- **Ownership of Resource Extraction Rights** that exceed 1% of any planetary commons (e.g., water tables, rare earth elements, carbon sinks).

2.2 – Legal Definition of "Wealth"
Includes:

- Real assets,
- Digital platforms,
- Intellectual property portfolios,
- Algorithmic training data,
- Corporate stock holdings,
- Private capital managed via trusts or foundations.

Valuations are determined by **independent civic-auditor panels** in cooperation with public disclosure requirements.

3. Responsibilities and Obligations
All Club members are required to fulfill **four core obligations**:

3.1 – Annual Contribution Mandate
Minimum annual contribution:

- **5% of total net wealth,** increasing by 1% per year after five years of Club membership.

Funds are directed to:

- Federation Universal Services Fund (clean water, housing, education),
- Climate Justice Reparations,
- Commons Infrastructure (e.g., open-source AI, digital identity systems),
- Indigenous Sovereignty Protection Grants.

Failure to contribute results in automatic penalty taxation (see Section 4).

3.2 – Commons Equity Transfer
All Club members must:

- Allocate **10% of their corporate equity** into a **Federated Commons Trust.**

This equity is:

Appendix D: Trillionaire Club Draft Proposal and Fra... 535

- Held by a global cooperative,
- Vested into climate and digital commons programs,
- Tied to voting mechanisms that represent **global citizen interests**, not shareholder profit.

3.3 – Transparent Disclosure and Civic Oversight

Club members must:

- Disclose financials quarterly,
- Submit to civic audits by randomly selected global citizen panels,
- Publish social impact, emissions, and human rights risk assessments of all investments.

Disclosures are:

- Publicly accessible,
- Reviewed by the **Trillionaire Oversight Tribunal**,
- Auditable by investigative journalists and NGOs with standing.

3.4 – Global Service Mandate

All members must serve a minimum of **60 days per year in global service roles**, such as:

- Federation Peace Corps deployment,
- Commons Advisory Panels,
- Citizen education initiatives on digital justice, climate science, or governance.

Members may not opt out. Nonparticipation triggers penalties and public flagging.

4. Enforcement, Transparency, and Penalties

The Trillionaire Club is enforced by the **Federation Tax Authority** and overseen by:

- **The Commons Court**, for legal noncompliance,
- **The Public Contribution Archive**, for civic transparency,

- **The Trillionaire Watchdog Coalition**, a rotating citizen oversight body.

4.1 – Noncompliance Penalties
Failure to meet obligations triggers:

- 10–25% wealth seizure,
- Loss of voting rights on corporate boards,
- Suspension from public markets under federation jurisdiction,
- Blacklisting from government contracts and research partnerships.

Persistent noncompliance results in:

- Legal asset freeze,
- Seizure and redistribution by Commons Recovery Board,
- Disqualification from future AI, space, and planetary technology licensing.

4.2 – Civic Review
Every five years, each Trillionaire Club member is evaluated by:

- Youth panels,
- Migrant coalitions,
- Commons stewards,
- Workers affected by Club member industries.

Reviews include:

- Public ratings,
- Policy recommendations,
- Requests for structural divestment or reparations.

5. Governance and Public Participation
The Trillionaire Club is governed **not by its members,** but by the **public.**

5.1 – The Federation Contribution Council (FCC)
Composed of:

- ⅓ citizen jurors (randomly selected),

Appendix D: Trillionaire Club Draft Proposal and Fra...

- ⅓ civic society delegates,
- ⅓ scientific and commons experts.

Duties include:

- Setting annual contribution targets,
- Evaluating compliance trends,
- Adjusting obligations based on climate, economic, and geopolitical stress indicators.

5.2 – Global Citizens' Portal
A public dashboard provides:

- Real-time tracking of Club member contributions,
- Equity transfers,
- Service hours,
- Compliance scores.

Citizens may:

- File noncompliance reports,
- Vote in performance polls,
- Propose contribution redirection for underserved regions.

5.3 – Trillionaire Charter Recitation
All members must publicly affirm this declaration:
"My wealth is not my kingdom.
My power is not my shield.
My role is to serve, repair, and reimagine.
I enter this Charter as a custodian of the future,
And I accept that I am accountable to all."

Wealth Without Contribution Is Not Freedom—It Is Failure
The Trillionaire Club is not punitive. It is restorative.
It asks of those who have gained most from globalization to **invest fully in global repair.**
It reminds us:

- That concentration of capital without conscience is collapse.
- That accountability is not just for governments—but for **anyone with world-shaping power.**

Appendix D: Trillionaire Club Draft Proposal and Fra…

- That the future is a shared inheritance—and **no one may hoard the key.**

ABOUT THE AUTHOR

JD Rossetti is a seasoned public affairs professional, which is a fancy way of saying he's spent over a decade navigating the world of government relations, legislative affairs, public administration, and policy analysis—without losing his sense of humor (or his hair... mostly). With a knack for advocacy, strategic planning, and community engagement, JD has dedicated his career to shaping public policy and making a real difference.

A former Washington State Representative, JD tackled big issues like education, infrastructure, economic development, and public health—because someone had to. He successfully secured funding for education, mental health initiatives, and broadband expansion, ensuring that students could learn, communities could thrive, and people could finally stream their favorite shows without buffering. As a School Board Director, he championed student success, technology integration, and budget oversight, proving that yes, numbers can be fun (sometimes).

JD holds a Master of Public Administration (MPA) from The Evergreen State College and a Bachelor of Arts in Public Affairs from Washington State University. Passionate about public service, policy innovation, and effective governance, JD continues to work toward policies that strengthen and support communities—one well-crafted policy (and dad joke) at a time.

www.ingramcontent.com/pod-product-compliance
Lightning Source LLC
Chambersburg PA
CBHW020529030426
42337CB00013B/786